Integrated Treatment for Co-Occurring Disorders

Integrated Treatment for Co-Occurring Disorders

Personality Disorders and Addiction

Sharon C. Ekleberry

Routledge
Taylor & Francis Group
New York   London

Routledge
Taylor & Francis Group
270 Madison Avenue
New York, NY 10016

Routledge
Taylor & Francis Group
2 Park Square
Milton Park, Abingdon
Oxon OX14 4RN

© 2009 by Taylor & Francis Group, LLC
Routledge is an imprint of Taylor & Francis Group, an Informa business

Printed in the United States of America on acid-free paper
10 9 8 7 6 5 4 3 2 1

International Standard Book Number-13: 978-0-7890-3693-3 (Softcover) 978-0-7890-3692-6 (Hardcover)

Library of Congress Cataloging-in-Publication Data

Ekleberry, Sharon C.
    Integrated treatment for co-occurring disorders : personality disorders and addiction / by Sharon C. Ekleberry.
       p. ; cm.
    Includes bibliographical references and index.
    ISBN 978-0-7890-3692-6 (hardbound : alk. paper) -- ISBN 978-0-7890-3693-3 (pbk. : alk. paper)
    1. Dual diagnosis--Treatment. 2. Personality disorders--Treatment. 3. Substance abuse--Treatment. I. Title.
    [DNLM: 1. Personality Disorders--complications. 2. Personality Disorders--therapy. 3. Diagnosis, Dual (Psychiatry) 4. Substance-Related Disorders--complications. 5. Substance-Related Disorders--therapy. WM 190 E365i 2008]

RC564.68.E55 2008
616.86'0651--dc22
                                          2008021689

Visit the Taylor & Francis Web site at
http://www.taylorandfrancis.com

and the Routledge Web site at
http://www.routledge.com

Contents

Contents

Contents　　　　　　　　　vii

For Bob. It couldn't have happened without him.

Preface

Over the course of many years I have provided training on co-occurring personality disorders and substance use disorders for a variety of human services staff. The participants in every audience describe this complex client population as their greatest professional challenge. Problematic clients in family medical practices, probation and parole agencies, and social and behavioral health services often have an underlying personality disorder that compromises the effectiveness of the services being offered. A co-occurring substance use disorder amplifies the difficulties experienced by these individuals, the people in their lives, and the service providers attempting to help them. My purpose in writing this book is to bring focus to the specifics of assessment and treatment for these co-occurring disorders and to suggest that greater adaptability, fewer self-sabotaging behaviors, and an abstinent lifestyle are all possible. There can be significant professional satisfaction in working effectively with the interplay of addiction and disorders of personality. It is my hope that service providers in the various treatment or service settings who must manage these challenges will obtain ideas and practical guidelines from the information provided here.

Throughout the book I have used the terms *dual diagnosis* and *co-occurring disorders* interchangeably. Neither is ideal, but both are useful. *Co-occurring disorders* is the more recent designation of choice; *dual diagnosis* is still in use. I saw no reason to eliminate one of them. I have also used the terms *substance dependence* and *addiction* interchangeably; both terms are useful as well.

This book addresses all the personality disorders in the *Diagnostic and Statistical Manual of Mental Disorders*, text revision (*DSM-IV-TR*), including the two placed in Appendix B for further study and possible inclusion in the *DSM-V*. Each of the personality disorders is covered in a separate chapter and is discussed in terms of essential features, self-image, view of others, relationships, issues with author-ity, behavior, affect, defenses, and the self-created world of the indi-viduals with the specific personality disorder. The substance use disorders section for each personality disorder addresses the impact of substances and drugs of choice. Although no specific psychoac-tive drug is associated with any of the personality disorders, person-ality-based vulnerabilities that impact substance use and drugs of choice can be addressed in the treatment process. Finally, integrated treatment is discussed in each chapter via engagement in treatment, treatment provider guidelines, professional ethics, assessment and treatment, treatment goals, and recovery activities.

I have provided many examples to clarify the concepts being discussed. To do so, I have changed identifying information and at times combined personality disorder–specific behaviors from two people into one example. The behavior remains accurate as described and applies to the personality disorder being discussed. The altera-tions were to fully obscure any possibility of identifying individuals through the content of the writing.

It is important to me to comment on the challenges of writing about personality and substance use disorders. Individuals with this type of dual diagnosis face continuing stigma. Because these disor-ders involve behaviors, attitudes, symptoms, and personality char-acteristics that are both personally disadvantageous and potentially unpleasant to others, I have attempted to clearly describe the rel-evant factors without adding to the stigma or sounding as though I were discrediting the individuals who have these concerns. Recov-ery is possible and worth the effort to achieve. I have attempted to be realistic and clear and to provide a message of optimism and hopefulness.

Finally, I would like to express my appreciation to the many people who made this book possible. To my husband, a psychologist, who was always willing to discuss and explore the concepts, complexities, and specifics of personality disorders co-occurring with substance use disorders. His ideas and thinking permeate every chapter of the book. To Peter Pociluyko for his generosity in editing the entire man-uscript. His ideas and corrections were invaluable and enormously appreciated. To Bruce Carruth, senior editor, for his support, ideas, and extensive knowledge and understanding of this complex popu-lation. To Ken Minkoff for his support, encouragement, and enthu-siasm. He made it all seem possible. To the many service providers who attended training sessions through the years and challenged me with their questions and allowed me to learn from their experiences. Finally, to the many clients whose courage, resilience, and determination served as my greatest teacher.

Foreword

During the past 10 years, there has been increasing recognition of the importance of addressing the issue of co-occurring mental health and substance use disorders as an expectation in every system, in every program, and in the case load of every clinician. Numerous textbooks, toolkits, research protocols, and manuals have been developed and promulgated to support the delivery of integrated services in all types of settings, and with nearly every type of client. Yet, in spite of this volume of effort, there is one area—until now—that has been significantly neglected: the population of individuals with co-occurring substance dependence and personality disorders. Just as a small example, for the past 10 years, I have regularly compiled and updated a bibliography of the best publications I could find on the treatment of individuals with co-occurring disorders. My most recent update has over 120 citations, but no general references on co-occurring substance use and personality disorders. Given that personality disorders are among the most common co-occurring mental disorders in individuals with substance use disorders, this is particularly striking.

There are no doubt many reasons for personality disorders to be underrepresented in the vast literature on co-occurring disorders. For one thing, it is much easier to discuss how to integrate approaches to Axis I disorders, which commonly respond to psychotropic medications, and which often have a range of specific evidence-based treatments that can be integrated into substance abuse care. Personality disorders are much more resistant to conventional treatment approaches, and, with the exception of dialectic behavior therapy for borderline personality, no widely available and well-known treatment modalities have been applied in the context of substance abuse treatment settings. Equally significant may be the fact that individuals with personality disorders, almost by definition, are more challenging to engage in positive relationships—or to state this another way, are more likely to engender negative feelings on the part of clinicians because of the very nature of their disorders. Consequently, the challenge of integrating services for individuals with personality disorders goes beyond helping the person engage in following a treatment regime (such as medication and symptom management) that will help the person be perceived positively by clinicians. Rather, the challenge involves addressing substance use disorders (which already involve behavior that may engender negative feelings) in the context of a dysfunctional personality style that may seem to be designed to thwart the best efforts of the clinician.

Given the dual challenge of writing about clients with these conditions and without clear or easy methods for "fixing" them, it is easy to see how the topic might be readily avoided. For this reason, I want to take this opportunity to convey my admiration and respect for Sharon Ekleberry and her willingness not only to address this difficult issue, but to address it with the diligence and the passion it deserves.

Sharon has been a leader in the field of dual diagnosis since before there was a field of dual diagnosis and has been accumulating material, strategies, and approaches to the issue of individuals with co-occurring substance use and personality disorders for nearly two decades. As a contributor to the Center for Substance Abuse Treatment's TIP 42, Sharon's work on personality disorders achieved a wider forum for recognition, but still not a place to be delineated in detail.

This work is clearly a labor of love and a product of intense dedication and effort. The book meets the challenge of working with individuals with co-occurring personality disorders. Rather than avoiding the difficulty and negative feelings that these clients stir up, Sharon describes the extent of the difficulty for each personality disorder directly and provides ample background to explain the underlying dynamics that may contribute to the overt behavior that is so frustrating for the clinician and (ultimately) the client alike. What is particularly remarkable is that in the middle of clearly describing negative behaviors, Sharon never loses focus on the importance of empathy and hope, and she never implies that these individuals cannot or should not be helped.

Working through this magnificent volume requires courage on the part of the reader. Anyone using this book has to be willing to be honest about their own feelings and reactions, and be further willing to go beyond those reactions to make contact with the souls of deeply troubled and isolated people, with very dangerous and destructive disorders, in order to reach them, touch them, and help them lead happier lives. Sharon Ekleberry has herself demonstrated enormous courage to produce this work. In so doing, she has provided us with an intellectual framework for such compassion and has herself become a model for such compassion. Let us all have the courage to join her on this path and follow her lead, so that these neglected, rejected, and often despairing individuals can have access to the dual recovery they deserve to achieve and that, with Sharon Ekleberry's guidance, they are able to reach.

Kenneth Minkoff, M.D.
Clinical Assistant Professor,
Harvard University
Senior System Consultant, Zialogic
Albuquerque, NM and San Rafael, CA

1

Integrated Treatment for Individuals with Co-Occurring Personality and Substance Use Disorders

Personality Disorders

Definition of Personality Disorders

Perhaps the most succinct definition of *personality* comes from the saying "wherever you go, there you are." Everyone has a personality style that is made up of personality traits or individualized patterns of behavior, attitudes, and emotions developed early in life in response to the challenges of living. Inherent in these patterns is the potential for flexibility of response, but there is also predictability. People are recognizable from situation to situation and across time (Heim & Westen, 2005; Millon, 1981; Millon & Davis, 1996; Oldham, 2005). Derksen (1995) suggests that the building blocks of the personality are biological, physiological, and genetic influences combined with temperament, environment, and experience.

Personality disorders are diagnosed when personality traits are inflexible and maladaptive and cause impairment in functioning across a wide range of personal and social situations. Individuals with a personality disorder are locked into long-standing cognitive, affective, interpersonal, and impulse-control patterns that lead to repeated antagonistic, disruptive, and self-defeating experiences (APA, 2000). The diagnosis of personality disorder must meet the following criteria:

- There is an enduring pattern that deviates markedly from the person's culture in two or more of the following:
  - Cognition (perception and interpretation)
  - Affect (range, intensity, lability, and appropriateness)
  - Interpersonal functioning
  - Impulse control
- The pattern is inflexible, pervasive, and leads to clinically significant impairment or distress.
- The pattern is of long duration. Onset is in adolescence or early adulthood.
- The pattern is not better accounted for as a consequence of another mental disorder, substance abuse, or medical condition. (APA, 2000)

Cognitive deviation can occur in individuals' perceptions of events or interpretation of those events. For example, individuals with a paranoid personality disorders are often acutely and accurately perceptive of both people and complex situations. However, these individuals tend to engage in the worst possible interpretation of what they perceive. A colleague who does not respond to a "good morning" greeting is being "purposefully" disrespectful rather than preoccupied or in need of that first cup of coffee. The interpretation leads to anger and possibly retaliative behavior that the bewildered colleague is unable to understand.

Affective deviance can be in the range of affect experienced, the intensity of affect, the lability of affect, or the appropriateness of affect. For example, individuals with a borderline personality disorder may experience a full range of affect but do so with a level of intensity that is difficult both for them to manage and for others to understand. For individuals with an avoidant personality disorder, negative feelings are experienced as intense, painful, and intolerable, so much so that avoidance of the precipitant of those feelings becomes fixed behavior.

It is in the realm of relationships or interpersonal functioning that the full cost of personality disorders becomes evident. The destructiveness of the narcissistic personality-disordered parent or the antisocial personality-disordered spouse or partner, the loneliness of the children of avoidant personality-disordered parents, and the hopelessness experienced in a relationship with a passive–aggressive personality-disordered companion are apparent and very painful to people around these individuals. For the personality-disordered individuals themselves, the impact of restricted, controlling, maladroit, or destructive interpersonal behavior varies. For example, people with a depressive personality disorder blame themselves for everything and experience unrelenting sadness in their relationships with others. On the other hand, individuals with narcissistic, antisocial, and passive–aggressive personality disorders absolve themselves of responsibility and comfortably blame others for their problems. Individuals with an obsessive–compulsive personality disorder believe themselves to be right and believe that their relationships would be fine if they could only get others to do what they should be doing. Unfortunately, these responses tend to contaminate understanding and make genuine growth in interpersonal skills difficult to achieve.

Impulse control varies across the personality disorders, from excessive to almost none. Individuals with antisocial or borderline personality disorders are often faced with the consequences of their impulsivity, for example, drinking, drugging, or shoplifting. Those with obsessive–compulsive personality disorders can bring a level of self-discipline to dieting that makes an impulsive cupcake or cookie an impossibility. These individuals are willing to delay gratification for themselves and for the people around them as well. Individuals with passive–aggressive personality disorders do not want to delay gratification and are furious with others who insist that they do so.

The *DSM-IV-TR* (APA, 2000) divides the 10 personality disorders into three clusters. Cluster A, the odd or eccentric cluster, includes paranoid personality disorder (PPD), schizoid personality disorder (SPD), and schizotypal personality disorder (StPD). Cluster B, the dramatic, emotional, or erratic cluster, includes antisocial personality disorder (APD), borderline personality disorder (BPD), histrionic personlaity disorder (HPD), and narcissistic personality disorder (NPD). Cluster C, the anxious or fearful cluster, includes avoidant personality disorder (AvPD), dependent personality disorder (DPD), and obsessive–compulsive personality disorder (OCPD). Appendix B includes depressive personality disorder (DpPD) and passive–aggressive (negativistic) personality disorder (PAPD) as categories needing further research for possible inclusion in the *DSM-V*. Dowson and Grounds (1995) note that the *DSM* categorical approach assumes that some members of each personality disorder are "better" examples of that category than others. A group of individuals who receive a diagnosis of a specific personality disorder are heterogeneous in respect to that disorder because there are many different combinations of the minimum number of positive criteria required.

Prevalence of Personality Disorders

Approximately 13 to 18% of the general population have personality disorders (Weissman, 1993, as cited by Gunderson & Gabbard, 1999). Grant et al. (2004), based on the National Epidemiologic Survey on Alcohol and Related Conditions, cite an overall prevalence of 14.79% of adult Americans with at least one personality disorder. Benjamin (1996) states that over half of the adults in mental health treatment are personality disordered. Tyrer, Casey, and Ferguson (1988) cite studies indicating that 69% of individuals with alcohol dependence and abuse also have a personality disorder. Dowson and Grounds (1995) note a study of alcoholic outpatients in which it was determined that 64% had a personality disorder. Personality disorders are associated with a high rate of consultations for physical symptoms that have no clear diagnosis; up to 34% of patients in primary medical care settings have been identified as having personality disorders. One of the most frequent reasons that primary care physicians refer patients for psychiatric care is the presence of a personality disorder, yet in many instances the referral is made without personality status being identified (Tyrer & Seivewright, 1988).

Treatability of Personality Disorders

Whether or not personality disorders are amenable to treatment is a matter of some controversy. The policies of many treatment programs state categorically that they do not provide services for people with personality disorders. However, these individuals rarely seek treatment for their personality; rather, they seek assistance with anxiety, depression, or legal problems secondary to substance use, so they make up a large percentage of the client population whether it was intended or not. Kane (2006) notes that personality disorders have been largely ignored or denied in psychiatric settings even though personality factors have a major impact on clinical response and outcome.

The National Institute of Mental Health in England (NIMHE) issued a report entitled *Personality Disorder: No Longer a Diagnosis of Exclusion* (2003b), in which it was stated that services will no longer be denied to individuals with personality disorder via the "treatability test." That is, individuals with personality disorder cannot be excluded from services because of a belief among mental health professionals that there is nothing these individuals can be offered that would help them recover and develop an improved ability to cope with everyday life (Kane, 2006). A NIMHE report entitled *Breaking the Cycle of Rejection: The Personality Disorder Capabilities Framework* (2003a) notes that when individuals with personality disorders seek help from community services, they encounter negative and rejecting attitudes from service providers that replicate and compound early life experiences. Only through evidence-based services provided by staff driven by compassion, optimism, and hope can this cycle of rejection be interrupted.

The NIMHE report entitled *The Ten Essential Shared Capabilities: A Framework for the Whole of the Mental Health Workforce* (2003c) describes the qualities and skills required of professionals to treat this client population so that they can respond more appropriately and compassionately, and with less inclination to be judgmental. The essential capabilities for professionals working with personality-disordered clients include:

- Positive collaborative relationship skills
- Respecting and valuing diversity
- Providing ethical and accountable care
- Challenging stigma and discrimination
- Promoting recovery—providing services with hope and optimism
- Negotiating achievable and meaningful goals based upon strengths
- Making a difference—providing evidence-based interventions
- Taking calculated risks to achieve goals
- Pursuing lifelong learning (NIMHE, 2003c)

Personality Disorder: No Longer a Diagnosis of Exclusion (NIMHE, 2003b) goes on to state that the provision of appropriate treatment for people with personality disorders requires clinicians to have system support and system supervision to alleviate burnout and exhaustion.

Substance Use Disorders

Definition and Criteria for Substance Use Disorders

The essential feature of substance abuse is a maladaptive pattern of substance use despite significant adverse consequences leading to clinically significant impairment or distress. One or more of the following must occur within a 12-month period:

- Failure to fulfill major role obligations
- Substance use when it is physically hazardous
- Recurrent substance-related legal problems
- Continued use despite persistent or recurrent social or interpersonal problems (APA, 2000)

The essential features of substance dependence are cognitive, behavioral, and physiological symptoms involving the use of substances, despite serious problems, which lead to clinically significant impairment or distress. It is defined as a maladaptive pattern of substance use that involves three of the following at any time in a 12-month period:

- Tolerance
- Withdrawal
- Use of larger amounts or for longer periods of time than was intended
- Persistent desire or unsuccessful attempts to cut down
- A lot of time spent obtaining, using, or recovering from the use of the substance
- Giving up important activities
- Continued use despite persistent physical or psychological problems that are caused or exacerbated by the substance (APA, 2000).

According to Miller (2006), substance dependence is a problem of motivation. In fact, it is a problem of competing motivations including craving, broken resolutions, restraint, yielding to temptation, compulsion, and loss of control. He believes that a motivational understanding of substance dependence helps make sense of the bewildering interplay of self-defeating and healing behaviors involved in relapse, response to legal trouble, and the transformational change observed in Alcoholics Anonymous (AA).

Unger (1994) suggests that one of the most puzzling and common occurrences in life is the experience of addiction, which he defines as any cycle of repetitive behavior from which people feel unable to free themselves. He suggests that this inclusive view of addiction comprises the "most common mental disorder" (p. 166) and the "most visible aspect of craziness in ordinary life" (p. 166). He describes addiction as:

- The individual experiences a state of diminished freedom.
- The self feels empty when not attached to the object of addiction.
- The condition of enjoyment cannot offer stable contentment.
- The experience of addiction has two mysterious factors:
    - Individuals are not certain why they crave the object of their addiction.
    - The craving is both intensely directed and capable of a sudden and apparently capricious redirection (e.g., switching from alcohol to sexual addiction).

Unger describes individuals with substance dependence or compulsive behaviors as believing that the expression of the addiction, for example, buying a new piece of clothing in a shopping compulsion, will result in satisfying their "most insatiable longings" (p. 167). There is, in fact, temporary satiation that passes quickly into dissatisfaction and the cycle begins again.

In this view, addiction is an intense, directed, changeable longing for a particular drug or experience that seems to promise a state of contentment, bliss, or freedom from craving. It does usually achieve this promise, but only for a short time. The dissatisfaction reignites, craving intensifies, and the drug or behavior once again becomes the most important thing in the lives of addicted individuals. Everything else can and will be sacrificed to access the object of addiction. Certainly, compulsive shopping or compulsive sexual behaviors can meet the criteria of engagement over longer periods of time than intended, persistent desire, preoccupation (i.e., substantial amounts of time involved in planning, experiencing, and recovering from the behavior), giving up other important activities in the dedication to seeking the compulsive behavior, and engagement despite persistent problems caused by or exacerbated by the behavior.

Royce and Scratchley (1996) state that addiction is a state involving the whole person; it is a way of living. Compulsivity, not physical adaptation, is central. They note that pathological gambling shows patterns of brain activity similar to drinking and using psychoactive drugs. The parallels in all addictive behaviors have become more evident as research reveals a common pleasure center in the brain.

The Power and Appeal of Psychoactive Drugs for Individuals with Personality Disorders

The power and appeal of mood-altering drugs has been known to psychiatry for a very long time. Freud described intoxicating substances as making it possible to keep misery at a distance. He believed that psychoactive drugs could not only yield immediate pleasure, but they could provide a greatly desired degree of independence from the external world. With the help of these drugs, anyone can withdraw from the pressures of reality and find refuge in a world that is easier on one's sensibilities than the real world (Khantzian, Halliday, & McAuliffe, 1990). The appeal of such power should be very apparent for individuals with personality disorders who seek an altered reality that, although not psychotic, sets up a world more agreeable or manageable than the reality that exists external to themselves. This changing of reality, for example, the narcissistic conviction that everything they do is admired by others or the avoidant conviction that they unappealing, is one of the most bewildering qualities for those who are in relationships with individuals with personality disorders. To add alcohol or other psychoactive drugs to the situation only enhances the inclination and the ability to ignore or alter aspects of reality that are not acceptable.

Integrated Treatment for Co-Occurring Disorders

The Relationship Between Substance Use Disorders and Personality Disorders

Severe levels of substance use disorders are associated with character pathology. In contrast to individuals without personality disorders, persons with personality disorders:

- Experience greater benefit from the pharmacologically induced effects of psychoactive drug use

- Are more likely to engage in substance use at an earlier age and polydrug use with greater frequency
- Are more vulnerable to having a compulsive and rigid substance use pattern
- Are more likely to develop substance dependence
- Are more vulnerable to relapse
- Have more difficulty working cooperatively and collaboratively with service providers (Beck, Wright, Newman, & Liese, 1993; Nace, 1990).

Ruegg and Frances (1995) suggest that substance misuse by individuals with a personality disorder results in the presence of greater personality disturbance and poorer treatment outcome; long-term abstinence is associated with remission of the personality pathology.

Personality disorders increase vulnerability to substance use disorders. Substance use disorders reduce what adaptability may be found in personality disorders. There are also commonalities between the two:

- Individuals with both personality disorders and substance use disorders use defenses to sustain a maladaptive pattern of preferred behavior and seek a way to escape from the pain of life. They dread the loss of their illusions and often seek others to either exploit or receive care and protection from. Their relationships are marked by a lack of reciprocity or equality. They are capable of betrayals that are devastating to their partners. The misuse of drugs or engaging in compulsive behaviors enhances the shield individuals with personality disorders can use to avoid understanding or accepting the poor fit of their expectations, behaviors, and attitudes to the demands of reality. Living as adults without accepting responsibility for themselves or the consequences of their behavior is a way of pretending that "reality does not apply." The impact of this turning from full adult participation in life results in increasingly severe consequences over time.
- In treatment for both personality disorders and addiction, service providers try to diagnose what clients are denying, minimizing, or trying to hide. Few individuals with substance dependence come into an intake assessment prepared to make a full disclosure of their patterns of substance use. Similarly, few personality-disordered individuals acknowledge their maladaptive and provocative behaviors. Both disorders are misrepresented by client self-report and involve the clients' insistence that the real problem lies elsewhere, usually in how they are being treated by others.

Diagnoses must be substantiated through observation, interpretation, extrapolation, and information from objective (tests) and nonclient (family or significant others) sources.

- Both personality and substance use disorders can be conceptualized as existing on a behavioral continuum from normal to pathological. Where individuals fall on either continuum is a matter of clinical judgment and often a matter of disagreement between the clients and the service providers. Even if the client agrees with the diagnosis (e.g., "Everyone knows I am narcissistic." "I know I drink too much."), the consequences of the behaviors are denied. Somehow, using substances or destructive interpersonal behavior just does not count.

- Personality disorders and substance use disorders frequently exist in multiple form. Individuals may evidence polysubstance use, and, if there were such a word, "polypersonality" disorders as well. Many individuals with a personality disorder meet the criteria for more than one. Clarity is difficult to attain, but recovery in both, in all their forms, requires an engagement in reality on its own terms and acceptance of responsibility for self.

- Individuals with personality disorders are so vulnerable to switching the object of their addiction that it becomes a significant factor in treatment. For example, individuals with borderline personality disorder, in the process of treatment, may become abstinent from psychoactive drug use only to engage compulsively in dangerous sexual behavior. They are not safe, they are not abstinent, and they are not in recovery, although they may have clean urine screens.

Treating one of these disorders without including the other substantially increases the risk for treatment failure. Conversely, improvement in one often has a positive effect on the other. The synergistic effects of treatment success enhance motivation for continuing treatment and pursuing recovery.

Personality Disorder as Primary Diagnosis or Secondary to Substance Use Disorders

In most cases of co-occurring personality and substance use disorders, the personality disorder precedes the substance use disorder. However, substance abuse or dependence may result in a pattern of behaviors that appear to meet the criteria for a personality disorder. Substances can produce a combination of toxic and organic effects on the brain; they can also cause and reinforce regressive behavior. This combination can result in disordered behavior that is secondary to substance abuse or dependence. The effect of chronic use of drugs or alcohol on personality functioning is marked by impulsivity, decreased frustration tolerance, self-centeredness (stubbornness, defiance, lack of empathy), grandiosity, passivity, and affect intolerance (Nace, 1995). Differentiating this drug-induced pathological functioning from a true personality disorder can be challenging. Usually, a thorough history with a focus on onset of symptoms, descriptions of behavior prior to using or during significant periods of abstinence, and input from significant others can assist in making the appropriate diagnoses. Beyond that, observation when abstinence has been achieved will reveal a significant drop in problem behaviors, or they will actually get worse. Generally, increased personality dysfunction during abstinence is an indication of a co-occurring mental health disorder.

It is also important to note that abstinence from psychoactive substances and medication for disorders such as depression or psychosis may reveal the presence of a personality disorder. There have been instances in which both substance dependence and a serious mental illness were being addressed and treatment progress remained frustratingly elusive. For one individual, recovery was repeatedly confounded by an unaddressed histrionic personality disorder. Every disastrous decision made by the individual, which invariably compromised her recovery, came from the attitudes, assumptions, and emotional vulnerability of the untreated personality disorder.

Integrated Treatment for Co-Occurring Personality Disorders and Substance Use Disorders

Integrated dual diagnosis treatment is a complex series of interventions addressing both substance use disorders and personality disorders. It is flexible treatment utilizing the knowledge base and intervention techniques of both mental health and addiction.

Mueser, Noordsy, Drake, and Fox (2003) propose that the principles of treatment for co-occurring disorders include integration, comprehensiveness, assertiveness, reduction of negative consequences, a long-term perspective, motivation-based treatment, and multiple psychotherapeutic modalities.

- **Integration:** Individuals with personality disorders and addiction are much more likely to achieve recovery when the services are integrated by the providers. Treatment that is consecutive or parallel requires clients, essentially, to serve as their own case managers. They must put the differing perspectives of substance abuse and mental health treatment into a coherent whole that supports them as they achieve recovery from both disorders.
- **Comprehensiveness:** Individuals are not alike in the type, severity, and level of dysfunction in their personality disorder or their addiction. Most require a wide range of services that change over time and level of recovery.
- **Assertiveness:** Unless personality-disordered dually diagnosed clients have legal consequences that mandate treatment, engaging these individuals can be very challenging. A flexible approach, utilizing outreach when necessary, can make a significant difference. On the other hand, depending on the personality disorder, service providers must avoid "doing all the work" while their personality-disordered dually diagnosed clients remain noncompliant with treatment requirements. This is a process of both responding with incentives for treatment and setting limits on client behavior.
- **Reduction of Negative Consequences:** It is imperative to assist individuals with paranoid, schizoid, schizotypal, borderline, avoidant, dependent, depressive, and obsessive–compulsive personality disorders to manage and limit the negative consequences of their behavior. For individuals with antisocial, histrionic, narcissistic, and passive–aggressive personality disorders, negative consequences may be the only effective leverage to bring them into the treatment process. This does not mean the process of treatment engagement does not apply, nor does it absolve service providers from developing skills in connecting to and motivating these clients. It means some individuals need, as is said in Alcoholics Anonymous, to "go back out and do more research" before they can accept treatment. The balance is a delicate one and requires a precision in diagnosing and observing the clients' responses and behaviors to determine what is the best possible approach to engage them in recovery behaviors.
- **Long-Term Perspective:** According to Mueser et al. (2003), this principle relates to the need for time-unlimited services. This is important, as both substance dependence and personality disorders are persistent and involve the ongoing risk of relapse. Adler (1990) referred to the personality-disordered treatment population as "chronic, non-psychotic clients." Treatment, to be effective, needs to be both integrated and not limited by number

of sessions. Unfortunately, public funding and private insurance are still inclined to see these individuals as at fault for both of their disorders and want treatment to be as brief and inexpensive as possible. Progress has been made in seeing addiction as a treatable disorder, but many people still believe that these individuals can "just say no." As for personality disorders, because these individuals range from being annoying to intolerable to other people, blame accrues to them for their behavior in a manner that is not currently common for individuals with serious mental illness.

- **Motivation-Based Treatment:** It is essential to work with the personality-disordered dually diagnosed clients according to their readiness for change, ambivalence, fear of change, and level of motivation. Otherwise, some of these individuals are likely to engage in intense and destructive power struggles that they will win by losing. They will sabotage their own progress to demonstrate that no one can tell them what to do or that the service providers are incompetent. They may end up "celebrating" their victory in a hospital or jail.

- **Multiple Psychotherapeutic Modalities**: Treatment should be offered for these individuals in as many formats as needed. Individual, group, family, multifamily, medication services, and facilitated involvement in peer support groups may all be useful at different points in their recovery.

Recovery from Personality and Substance Use Disorders

Treatment is what professionals offer; recovery is the personal journey that individuals undertake for themselves. Interventions that facilitate and promote recovery assist dually diagnosed individuals to develop long-term sustaining activities that will help them consolidate gains made in treatment. Recovery from co-occurring personality and substance use disorders is a process of change through which individuals achieve improved health, wellness, and quality of life. It is a journey of personal growth, gaining strength, understanding, and wisdom. Recovery requires hope, responsibility, diligence, daily involvement, and action (Hendrickson, Schmal, & Ekleberry, 2004). Daley and Thase (1995) propose that co-occurring recovery also involves realistic expectations, active participation, honesty, patience, persistence, self-reflection, commitment, accepting help, making mistakes and learning from them, and building inner strength.

2

Cluster A
Paranoid Personality Disorder and Substance Use Disorders

Paranoid Personality Disorder Defined

Essential Features

An essential feature of paranoid personality disorder (PPD) is a pattern of pervasive distrust and suspiciousness of others (APA, 2000). Prominent features of PPD include hypersensitivity to signs of deception and an inclination to stay free of relationships in which the power of self-determination might be compromised (Millon & Grossman, 2007a). Individuals with PPD demonstrate a cognitive rigidity that isolates them from corrective environmental feedback; they become increasingly convinced that their distorted worldview is accurate as they do battle with the hostile forces they see around them.

Paranoia can be seen as existing on a continuum that goes from normal vigilance toward potential threat in the environment to transitory paranoid behavior and interpersonal suspiciousness (PPD) to delusional states to full paranoid schizophrenia. The personality disorder is distinguished from the psychotic disorders by the lack of delusions and hallucinations (Sperry, 2003). It is less clear when wariness and suspiciousness have become severe enough to be considered a personality disorder. Vigilance can and should be heightened when there is potential for personal danger; it is a survival behavior in war and times of political unrest. There was a poster in the 1960s that said, "Just because you are paranoid doesn't mean that people aren't out to get you!" It was a rather humorous take on the need for "paranoia" when in conflict with authorities.

The dilemma in naming a personality disorder "paranoid" is that paranoia is a symptom of several Axis I and Axis II disorders. Rawlings and Freeman (1997) note that at least five mental disorders contain paranoia constructs: PPD, schizotypal personality disorder, borderline personality disorder, the paranoid type of schizophrenia, and the persecutory type of delusional disorder. Symptoms of paranoia can also be associated with the use of various substances and must be distinguished from chronic cocaine use. It has been suggested that PPD be renamed the "vigilant" (Millon, 1981) personality disorder to make the Axis II variant easier to separate from the psychotic disorders on Axis I. Peter Pociluyko has suggested the term *hypervigilant* to differentiate the personality disorder from nonpathological vigilance (personal communication, July 2007).

In clinical settings, individuals with PPD can be misdiagnosed as having an antisocial personality disorder and approached with misguided confrontation that ignites their inclination to fight authority even at the expense of severe negative consequences. These individuals have left treatment programs that required going back to jail just to demonstrate that service providers cannot push them around. The arrogance, secretiveness, and hostile style of people with PPD can be misconstrued as antisocial disdain for regulations when it is actually the intense conviction that authority is corrupt and controlling and must be stopped.

Whereas the *DSM-IV-TR* (APA, 2000) states that the prevalence of PPD is up to 2.5% in the general population and is more commonly diagnosed in males, Grant et al. (2004) note, in the National Epidemiologic Survey on Alcohol and Related Conditions, that PPD is the second most prevalent personality disorder (4.41%) in adult Americans and that the risk is significantly greater among women than men.

Self-Image

Individuals with PPD experience a polarity in their self-image. Even though their behavior may be grandiose and arrogant, with persistent ideas of self-importance (Millon & Grossman, 2007a), they are vulnerable to shame and alternate between the impotent, despised self and the omnipotent, vindicated self (McWilliams, 1994). They are secretive about this vulnerability; they do not want others to know it exists.

Individuals with PPD view themselves as blameless and mistreated (Beck, Freeman, & Davis, 2004). They try to exert power over others by declaring themselves to be irreproachable and seeing themselves as fighting on the side of the angels. They are vengeful and pursue conflict with great tenacity, never seeming to tire in their quest for self-vindication; they acquire an inordinate fondness for righteous causes (Kantor, 1992).

View of Others

Individuals with PPD assume others will exploit, control, or deceive them; they are preoccupied with doubts about the loyalty of others and often feel that people have deeply and irreversibly injured them (APA, 2000). These individuals are consumed by their mistrust and their anticipation of treachery and betrayal. They expect the worst of others and are apprehensive, suspicious, uncompromising, and argumentative. They are on guard against a hostile world (Beck et al., 2004; Oldham & Morris, 1995). The motives of others are routinely interpreted as malevolent; for example, individuals with this personality disorder may assume that a compliment on a new outfit is a criticism of how they usually dress. Even offers of assistance can be misinterpreted as meaning that they are helpless or feeble. A man with PPD at a supermarket, when asked if he needed help with loading his groceries into this car, was furious because he thought the employee asking the question (a store policy) was suggesting that he was too old and too weak to do it on his own.

Relationships

Relationships are problematic for individuals with PPD. They are argumentative and can easily provoke hostility in others. They engage in hair-trigger responses to trivial behavior (Kantor, 1992) and are antagonistic and sarcastic toward those who betray or disappoint them (APA, 2000; Meissner, 1994). These individuals are frequently domineering (Matano & Locke, 1995), inordinately quick to take offense, slow to forgive, and ever willing to counterattack (Fenigstein, 1996). They expect that friends and associates will attack or ignore them when they need help (APA, 2000). In fact, relationships may become so difficult that they convince themselves they are the masters of their own fate and can go it alone (Millon & Grossman, 2007a).

In family relationships, individuals with PPD may demonstrate their fear of the world by being overly restrictive of their partners' or children's activities. They may limit who can visit their home and can easily get into escalating arguments with neighbors about property lines, trees, noise, or other aggravating behaviors.

The diagnosis of PPD contains a wide range of levels of dysfunction and severity. Some individuals with PPD are sufficiently functional to be able to preserve relatively cohesive relationships. Many authors note the possibility of individuals with PPD with symptoms that manifest at a level of subtlety that allow them to function within a marriage and maintain adequate, if tenuous, work relationships.

Issues with Authority

Individuals with PPD have recurrent conflicts with authority figures. They fear domination and loss of independence. McWilliams (1994) suggests that individuals with PPD are vulnerable to shame and humiliation as a result of parental criticism and punishment; many people with PPD grew up around adults who could not be pleased. Individuals with PPD, as adults, attempt to exert interpersonal power to avoid the anticipated destructive consequences coming from interaction with people in authority (Meissner, 1994). They are inclined to engage people they see as having influence in a series of complaints, contentious confrontations, and litigation. They welcome opportunities to force people in authority, in particular, to admit they were wrong. An individual with PPD and alcoholism, who worked for a towing company, was incensed with a man who was attempting to reclaim his car. The car should not have been towed; it had diplomatic plates. In refusing to release the car unless the fines were paid, the individual with PPD stated emphatically that diplomats should have to park legally like everyone else. He was so outraged that he had a fight with both the diplomat and the local police; he was arrested for assault and found himself in court, where he argued so vehemently and relentlessly about the unfairness of the immunity granted to individuals with diplomatic license plates that the judge found him to be in contempt and he spent a few days in jail. When he talked about the event several years later, he clearly still relished the chance to take on the legal system and show them the error of their ways. Going to jail was a small price to pay for being "right." These individuals interpret negative consequences that arise from their own actions as further proof that those around them are malicious and corrupt. This is so dominant a feature in PPD that Benjamin (1996) considers deferential behavior with authorities to be an exclusionary criterion for the diagnosis of PPD.

Behavior

Paranoid traits may be manifest to some degree in a significant portion of the normal population. Indications of a paranoid style are frequently quite subtle; the paranoid features may form a latent portion of the personality that emerges under stress (Meissner, 1994). McWilliams (1994) writes that individuals with PPD can have any level of ego strength, identity integration, reality testing, and object relations. They are often seen as energetic, ambitious, hard-working, and competent. They tend to be intellectual as well as inflexible, stubborn, and unwilling to compromise.

However, the more disturbed these individuals are, or the more severe the paranoid personality disorder, the more dangerous their behavior can be (McWilliams, 1994). They may be easily aroused to agitated contentiousness. They can appear tense, guarded, and ready to counterattack. They are inclined to criticize and devalue others, yet any criticism of them is unacceptable.

Beck et al. (2004) note that whereas individuals with PPD anticipate betrayal and deceit from others, they may be deceptive, hostile, disloyal, and malicious themselves. They displace responsibility from self to others via an inclination to project and to blame. They tend to define and understand problems in terms of external circumstances, forces, and persons rather than in terms of internal difficulties, problems, or limitations. They then scan the environment for minimal clues that validate their preconceived ideas (Meissner, 1994).

Overall, behaviors associated with the paranoid personality disorder are:

- Vindictiveness and suspiciousness
- Irritability
- Hypervigilance
- Resentment of authority
- A strong reaction to humiliation
- A tense and abrasive style
- Self-righteousness and arrogance
- Exaggerated competitiveness
- A fondness for righteous causes
- Grandiose rescue fantasies
- An unusually strong need to be self-sufficient and independent
- Difficulty expressing warmth
- Pathological jealousy (Beck et al., 2004; Fenigstein, 1996; Kantor, 1992; Stone, 1993)

Affect

Underneath the abrasive and arrogant behavior of individuals with paranoid personality disorder lies fear, self-righteous rage, and dread. The hostile environment in which they believe they live places them in constant jeopardy. At times they may believe they can protect themselves, but often, although they will not admit it openly, they are afraid and unsure. They can rarely relax, and contentment or satisfaction eludes them. The more they have of what they want in life, the more vigilant they must become. They ward off the (sometimes real, sometimes projected) envy and maliciousness of others who might want to take anything of value for themselves. Only when they can believe they have a situation under control is an element of safety introduced into their affective experience. This is a powerful motivator and should be considered in any attempt to confront these individuals in the treatment process.

Defenses

Individuals with PPD are uncomfortable with dependency and become anxious when coerced by external authority. Their defensive structure requires an ongoing experience of independence, superiority, and autonomy (Millon & Davis, 1996). They may react to empathic statements from service providers with a powerful, punishing anger if they experience gentleness and support as demeaning and infantilizing. Or they may simply become condescending about what they perceive as the "feel good" approach of mental health clinicians.

These individuals actively disown undesirable personal traits and motives by projecting them onto or attributing them to others. Even while people with PPD avoid awareness of their own unattractive behaviors and characteristics, they remain extraordinarily alert to, and hypercritical of, similar features in other people.

Individuals with PPD engage in an active fantasy wherein they create a self-enhanced image and a rewarding existence apart from others (Millon & Davis, 1996). Their fantasies ameliorate their loneliness and impoverished relationships.

Individuals with PPD maintain their sense of balance, internal and external, through rigid adherence to an inelastic set of defenses and methods of need gratification. Extreme or unanticipated stress can precipitate a crisis that is out of proportion to the situation (Millon & Davis, 1996). They are determined to control themselves, people, and events to reduce stress and enhance security.

The Self-Created World (Altered Reality) of PPD

Individuals with PPD create and sustain an altered reality that, although not psychotic, sustains their beliefs about themselves and others. This reality keeps the world at a distance (much as psychoactive drugs do) and allows a perception of continuity and predictability to exist at the expense of authenticity and relatedness to others. For individuals with paranoid personality disorder, the altered reality is composed of believing that:

- Being on the side of the angels gives them the right to fight corrupted authority.
- People should pay for what they do or try to do.
- No one can surprise you if you see him coming.
- People have to be watched; they will exploit and deceive if not stopped.
- "Never let them see you bleed" is good advice.
- Trusting others is a way to self-destruct.
- Differentiating good people from bad people is not too hard when you know that everyone is only out for himself; whoever said "kill

them all and let God sort them out" knew what he was talking about.

• People will respect what they fear; being soft only lets people do what they want and take what they want.

Substance Use Disorders and PPD

Co-Occurring Substance Use Disorders and the Impact of Drugs on PPD

Individuals with PPD have one important mitigating factor against vulnerability to addiction: They fear the loss of control that accompanies drug use, detoxification, and withdrawal. Some of these individuals may also resist drug involvement due to the intensified sense of mistrust and vulnerability accompanying drug acquisition (Hendrickson et al., 2004).

On the other hand, there are individuals with PPD who are both strong and capable enough to survive in the world of dealing drugs. In this case, they may also be contemptuous of the weakness demonstrated by individuals addicted to drugs. It would never be a good idea to try to cheat or steal from a drug dealer with a PPD.

However, the aversion to loss of control may not protect individuals with PPD from drug use if their paranoid defenses break down or become less effective against the direct experience of vulnerability, weakness, inferiority, and inadequacy (Meissner, 1994). If alcohol, methamphetamine, or cocaine, for example, reinstates the paranoid defenses, and these individuals can reliably control or avert descent into feelings of despair and worthlessness, then addiction becomes a substantial risk. The more fragile the inner organization of the paranoid personality-disordered individual, the more need there is for stabilization from external sources. Drugs and alcohol can be the answer to the wish to be "someone" and to feel powerful (Meissner, 1994). Stimulant drugs can ignite their own paranoid thinking. Yudofsky (2005) states that dependence on alcohol and other drugs compounds the disabling symptoms of individuals with PPD and that treatment of these comorbid conditions constitutes a therapeutic priority.

Drugs of Choice for PPD

Amphetamines were given to Japanese, English, and American World War II combat soldiers to allow them to ignore fatigue, have a sense of invulnerability, and heighten their inclination toward aggression (Kuhn, Swartzwelder, & Wilson, 1998; Winger, Hofmann, & Woods, 1992). In a sense, individuals with a PPD are at war with the world. The effects of any of the central nervous system stimulants will help these individuals feel alert and strong enough to be effective in their own unending personal battles. Unfortunately, use of stimulants can also exacerbate paranoid thinking and misinterpretation of the level of threat in the environment.

Richards (1993) suggests that drugs of choice for individuals with PPD will intensify self-aggrandizement; these include cocaine, marijuana, amphetamines, extreme alcohol intoxication, or chronic alcohol abuse. Benjamin (1996) also notes PPD attraction to the "dominance drugs," for example, alcohol, cocaine, and amphetamines, because they give a sense of power and control. These drugs easily impart the longed-for sensations without requiring that the user demonstrate the social skills and awareness of social complexities that would implement interpersonal dominance in reality; they offer an illusory short-cut to power.

Should these individuals be attracted to central nervous system depressants such as heroin or benzodiazepines, they are likely to use only in familiar environments or when they are alone, so that the loss of capacity to be vigilant does not become overwhelmingly threatening. Soothing fear and tension with these drugs may offer relief from the unending vigilance and the energy it requires.

Integrated Dual Diagnosis Treatment for PPD

Engaging in Treatment

Few individuals with a Cluster A personality disorder are inclined to seek treatment. The fact that many individuals with PPD come in for services as a result of pressure from their families or involvement with the legal system can serve as a potential tool for engaging them in treatment. They may be inclined to accept substance abuse treatment to acquire freedom from external sources of constraint, that is, the presence of probation officers in their lives. Service providers can point out loss of autonomy as a negative impact of drug and alcohol use. Such an approach can initiate the process of motivational interviewing so that these individuals can come to see and accept the reality of their circumstances and the need for and the benefit of change (Miller & Rollnick, 2002).

Treatment Provider Guidelines

Beck et al. (2004) believe that a key issue for individuals with PPD coming into treatment is the fear of being manipulated, controlled, or demeaned. Any experience of mistreatment, particularly from those who are seen as powerful, will be interpreted as intentional and malicious—and deserving of retaliation. Therefore, the challenge is to engage clients with PPD in collaborative working relationships based upon trust. Even though the development of a working alliance can be difficult, many individuals with PPD are able to attach to and trust services providers when their (inevitable) testing behavior is met with honesty, openness, and a willingness to interpret anger without behaving with hostility. These individuals may ask questions when they know the answers; evasion or deflection will result in suspicion and failure to establish rapport.

One man with PPD, noting that his therapist was distracted and sleepy during a session, said nothing, only to return a week later with the statement: "You weren't doing too well last week, were you?" The therapist, sensing that the answer to this question was important, said: "No, and I am sorry. It was hot in the office and I was not feeling very well last week. I apologize for not saying something at the time. I'm fine now and can give you my undivided attention today." The PPD client relaxed and said nothing further—during that session or any other. All he needed was to know whether the therapist would be honest or attempt to refute the client's observation with something like, "I wonder why you would feel I was not there for you" or any other interpretation that implied the client could not see what was right before his eyes. Because the therapist acknowledged the problem and apologized, the client was able to be a little more trusting.

Direct confrontation and refutation of paranoid assertions are counterproductive. Rather, clinicians can introduce an element of doubt, for example, half-agree but half-wonder if a more benign interpretation of the world or the event could be made (Stone, 1993). Agreeing but suggesting alternatives can also help the service provider avoid "knowing too much." Clients with PPD will not necessarily welcome skilled interpretation. They may feel uncomfortably transparent and see the service providers as intrusive. Richards (1993) points out that too much insight may be seen as sadistic by individuals with PPD and result in retreat or retaliation toward clinicians. A not infrequent paranoid response to a skilled interpretation from a talented clinician is, "Who told you that?" It can be intolerable to them to think that they allowed service providers to see what they believed they could keep hidden from sight.

Benjamin (1996) notes that harshness must not be met with harshness, even though these individuals are exceptionally able to provoke hostility from others. Moreover, service providers need to find a manageable method to call these clients' attention to their provocativeness, or they will continue to be on the receiving end of anger and abuse from others. Service providers must be able to calmly accept these clients' powerful hostility, maintain strict boundaries, and allow their own personal strengths to be conveyed in the treatment process (McWilliams, 1994).

Professional Ethics and the Paranoid Personality Disorder

Individuals with PPD, among all the personality disorders, need the most interpersonal distance from others because of their fear of the consequences and hidden motives of attachment behavior (Richards, 1993). Given the inclination these individuals have toward litigation, service providers must adhere to strict boundaries and conservatively interpreted ethical behavior as they attempt to develop a therapeutic relationship. The vigilance of these clients allows them to observe any fault or failure on the part of service providers, and they are inclined to vindicate themselves through the search for retribution. Breaking or bending the rules, for whatever reason, could lead to serious consequences for those working with clients with PPD.

One individual with PPD and alcohol dependence, a man who completed his law degree but was never able to pass the bar exam, set aside one bedroom in the small two-bedroom apartment he lived in with his wife and small son strictly as an office that contained all the paperwork on all the lawsuits he currently had in active status. His small son had his bed placed in the first bedroom, where his parents slept. Because he had been referred for both mental health and substance abuse treatment from Child Protective Services (CPS) following abuse of his son, and he had already filed a lawsuit against the social service agency, there was little doubt that he would find some reason to sue his new treatment providers. When working with this man or other individuals with PPD, clinicians would do well to ask themselves if their actions, decisions, behaviors, documentation, treatment planning, and treatment reviews are items that they would feel comfortable discussing in court.

Because these individuals tend to be abrasive, arrogant, and self-important, service providers can tire of the demand to be supportive without showing reactivity to the hostility. Peer supervision or consultation can assist in maintaining balance toward PPD dynamics. Nonreactivity, however, does not mean allowing individuals with PPD to behave abusively toward service providers. Limits should be set on PPD behavior. Nonreactivity means not meeting aggression with aggression; it means interpreting the PPD behavior without hostility, anxiousness, or a punishing affect.

Assessment and Treatment

Individuals with PPD are so reactive to confrontation that they may leave treatment despite potential negative consequences, for example, violation of probation and a return to jail. One dually diagnosed woman with PPD and drug addiction (assessment done by previous providers) stormed out of an intake session at a mental health center saying loudly in the lobby on her way out, apparently to no one in particular, "I'd rather be in jail than put up with your (expletive–expletive)!" She meant it and, indeed, did go back to jail. When people are willing to bring harm upon themselves in a determined effort to control the behavior of service providers, it can be very difficult to engage them in a collaborative relationship. Therefore, assessment must be done with both a careful approach and nonprovocative wording. Direct and early confrontation will provoke hostility and escalation of dysfunctional defenses.

It may be difficult to identify the intolerance and self-destructive response to confrontation in these clients because they can so easily confront others. They do not appear particularly fragile. On the contrary, they can appear tough and antisocial. Because substance abuse assessment requires direct questions about drug and alcohol use, assessing the individuals' tolerance for seeing themselves in a negative light is important. People with PPD may develop, in response to confrontation, an intractable view of service providers as being of malicious intent and impossible to trust. The damage can be considerable and both assessment and treatment rendered ineffective. It is preferable to guide these individuals to talk about their experiences with substance use by reflecting back to them what they have said and asking them what these experiences were like for them, for example, blackouts.

Early in treatment, individuals with PPD may respond most constructively to a psychoeducational approach that limits personal issues to self-reflection rather than sharing with others. Providing education regarding drugs and alcohol may initiate a cognitive recognition and acceptance for individuals with PPD that they do not want these substances in their lives doing them harm—all without confrontation or igniting paranoid defenses.

Sperry and Carlson (1993) note that antipsychotic medications, particularly those selected for their impact on delusional disorders, may be helpful. Janicak, Davis, Preskorn, & Ayd (1993) state that there have been a few controlled studies and anecdotal information that low-dose antipsychotics may benefit individuals with PPD when used in conjunction with therapy. SSRIs (selective serotinin reuptake inhibitors) have been effective for the symptoms of suspiciousness and irritability (Sperry & Carlson, 1993). However, it is likely that individuals with PPD will distrust medication and respond quite negatively to unpleasant side effects. It is not likely that these individuals will be compliant with a suggestion that they take antipsychotic medication. They would be more inclined to take antidepressants if they are experiencing depression. Pressuring these individuals to accept medication they dislike or distrust would not be beneficial to them or facilitate the treatment process. Unless the symptoms are so severe that other treatment modalities are ineffective, medication may best be left for consideration only when the clients with PPD ask about it for specific target symptoms.

Treatment Goals

Although individuals with PPD may need help with feelings of infe-riority and vulnerability to shame, this focus in treatment may be intolerable. It is more likely to be acceptable to form treatment goals to increase a sense of competence and effectiveness. It is important, though, that treatment goals be stated in terms of positive gains for self rather than changing behaviors aimed against others, for example, to stand up for self against unreasonable and impossible people. Although this may seem like a good idea to these clients, the conceptualization of the goal invites paranoid interpretation of the behavior of others.

Goals of treatment do need to include increasing benignity of per-ception and interpretation of reality; in particular, these individu-als need to learn to interpret interpersonal cues without distortion and preconceived conclusions (Sperry & Carlson, 1993). They must reduce their use of "anticipatory retaliation"; they elicit hostility and counter-aggression in others when they engage in preemptive strike behaviors (Benjamin, 1996).

In co-occurring disorders treatment, individuals with PPD may be inclined to work toward abstinence to regain autonomy. Freedom from legal constraints or the reduced potential for loss of a relation-ship can become a motivator for abstinence. Service providers might ask, "What will the judge or your partner need to see to be convinced that you no longer need treatment? What would have to be different to persuade them?"

Some treatment programs require abstinence as a prerequisite for treatment. Other programs are structured so that relapse, or sub-stance use, results in termination from treatment. Both approaches are likely to be less than helpful for addicted paranoid personality-disordered individuals. Abstinence as a prerequisite for treatment may result in a failure to engage; individuals with PPD resist domi-nation, and such an ultimatum may send them into a flight toward autonomy; that is, "You can't tell me what to do." Discharge for use is likely to be interpreted as an abuse of power and seriously inter-fere with the rapport needed for successful reengagement in the treatment process. Use must be addressed, but, most effectively, in terms of the power the psychoactive drugs and alcohol have, and that strength and resolve must be brought to the process of recovery. It is important that the service providers and individuals with PPD form an alliance against the betrayal of alcohol and other drugs; power struggles must be avoided regarding use of substances. Programs that have sufficient flexibility to utilize harm reduction techniques can give these individuals time to trust the service providers and to realize that the treatment goals actually do address what is best for their well-being.

Recovery Activities for Individuals with PPD and Addiction

Matano and Locke (1995) note that addicted clients with PPD have a hard time relinquishing autonomy and control to a higher power in AA. These individuals may also have difficulty being in groups where people are sharing personal information and they are expected to do the same. Service providers can share examples of people listening to and learning from others who have developed the internal strength to achieve and maintain sobriety. If taking in information works best, then that too can be a valuable path to recovery. No one is required to share when it is uncomfortable.

In contrast to reliance on an external source of strength, Richards (1993) believes that individuals with PPD may be able to leverage considerable self-control against urges to use once engaged in recovery and stabilized. This may appear contradictory to the principles of the recovery community, that is, the importance of turning to a power greater than the self. However, if individuals with PPD are intolerant of dependency or feel too crowded by attachment to groups, self-help or self-generated strength may be enough, or may be the best that individual has to bring to a program of recovery.

3

Cluster A

Schizoid Personality Disorder and
Substance Use Disorders

Schizoid Personality Disorder Defined

Essential Features

According to the *Diagnostic and Statistical Manual of Mental Disorders*, IV-text revision (*DSM-IV-TR*; APA, 2000), an essential feature of schizoid personality disorder (SPD) is a pervasive pattern of social detachment and restricted expression of emotions. These individuals appear to lack a desire for physical intimacy or sexual experiences. They spend time alone and select activities that do not include interaction with others. They may have particular difficulty expressing anger, even when directly provoked. They often react passively to adverse situations and may not respond appropriately to important life events. These individuals may experience brief psychotic episodes in response to stress. The most frequent co-occurring personality disorders with SPD are schizotypal, paranoid, and avoidant personality disorders (AuPD). Whereas the *DSM-IV-TR* states that SPD is diagnosed with slightly more frequency in males, the 2001–2002 National Epidemiologic Survey (Grant, et al., 2004) states that there was no sex difference in the risk of SPD.

Both the *DSM-IV-TR* (APA, 2000) and Bowler (2007) note that there can be substantial difficulty differentiating individuals with SPD from those with Asperger's disorder. It is suggested that, although there is extensive overlap between the two, individuals with Asperger's disorder show more severely impaired social interaction and more stereotyped behaviors. Asperger's disorder is noted for the development of restricted, repetitive behaviors and a lack of social reciprocity that is not so much based upon indifference or lack of interest, but is manifested by an eccentric determination to pursue a specific topic regardless of the interests of the other people involved in the conversation.

Self-Image

Beck et al. (2004) suggest that individuals with SPD view themselves as loners who prize independence and solitude. There is some question as to whether or not schizoid withdrawal from others is preferred or is generated from interpersonal anxiety. If the apparent lack of overt interpersonal anxiety is covertly experienced, the differentiation between SPD and AuPD becomes more problematic. SPD is currently defined by imperviousness to joy, anger, or sadness, inability to experience pleasure, and low interest or involvement with self or others (Millon & Grossman, 2007a). Individuals with APD, on the other hand, control affect, withdraw from pleasurable activities, and avoid others in the name of anxiety management. Both may seek isolation, but individuals with SPD tolerate the separation with comfort, and individuals with AuPD are distressed, agitated, and lonely (Millon, 1981).

Millon and Grossman (2007a) believe that individuals with SPD are complacent, with little awareness of their feelings. Although there may be minimal anxiety, Magnavita (1997) notes that people with SPD recognize their differences from others. He described a client with SPD who was distressed by the thought that there was something wrong with him; he could not enjoy life and seemed to be living inside of a shell. This individual knew that he troubled his wife with his quietness. Siever (1986) describes individuals with SPD in treatment who say that life passes them by; they see themselves as "missing the bus" and complain of observing life from a distance. Akhtar (1992) suggests that the individuals with SPD have a self-concept that may be overtly compliant, noncompetitive, and self-sufficient, but they may covertly see themselves as cynical, inauthentic, and depersonalized.

View of Others

The presence of other people does not appear to bring solace or comfort to individuals with SPD. People are a source of demands, unmet needs, and intrusion. These individuals prefer solitude; their comfort and peace come from involvement in activities without the added complexity of relating to others. Even if individuals with SPD believe it is expedient to fit in with others, they tend to feel awkward; they want to maintain a safe distance from the rest of humanity (McWilliams, 1994).

One residential program within a large mental health center in an urban community placed two women with borderline personality disorder (BPD) with a third woman with SPD in a supported living situation. These women were not able to get along, and soon the two women with BPD became unwilling to have the "odd" roommate continue to live with them. The two women with BPD could not understand nor could they accept that the third individual was bewildered by their demands to socialize. She preferred watching television alone in her room and would try to avoid excessive interaction with her lively and emotionally demanding roommates. The experiential and expressive emotional differences between them created a chasm too wide and too unnerving to allow them to sustain the living arrangement. To the woman with SPD, her roommates were demanding, angry, domineering, and critical people who refused to leave her in peace. She was glad, in the end, to move out of that apartment.

Another woman with SPD shared an apartment with a roommate in a situation that worked out very well. They worked different shifts; one worked during the day and was home in the evening; the other worked in the evening and was home during the day. They were able to go days without seeing each other, and both were satisfied with the arrangement.

Relationships

Individuals with SPD have a profound defect in their ability to respond to others in an emotionally meaningful way (Frances, First,

& Pincus, 1995). They are aloof, introverted, and reclusive; they appear interpersonally indifferent, unengaged, and remote. Social communication is perfunctory and formal (Millon, 1996). Magnavita (1997) suggests that this distance from others restricts individuals with SPD in their capacity to receive feedback—the information that could increase their self-awareness and allow them to grow in their capacity to relate.

Individuals with SPD evidence little desire for sexual experiences. They may marry but then are sexually apathetic with their partners (despite being functional and orgasmic). Sex can mean closeness and enmeshment. For these individuals, abandonment is a lesser evil than engulfment; personal space can become a greater need than maintaining relationships with the people they care about (McWilliams, 1994). Guntrip (1969; as cited in Akhtar, 1992) suggests that individuals with SPD feel lost without the people to whom they are attached, but when they are with them, feel swallowed, smothered, and absorbed. Thus, these individuals seek relationships for security but break out again to gain freedom and independence. Clearly, individuals with SPD are going to be most comfortable with others who demand little intimacy and make few emotional demands. Kantor (1992) believes that true SPD involves reticence and interpersonal withdrawal because of anhedonia, that is, the compromised capacity for relating due to an inability to anticipate or experience joy in human relationships. They may live or work in a group setting, for example, religious or counterculture groups, which allows them to maintain superficial contact without intimacy (Siever, 1986). Dietary and health fads and philosophical movements that do not require personal involvement can be engrossing to individuals with SPD. They may become very attached to animals (Sadock & Sadock, 2004).

Although individuals with SPD can form enduring relationships with people who are assertive enough to get past their reticence, they do not fully participate in those relationships. One man, married to a woman who had been diagnosed with SPD, commented that living with her is "almost as good as living alone." Another man with SPD, while being assessed in an alcohol and drug program, reported that he set up a room in the basement of the home he shares with his wife and children so he could be alone and smoke marijuana. This is the identical pattern he had as an adolescent when he withdrew to his basement bedroom every evening for the same reasons. He states that his wife, a member of AA, "does all the people stuff." He has very limited sexual contact with his wife and simply refuses to participate in any social activities she may plan or suggest.

Issues with Authority

Individuals with SPD do not frequently come in contact with society's authority figures. They are inclined to go their own way but do so without obvious defiance or a need to demonstrate their independence. Thus, they may be nonconforming but keep a low enough profile to avoid sanctions, whether at work or in society in general. They feel themselves free of any particular internal pressure to do as others do or follow the rules made and enforced by others. They just have no need to point this out to authority and trigger sanctions. The intent is not defiance; it is detachment from the need to please others or conform to social norms. On the other hand, they are quite sensitive to intrusion and withdraw from external pressure when possible.

Behavior

Beck et al. (2004) state that individuals with SPD appear dull, uninteresting, and humorless to others; they are often ignored. Whereas their speech is laconic and meager, what they say is rarely abnormal (Kantor, 1992).

Individuals with SPD are unaware of the feelings and thoughts of others. Although they are not intentionally unkind, they appear to be unresponsive to praise, criticism, or feelings expressed by others. They are preoccupied with tangential matters and seem to have a fundamental incapacity to sense the needs of the people around them. They do not need to communicate and are generally under-responsive to most forms of stimulation or reinforcement. When others relate or attempt to get to know people with SPD, they are frequently bewildered by the nonresponse and benign indifference they encounter (Frances et al., 1995; Millon, 1996; Millon & Grossman, 2007a).

Individuals with SPD may live as adults with their elderly parents without significant discomfort, interaction, or concern. If they have jobs that suit them, they can stay for many years. They may work as stock clerks during the midnight shift in retail, work with computers, or become long-distance truckers. They do well in jobs where interaction with others is minimal and they are not too closely supervised. If they are detached from a supportive family and have become involved with drugs and alcohol, they may become homeless and refuse outreach services designed to engage them in co-occurring disorders services or move them into shelters or other supported living programs.

Affect

Individuals with SPD are affectively constricted. They appear to be unable to experience pleasure, sadness, or anger in any depth. They are low in emotional arousal and reactivity; they are imperceptive and apathetic. Their inner emotional experience tends to be undifferentiated and unarticulated. Even their language shows a deficit in the range and subtlety of emotionally related words (Millon & Grossman, 2007a).

Although these individuals do not particularly struggle with shame or guilt, they can be quite anxious about basic safety (McWilliams, 1994). Emotional distress may be experienced when there are unusual social demands or responsibilities or when their stimulation level becomes excessive (Millon, 1996). Under ordinary circumstances, these individuals do not appear to be motivated or energized by their affective responses; their engagement with the external world tends to be cognitive or intellectual.

Defenses

Individuals with SPD utilize defenses to detach and form an emotional barrier; they engage in intellectualization, conflict avoidance, and withdrawal (Magnavita, 1997). Millon and Grossman (2007a) also note the SPD use of intellectualization. They suggest that these individuals tend to be abstract and matter-of-fact about their emotional and social lives; they engage in few complicated unconscious processes. Their lack of reactivity results in little need for complex intrapsychic defenses.

McWilliams (1994) believes that another SPD defense is withdrawal into fantasy. The external world feels so full of consuming threats against security and individuality that people with SPD manifest a tendency to withdraw and seek satisfaction in daydreams. If they come to trust a service provider, they may reveal many fantasies, imaginary friends, and fears of unbearable dependence (Sadock & Sadock, 2004).

The Self-Created World (Altered Reality) of SPD

Individuals with SPD create and sustain an altered reality that is not psychotic but allows them to keep unpleasant aspects of reality at a distance. They must sacrifice authenticity and connection to others to shelter themselves but are very resistive to any challenge of these ideas and interpretation of events. For individuals with SPD, the altered reality is composed of believing that:

- People will try to crowd you. They want too much.
- Relationships are not always worth the trouble they cause.
- I am a loner.
- People seem to get upset when you don't tell them what they want to hear. Sometimes it is easier just to make them think you see things their way. Then they will leave you alone.

Substance Use Disorders and SPD

Co-Occurring Substance Use Disorders and the Impact of Drugs on SPD

The impoverished social connections experienced by individuals with SPD limit their exposure to the drug culture. They have marginal skills and limited inclination to learn how to obtain illegal drugs.

On the other hand, these individuals are easy prey for more aggressive personalities. On the street, in jail, in colleges, or in treatment settings, they can be marked for induction into the use of drugs and taught how to obtain what they may come to need. Individuals with SPD do not pick up interpersonal cues well enough, nor are they interpersonally dominant enough to avoid victimization. In jail, these individuals may need protection from the general population. In treatment settings, observation of interaction with other group members may be needed. Although these individuals may not welcome such protection, the attempt is worthwhile, as it is in these settings that individuals with SPD can discover, experiment with, or learn to obtain drugs with which they had no previous familiarity.

Even if these individuals can access illegal drugs, they are disinclined to use them in public or social settings. Because individuals with SPD are likely to use marijuana or alcohol in isolation rather than for social disinhibition, they are not particularly vulnerable to negative consequences in early use. They are also inclined to consider their use to be nobody's business but their own. If they are coerced into treatment due to legal difficulty or family pressures, they may comply with program directives but maintain an internal certainty that they will return to drug use as soon as external sanctions are removed. Essentially, individuals with SPD are highly resistant to influence but are not particularly inclined to engage with authority figures in an active struggle against demands for compliance; they will simply wait until they are free of external pressure to return to their preferred behavior.

Drugs of Choice for SPD

Although no single pattern of substance use can be identified for any specific personality disorder, individuals with SPD may be attracted to psychedelics. Milkman and Sunderwirth (1987) suggest that, from a psychological perspective, drug choice depends on a positive fit with an individual's usual style of coping. The drug of choice can function as a pharmacological defense mechanism. For individuals with SPD, there is the possibility of an addiction to compulsive fantasy and an inclination to seek drug experiences with the psychedelics that provide imaginative transport such as LSD, psilocybin, and peyote.

Marijuana may be the most ego-syntonic drug for individuals with SPD. It allows a detached state of fantasy and distance from others, provides a richer internal experience than these individuals can normally create, and reduces an internal sense of emptiness and awareness of their failure to participate in life. Even if they are in treatment, a drug that meets these needs would be of greater value to these individuals than the interpersonal, and therefore troubling, relationships with counselors or group members. Walant (1995) believes that effective treatment must address addicted individuals' inclination to collapse all needs into one object of attachment: drugs. Individuals with SPD need to shift their focus away from the valued drug experience to the real world with real people.

Alcohol, readily available and safe to obtain, is another obvious drug of choice for individuals with SPD. Some use both marijuana and alcohol and see little point in giving up either. Although not likely to be argumentative, they may hold the conviction that marijuana should be legalized and both law enforcement and treatment personnel are misguided and unnecessarily coercive in their attempts to stop the use of marijuana in society.

Integrated Dual Diagnosis Treatment for SPD

Engaging in Treatment

Few individuals with a Cluster A personality disorder are particularly inclined to seek mental health, substance abuse, or co-occurring disorders treatment. Richards (1993) notes that individuals with SPD have few complaints and do not seek an interpersonal context for solving their problems. These individuals can be society's misfits and can spend a lifetime in single rooms in interpersonal isolation. If they come into treatment, they are often forced to do so by family or the legal system.

In treatment, clients with SPD challenge service providers, not with hostility, distrust, or aggression, but with the absence of response. They do not reciprocate feeling for feeling; they are not responsive to praise, criticism, or other kinds of emotional leverage used between people when one is attempting to influence the other. It is the apparent immunity to influence that can leave service providers feeling frustrated and ineffective. However, the lack of affective bonding or responsiveness does not mean insensitivity or imperviousness. In clinical settings, when placed in a group where they are not pressured to engage at a level they cannot endure or sustain, these individuals can become attached in their own way and will attend regularly. It appears that they can value contact if the intensity is controlled and safety ensured.

Treatment Provider Guidelines

Even though individuals with SPD are likely to relate to service providers only in a limited way, McWilliams (1994) believes that clients with SPD can be cooperative with, and appreciative of, the treatment process when they are received with consideration and respect. These individuals fear engulfment and need safe interpersonal distance. They may feel empty, lost, and unable to express their thoughts in treatment. Service providers need to communicate that the limited expression of cognitive or affective content from these individuals is intelligible and can form the basis of a connection between them. Accepting their silence affirms them as individuals of worth.

Clients with SPD have difficulty maintaining a connection to treatment providers between group or individual sessions. It is possible, because clients with SPD do not provoke hostility, experience multiple crises, or make many demands, for service providers to detach as well. These clients may be forgotten in supervisory sessions or staff meetings because they evoke few feelings or concerns. Both the clients with SPD and their service providers may permit a treatment stance of minimal involvement with few treatment interventions directed toward specific goals or needed changes.

Within individual or group sessions, patience is required for service providers to maintain an empathic stance and to establish a therapeutic bond with these clients (McCann, 1995). Their lack of responsiveness, a frustrating incapacity to relate, and a general and pervasive lack of empathy does not make interaction particularly interesting or rewarding for service providers. It is important that clinicians not fall into a bored, disconnected intolerance.

Service providers are likely to have to structure treatment sessions and reward schizoid personality-disordered individuals' attempts to establish interaction or make contact (Craig, 1995; Hyer, Brandsma, & Shealy, 1995). If affective experience or expression is intolerable to clients with SPD, initial focus on cognitive understanding of interpersonal, emotional, or addiction issues may be effective and a method of establishing a connection.

Professional Ethics and SPD

It can be a challenge to remain connected to clients who are not attached in return. It can be difficult to remember that whereas SPD clients may be nonexpressive and detached, they may also despair and put themselves at risk. These individuals can literally be dismissed from the conscious scanning service providers do for client vulnerability. They can be relegated to near invisibility, and the ethical consequences can be serious. Not only is it possible to fail to engage with these clients with the same energy that might be used with more connected clients, but crisis intervention can be delayed because of service provider lack of awareness of SPD vulnerability. Clients with SPD can lose jobs, important supportive relationships, or a sense of security in a difficult world. They can respond to intractable problems by withdrawing, but if the press of a negative reality is severe enough, they can turn to self-destructive or self-defeating behaviors to cope.

Assessment and Treatment

In assessing individuals with SPD, consider possible psychotic processes; determine whether there is evidence of hallucinations, delusions, or a thought disorder. If symptoms of psychosis are present, treatment must be designed for serious mental illness, and the accurate diagnosis is likely to be on Axis I.

Zimmerman (1994) suggests the following questions in assessing for SPD:

- Do you have close relationships with friends or family? If yes, with whom? If no, does this bother you?
- Do you wish you had close relationships with others?

- Some people prefer to spend time alone. Others prefer to be with people. How would you describe yourself?
- Do you frequently choose to do things by yourself?
- Would it bother you to go a long time without a sexual relationship? Does your sex life seem important, or could you get along as well without it?
- What kind of activities do you enjoy?
- Do you confide in anyone who is not in your immediate family? Whom do you talk to the most?
- How do you react when someone criticizes you?
- How do you react when someone compliments you?
- In the assessment process, do these individuals make eye contact, smile, or express affect nonverbally?

Beck et al. (2004) note that individuals with SPD appear to have defective perceptual scanning, which results in missing environmental cues. The defective perceptual scanning is characterized by a tendency to miss differences and to diffuse the varied elements of experience. Perceptions of events are mixed, disorganized, and undifferentiated (Millon & Davis, 1996). This increases the schizoid personality-disordered individual's reluctance to seek intimacy and encourages severely limited interpersonal experiences. The impact of the resulting isolation is insufficient opportunity to learn social skills and failure to correct unusual behavior. Socialization groups offer corrective learning experiences with others; they also involve lower interpersonal intensity than does individual treatment. Therapy for mental health issues is often educational in design and aimed at teaching social appropriateness, social customs and manners, and social comfort (Stone, 1993). Group treatment focused on substance abuse or dependence can have the secondary benefit of permitting these individuals to interact and to learn interpersonal skills. Group experiences are most likely to be beneficial when they are accepting and emotionally nondemanding. Co-occurring disorders groups would need to address both interpersonal detachment and the indifference these individuals experience to requirements for abstinence.

Educational strategies may be effective in working with individuals with SPD to identify their positive and negative emotions. They can use affect or feeling identification to learn about their own emotions, the emotions they elicit in others, and possible feeling states of people with whom they relate. This process can assist in developing the capacity for empathy (Will, 1995).

Intervention with individuals with SPD may include exploring their self-concepts, their values, and their sense of where they belong in the world. Questions framed to be neutral or intellectual are more effective. Confrontation should be minimal regarding either personality or substance use issues. Intensity of service provider affect or contentious interaction could lead to client withdrawal. These individuals are effective in emotionally and psychologically retreating from uncomfortable situations without physically leaving the situation. Service providers need to pace the dialogue with clients with SPD so there are periods of silence and reflection. Rapid-fire interaction is unlikely to be helpful or comfortable for these individuals.

It may be necessary to have harm reduction rather than abstinence as an initial goal. To this end, psychoeducation is valuable because it can be received and processed at an intellectual level and includes reality-based reflections on the consequences of drug use. Motivational interviewing (Miller & Rollnick, 2002) is very helpful because the focus can be primarily cognitive and allow individuals with SPD to reconsider their drug behaviors and make decisions in an interactive process that is accepting and manageable. These individuals are often able to utilize intellectual concepts that can facilitate attitudinal change and lead to more positive behaviors.

Treatment Goals

Individuals with SPD do not often seek mental health services. They are usually more or less satisfied with what is regarded by others as an impoverished existence. If, however, family insistence or legal circumstances bring individuals with SPD into treatment, treatment goals should be supportive and practical, aim at achieving reductions in social isolation, and promote effective adjustment to social circumstances (Kalus, Bernstein, & Siever, 1995; Oldham & Morris, 1995).

Treatment goals that address drug and alcohol use must be practical and realistic as well. These individuals quietly resist behavioral guidelines they do not like and do not intend to adhere to, for example, abstinence. Even if they do not directly argue with service providers, they may be determined not to discontinue their drug use. It is important to be direct and open about the realistic possibilities of any treatment goal and to stress that the choice for behavioral, attitudinal, or affective change always remains with the clients.

Recovery Activities for Individuals with SPD and Addiction

Mental health recovery activities include anything that engages individuals with SPD in social or interpersonal interaction. Social skills groups can be used to prepare clients with SPD for group membership in the alcohol and drug recovery community. If they can develop the confidence that their interactive style is acceptable enough for them to successfully participate in an assisted group setting, they can transfer both the social skills and the confidence to fuller integration in community settings.

Substance use recovery activities are most successful if individuals with SPD can find peer support groups that do not attempt to force interaction or connection before comfort is established and if there can be flexibility in seeking abstinence as a goal. Because they may have some difficulty with socializing within the 12-step community, these individuals may find a better fit with Dual Recovery Anonymous should they be in a community large enough to offer this option. AA or NA meetings are held in community mental health centers in some areas. Due to member composition, which often includes other people with co-occurring disorders, these meetings are more likely to be accepting of unusual behavior in their participants. Not all individuals with SPD need this special consideration, but the more severe the personality disorder, the more likely it is that service providers need to foster attendance and assist in the group selection process if 12-step groups or other peer assistance groups are to be a successful option. Recovery is more likely if clients with SPD can be guided in how to both accept others and be accepted in a group setting.

Co-occurring disorders recovery is sought by individuals who can acknowledge that they have both a mental health disorder and a substance use disorder. It is often challenging enough for people to accept that they have one or the other; accepting both can be much more difficult. Particularly for individuals who have a personality disorder, recognizing a substance use disorder may be easier. It is challenging indeed to concede one's own personality liabilities and maladaptive qualities. Fortunately, seeking addiction recovery can often have an equally positive impact on the personality disorder. Individuals with personality disorders usually have interpersonal and maturation deficits. This is not an unusual situation for individuals with addiction. Self-help involvement, learning from peers, and following the spiritual or psychological guidance of the various peer-led support groups can result in an increase in relating skills and enhanced maturity as well as a full or partial recovery from substance use disorders.

4

Cluster A

*Schizotypal Personality Disorder
and Substance Use Disorders*

Schizotypal Personality Disorder Defined

Essential Features

An essential feature of schizotypal personality disorder (StPD) is a pervasive pattern of social and interpersonal deficits. These individuals are acutely uncomfortable with others and have a limited capacity for close relationships. StPD also includes cognitive or perceptual distortions. These individuals often have a preoccupation with paranormal phenomena, special powers, and magical control. There may be ideas of reference involving incorrect interpretations of casual incidents (APA, 2000).

StPD encompasses a combination of peculiar behavior, speech, thought, and perception. Individuals with StPD are usually withdrawn and display eccentric beliefs, paranoid tendencies, idiosyncratic speech, perceptual illusions, unusual appearance, inappropriate affect, and social anxiety (Frances et al., 1995).

Whereas the *World Health Organization ICD-10 Classification of Mental and Behavioural Disorders* (*ICD-10*; WHO, 1992) definition of StPD is similar to that found in the *Diagnostic and Statistical Manual of Mental Disorders, IV* (*DSM-IV*; APA, 1994) and the *DSM-IV-TR* (APA, 2000), it has been removed from the personality disorders category and placed with the schizophrenia spectrum disorders. According to the *ICD-10*, StPD is a disorder characterized by eccentric behavior with anomalies of affect and cognition similar to those seen in schizophrenia. Other symptoms of StPD are:

- Anhedonia
- Odd or eccentric appearance
- Interpersonal discomfort and social withdrawal
- Odd beliefs or magical thinking
- Paranoid ideas without true delusions
- Ruminations
- Perceptual disturbances
- Odd speech
- Transient quasi-psychotic episodes

StPD was introduced in the *DSM-III* in 1980. The term *schizotype* was first used by Sandor Rado in 1953 as a combination of schizophrenic and genotype. The concept comes from the awareness that there are nonpsychotic but eccentric and dysfunctional personalities who are considered to have attenuated expressions of schizophrenia. Rado noted that schizotypal individuals have difficulty integrating pleasurable experiences and a distorted awareness of the bodily self (as cited by Ingraham, 1995).

Individuals with StPD have poorly regulated cognitive controls that are particularly vulnerable to disruption when experiencing interpersonal affective stimuli. Cognitive slippage can occur even with low levels of anxiety; when this happens, speech becomes digressive, vague, and difficult to follow. Although the ideational and perceptual abnormalities of StPD do not cross the clinical threshold of delusions and hallucinations, the symptoms of social withdrawal and constricted affect may be as pronounced as those observed in many individuals with schizophrenia (Siever, 1986; Walker & Gale, 1995).

Both the schizoid and schizotypal personality disorders show interpersonal reserve and semi-isolation. However, individuals with StPD demonstrate strange and eccentric beliefs and habit patterns; according to Kantor (1992), StPD has a schizoid tree trunk with odd, quirky branches.

StPD is more prevalent among the first-degree relatives of individuals with schizophrenia than among the general population (APA, 2000). Research supports the idea of familial transmission of schizotypal personality disorder similar to that of other schizophrenia-related disorders (Siever, Bernstein, & Silverman, 1995).

Self-Image

Individuals with StPD have an estranged self-image; they see themselves as forlorn and alienated from the world. These individuals ruminate about life's emptiness and meaninglessness. To themselves, they seem insubstantial, foreign, and disembodied. Some people with StPD see themselves as "more dead than alive" and feel threatened by nonbeing (Millon, Grossman, Millon, Meagher, & Ramnath, 2004).

Individuals with StPD know that their relationships and their vocational experiences are prone to disruption and failure. They begin to isolate and increasingly see themselves as not fitting into the society in which they live. Interpersonal feedback usually confirms that they do not experience the world as others do. They can rarely find affirmation or validation for themselves in their interactions with others.

View of Others

Individuals with StPD view others as potentially dangerous. Under stress, or if the degree of personality-disordered symptoms is severe, these individuals can become vulnerable to paranoid thinking. They fear being controlled by others but can sometimes manage this fear via a belief that they can magically influence people.

The intense social anxiety associated with StPD has to do with distrust rather than a negative self-appraisal (Sperry, 2003). Their inability to achieve interpersonal safety, comfort, or satisfaction may become so severe that they just want to be alone; they can withdraw and show substantial hostility toward others (Benjamin, 1996; Millon & Grossman, 2007a; Millon et al., 2004). Unfortunately, interpersonal isolation and peculiarity become mutually exacerbating conditions. The more isolated persons with StPD are, the more peculiar they become; the more peculiar they become, they more they are interpersonally maladroit and inept.

Relationships

Individuals with StPD have substantial difficulty meeting people, so they seldom have the opportunity to develop relationships outside of their immediate family. When they are involved in socializing, they can become so agonized by their own inconsolable anxiety that the effort is simply not worth the discomfort. This does not mean they do not want relationships, but they may have to revert to fantasy to manage loneliness. A middle-aged woman with StPD developed complex and ongoing romantic ideas about her chiropractor that she discussed at length with her therapist. Every interaction between the client and the chiropractor was scrutinized for meaning and any possible indication of his feelings for her. His every word, apparent mood, and behavior were grounds for speculation and either hope or anxiety. It was apparent that indications of romantic attraction from this man existed entirely in the imagination of the individual with StPD. Her infatuation was benign but, the potential for her to escalate into an imagined attachment that he could "betray" (by her interpretation) placed the man in some jeopardy in a situation that he knew nothing about. Her real relationships with her older brother and her mother were barren, nonreciprocal, and without emotional sustenance, so any suggestion that the chiropractor was not really involved with her resulted in powerful anger and feelings of emptiness. Although she was in her late forties, her infatuation was marked by an adolescent style that included intensity and amplified responses to any challenge about the relationship or any indication from the chiropractor that he was becoming uncomfortable with her behavior.

Issues with Authority

Individuals with StPD are interpersonally unusual, with eccentric mannerisms, unusual dress, peculiar behavior, and distrust of being controlled; they are likely to both attract attention and be unable to manage their behavior in the presence of authority. Accordingly, they are likely to be able to function only in marginal jobs with limited oversight by supervisors, who are nearly always experienced as alarming. They are also likely to be unable to manage their behavior in public settings and may find themselves in difficulty with the police, particularly if they are also using alcohol or other drugs. Authority figures are distrusted and intensely anxiety-provoking; their presence may lead to even more bizarre and socially unacceptable behavior. On the other hand, if the authority figure becomes a trusted helper—as can happen with service providers—they may form a genuine, if rather odd, attachment and enjoy the contact.

Behavior

Individuals with StPD engage in a variety of persistent and prominent eccentricities of behavior, thought, and perception that mirror, but fall short of, clinical schizophrenia (Millon & Grossman, 2007a). They are socially awkward and are perceived by others as bizarre. Their unusual qualities attract attention and elicit responses from others that range from amusement to bewilderment.

These individuals are unable to differentiate the salient from the tangential, causing them to attend to a different aspect of an event or interpret events differently than others; for example, they may digress into a heated discourse on Mexican political corruption when another guest compliments a hostess on the tacos served at a picnic. They may also ascribe special significance to incidental events; for example, the Mexican picnic theme might indicate some significant event about to occur in that country. The overall impact of this variance in attention, interpretation, or attribution of meaning to everyday events renders them peculiar to observers (Millon & Davis, 1996). Other people may find themselves doing a "double-take" when experiencing the "slightly left of center" logic that is associated with schizotypal personality disorder. One woman, in her forties, with StPD, came to a session with her therapist one afternoon in a very cross mood. She said she was angry because when she took mid-morning walks in her neighborhood, she could see many cars parked along the streets. She said, "There are so many cars that obviously no one needs or is using, why can't I drive one of them?" This individual did not know her logic was unusual, and it was difficult for her to understand why people responded to her as they did—why they seemed to be either amused by or disapproving of her. At the time of this exchange, she had severely limited her contact with others because of her growing interpersonal discomfort.

At other times, the oddities of schizotypal responses are simply social anxiety and having few skills at polite interchange with others. One young man with StPD, when the father of a fellow group member passed away, attended the funeral. When the son thanked the young man for coming, his response was, "Sure, anytime."

Affect

Individuals with StPD tend to display one of two predominant affective states. The first is insipid, drab, apathetic, sluggish, and joyless. The second is timorous, excessively apprehensive, ill at ease, agitated, and anxious (Millon & Grossman, 2007a; Millon et al., 2004).

Kantor (1992) believes that the inappropriateness of affect associated with StPD may result from missing a primary idea in social interaction and reacting instead to a secondary or peripheral matter. For example, an individual with StPD at a funeral may compliment a bereaved widow on her lovely dress and talk about the best places to shop for bargains. The affective responses of individuals with StPD will be unusual—and apparently insensitive—if they are attending to irrelevant or peripheral details instead of focusing on central issues.

Defenses

Individuals with most of the personality disorders have an inherent tendency to live in the past, or in fantasy, with too little input from the here and now. This produces a characteristic immature quality in these individuals. To this, in StPD, is added an inclination to create illogical theories that are wishful, capricious, and magical. These odd beliefs are "soft" delusions in that they are modest, trivial, and surrealistic; they create a dreamy eccentricity in individuals with StPD (Kantor, 1992).

Oldham and Morris (1995) suggest that many people with StPD need to believe that they have extraordinary, supernatural powers to give meaning to their impoverished sense of self. Millon and Grossman (2007a) propose that individuals with StPD are overwhelmed by the dread of total disintegration and nonexistence; the self-made reality of superstition, suspicion, and illusion counters the threat of nonbeing.

Individuals with StPD are ineffective and uncoordinated in regulating their needs, tensions, and goals. Their inadequate defenses lead to a disorganized and often direct discharge of primitive thoughts and impulses. They are unable to effectively sublimate their energy into reality-based activity and have few successful achievements in life. The disorganized and ineffective defenses leave these individuals vulnerable to being overwhelmed by excess stimulation (Millon et al., 2004).

The Self-Created World (Altered Reality) of StPD

Individuals with StPD create and sustain an altered reality that, while not psychotic, shelters their beliefs about themselves and others. Much like alcohol and other psychoactive drugs, these ideas blur reality and allow the world to seem to be a predictable place even though there is a significant loss of authenticity and relatedness to others. The altered reality of StPD is composed of thoughts, beliefs, or wishes such as:

- Transcending reality lifts the spirit above the clouds.
- It is sad that most people are transfixed by the ordinary and mired in the trivial details of daily life. I have a seeking mind—open to the universe; the smallest thought can transport me to another level of consciousness.
- It seems like, if I concentrate very hard, I can make the people around me feel just a little bit better, or a little worse, if I am in a bad mood.
- I push away negativity. I invite the loving universe into my soul.

Substance Use Disorders and StPD

Co-Occurring Substance Use Disorders and the Impact of Drugs on StPD

Drug use can result in destabilization for individuals with StPD— very much like what can happen to people with schizophrenia. Substance abuse or dependence may not be necessary for negative consequences; use alone can precipitate a crisis. When there is sufficient psychiatric stability to sustain considerable alcohol or other drug use, these individuals often do not have enough social or interpersonal support to effectively interrupt drug use or to support an abstinent lifestyle. They are inclined to use alcohol and other drugs to either connect to an accepting social environment or manage their interpersonal anxiety. If substance use is core to their social connections, or if they cannot imagine socializing without the help of drugs, abstinence is going to carry the burden of interpersonal loss and heightened anxiety.

Individuals with StPD may use drugs to escape feeling odd and disenfranchised. Heavy use of narcotics or sedative hypnotics can mask symptoms; giving up drugs could reveal to these individuals the full force of the social, interpersonal, cognitive, and affective symptoms of their personality disorder. Service providers who do not recognize the costs of abstinence may push too hard, too soon, and with considerable insensitivity to the level of need felt by individuals who use drugs to manage their fear, their oddness, and their interpersonal losses. Individuals with StPD may feel like the demand for abstinence within a treatment program is more than they can possibly manage; the very structure of the services will induce treatment failure.

Drugs of Choice for StPD

Individuals with StPD may have difficulty establishing connections to obtain illegal drugs. If they are able to connect to a source for drugs, they are extremely vulnerable to exploitation and abuse or violence. If they can access drugs, they are likely to be attracted to psychedelics and risk ego fragmentation and failure of their limited defenses. Nevertheless, marijuana, LSD, peyote, and other hallucinogens can be used to facilitate a fantasy state that is distant from the troubling real world. Walant (1995) suggests that LSD can provide weird perceptual distortions that can actually alleviate anxiety about the personal strangeness that is not drug induced. Thaddeus Golas (1972, 1979), the author of *The Lazy Man's Guide to Enlightenment*, said that people choose the state of consciousness they prefer by the drugs they use. He saw LSD as a means to access spiritual levels of consciousness; LSD transports to a timeless place and gives users all the divine intelligence they can handle. For individuals with StPD, how much more appealing must this transcendence to a higher level of consciousness be to feeling odd and disabled.

Alcohol may become the drug of choice because of its accessibility. With the capacity of alcohol to disinhibit, individuals with StPD may be able to drink to release an already heightened capacity for fantasy and unusual beliefs about who they are and what they can do.

Integrated Dual Diagnosis Treatment for StPD

Engaging in Treatment

Few individuals with a Cluster A personality disorders are inclined to seek treatment; they are often forced into receiving services by family or the legal system. Substance abuse or dependence may be the visible or apparent problem, and the personality disorder is either unidentified or the behaviors associated with the personality disorder are assumed to be caused by or secondary to the substance use disorder. Understanding the interaction of personality disorder dynamics with the function of substance use will form the core of effective intervention. Once in treatment, individuals with StPD may respond positively to an environment structured to allow them greater personal and interpersonal success. Being able to experience positive connections to others is particularly essential if substance use is connected to socializing, and abstinence requires loss of relationships, or what seem like relationships, no matter how destructive they may be.

Treatment Provider Guidelines

The result of the impaired social interaction and lack of social skills for individuals with StPD is an ongoing loss of contact with reality. Interaction with individuals with StPD can elicit surprising statements and peculiar ideas; clinicians must be empathic and show understanding to demonstrate that they can enter the StPD secret world (Sperry, 2003). With the development of trust, the relationship with treatment providers can serve as a basis for reality testing and a corrective experience for eccentricity and bizarre thinking. Psychoeducational techniques can be effective with service providers functioning as an auxiliary ego (Stone, 1993).

Clients with StPD are inclined to engage treatment providers in circuitous, belabored, odd, and meaningless discourses on subjects such as "artistic endeavor and the use of drugs" or "dual diagnosis counselors as agents of social control." Treatment providers can become bored or frustrated and begin to withdraw. Yet individuals with StPD often cannot structure treatment sessions; the focus and content needs to come from service providers so that the therapeutic tasks can be achieved and neither client nor clinician becomes over-whelmed and defeated.

Professional Ethics and StPD

The challenges involved in working with individuals with StPD are much like those clinicians face in working with clients with Axis I serious mental illness. Therapeutic interventions often need to be more directive and structured. However, providing focus and structure is not the same as taking over the treatment and diminishing client choice. The necessity of managing the treatment process can elicit service provider overcontrol. Respecting client autonomy, to the maximum extent possible, can recede under the well-meaning pressures of clinician protectiveness and paternalism. This is rarely the situation with individuals who are more aggressive or more able to manage than is the case with individuals with StPD, particularly when they enter treatment in crisis. The concept of providing services in the least restrictive manner applies even if all services are outpatient. A lack of respect can be implied and communicated whenever clinicians treat clients as being incapable of making their own choices. Client choices to drink, to use, to work or not, to have relationships that appear unstable or undesirable all belong to the individual who is making them. Service providers can share their concerns and use motivational interviewing to reflect on previous consequences or note potential consequences of the behaviors (Miller & Rollnick, 2002), but attempts to control are inappropriate and unethical except in circumstances where individuals are dangerous to themselves or others. This can be very difficult when service providers sincerely believe they are right and their clients would be better off if they would just listen or follow advice. Parents of adolescents know the feeling well. People cannot and should not be protected from learning on their own. Being a client is not the same thing as giving up the right to make choices or make mistakes.

Another concern in working with individuals with StPD has to do with service providers' vulnerability to becoming either bored or overwhelmed. If service providers begin to experience drowsiness or anxiety, they may withdraw from the treatment process and allow a pointless drift and lack of attention to working toward therapeutic goals. In a group, either lack of participation or distracting behaviors may not be confronted. Clinicians may feel the need to protect themselves from the feelings they experience when working with these individuals, and treatment progress becomes less and less likely.

Essentially, the demands on service providers include focused treatment, respect for client autonomy, and sustained appropriate involvement when working with individuals with StPD.

Assessment and Treatment

In assessing individuals with StPD, consider possible psychotic processes; determine whether there is evidence of hallucinations, delusions, and a thought disorder. If symptoms of psychosis are present, consider an Axis I diagnosis.

Even if there are no indications of psychosis, treatment is most effective when structured, supportive, and focused on teaching social skills. When these individuals relinquish their activities, they regress into an unmotivated state; they may deteriorate and become increasingly less functional without the feedback process that accompanies interpersonal interaction (Millon & Grossman, 2007a; Millon et al., 2004). Increasing their capacity to develop and maintain a social network is an effective therapeutic strategy (Beck et al., 2004).

One source of the cognitive peculiarity for individuals with StPD is emotional reasoning. This is a process wherein they believe that a negative external situation exists because they have a negative emotion; for example, if the individual with StPD is uncomfortable with another person, that person must be hostile or dangerous (Sperry, 2003). These individuals can be taught to recognize when they are distorting reality. Just because they "feel it" does not necessarily mean it is real or true. Clients with StPD can learn to evaluate their thoughts against environmental evidence rather than their feelings. This reduces emotional reasoning and the drawing of incorrect conclusions about interpersonal situations (Millon et al., 2004).

Individuals with StPD may believe they are responsible for external situations when this is not the case. Structured, focused reframing of environmental cues that normalize the interpretations these individuals make in regard to the behavior of others allows them to function with greater stability both socially and vocationally. Use of solution-oriented questions to focus on personal efficacy can be helpful; for example, "When things are going well for you, what are you doing to help make this happen?"

Hypochondriasis is another problem for people with StPD. However, if they can become more successful interpersonally, many of the physical symptoms will diminish (Sperry, 2003; Stone, 1993). Although this may be a benefit of treatment, physical symptoms should still be evaluated by a physician to ensure that medical care is not needed.

Not pushing individuals with StPD too hard in treatment can prevent their experiencing severe anxiety and having paranoid reactions. Confrontation or attempts to pressure these individuals to "drop their denial" can be harmful and is usually contraindicated. A supportive approach is often the only kind of therapeutic intervention they can tolerate (Millon & Davis, 1996). Supportive treatment utilizes sympathetic listening, education about the world, giving advice, assisting with problem solving, and the quiet establishment of relatedness that relies upon regular contact and nonjudgmental acceptance. Expectations must be in harmony with clients with StPD even if their goals fall short of an ideal life (Stone, 1996). This applies to both the symptoms of StPD and the possible necessity of a harm-reduction approach to drinking and drugging. Individuals with StPD rarely can achieve and sustain abstinence as a prerequisite to treatment. If continued substance use or relapse results in treatment termination, many of these individuals experience treatment failure and loss of hope because the challenges of their personality disorder compromise their capacity for abstinence.

Individuals with StPD may benefit from a medication evaluation. These individuals have responded positively to low-dose neuroleptics, which can reduce the tendency to blame others, unwarranted suspicion, outbursts of rage, and repeated interpersonal conflict. These individuals are inclined, however, to experience medication as causing odd side effects, and compliance can become a problem (Ellison & Adler, 1990). High-functioning individuals with StPD who display oddities of speech but who do not have psychotic episodes may not require medication (Stone, 1996).

Treatment Goals

Personality disorders derive in part from patterns of behavior and thought that appear to have begun very early in life. It is understandable that personality disorders are hard to modify and slow to change. However, progress can and does occur. The treatment goal in working with all of the personality disorders is the same: gradually exchanging new, more adaptive habits of thought and behavior for preexisting, maladaptive habits (Stone, 1993).

Improvement for many clients with StPD is most likely in occupational activities, reality testing, and participation in enjoyable activities. It is much more difficult to see progress in social or intimate relationships. Treatment can help identify spheres of life toward which some positive inclination exists. While enthusiastic involvement may be difficult to achieve, increased participation in activities can provide a window of reality-based experiences that may preclude the need for less constructive internal gratifications (Millon & Davis, 1996; Millon et al., 2004; Stone, 1996).

One important treatment goal is to teach individuals with StPD to recognize their bizarre thoughts, to label these thoughts as symptoms, and to reduce their behavioral and emotional responses to these thoughts (Beck et al., 2004; Will, 1995).

Another treatment objective for individuals with StPD is to develop and maintain social relationships through social skills training, cognitive reorientation, and environmental management (Millon & Davis, 1996). Particularly in group settings, clients with StPD can develop connections with others that, although limited and rather fragile in the beginning, become of considerable value and offer substantial growth potential.

One of the National Institute of Drug Abuse (NIDA, 2000) principles of effective drug-abuse treatment involves a focus on the multiple needs of individuals, not just substance use. Treatment must also address associated medical, psychological, social, vocational, and legal problems (Hoffman & Froemke, 2007). Individuals with StPD are likely to have serious concerns in all of these areas given the nature of the personality pathology and the extra burden substance use puts on their limited coping skills. DiClemente (2003) proposes that individuals who can make their lives work by achieving some success and developing relationships reduce their vulnerability to substance use disorders and relapse. Treatment gains in interpersonal, vocational, and personal efficacy yield benefits for recovery from both the personality and the substance use disorder.

Recovery Activities for Individuals with StPD and Addiction

For individuals with StPD to engage in successful recovery activities, they must find groups or other connections within which they can socialize, find acceptance, and experience positive interaction. The aspects of StPD that appear to remain stable over time, such as odd beliefs and ideas of reference (McGlashan et al., 2005), can make them very vulnerable in a group that is not accepting of unusual behaviors or personal qualities. If these individuals live in a large metropolitan area and no Dual Recovery Anonymous or Double Trouble groups exist, it is worthwhile to facilitate or encourage them to begin one of their own. Also, 12-step groups that meet in mental health centers often are more accepting of unusual behaviors, speech patterns, or attitudes and can become a base of operation for these individuals.

Opportunities for social interaction in an accepting environment can foster the acquisition of social skills and the development of relationships, both of which counter the isolation and the social anxiety of individuals with StPD. It is imperative that socialization possibilities be formed in drug-free settings if alcohol or other drugs have been the only available avenue to interpersonal interaction. It is counterproductive to push individuals with StPD to give up their drug-using friends without substituting other opportunities for connection.

Another consideration in fostering recovery activities for addicted individuals with StPD is the intensity of their attraction to magic, transcendence, special powers, or the occult. If drugs have allowed them to transcend what they consider to be pedestrian levels of consciousness, they will be loath to give up their access to the paranormal or apparent special abilities. It is possible to substitute meditation for psychedelic drugs, Wicca activities for drug-induced trance-like experiences of the occult, and other means that permit these individuals to engage in what is likely to be very important to them. It is imperative that the connections to the world that are meaningful be sustained, or achieving abstinence will involve too much sacrifice. If recovery increases isolation or reduces sustaining involvements, it becomes much more difficult to maintain. Conversely, if recovery activities meet social and philosophical or spiritual needs, abstinence carries rewards and becomes increasingly valued. Any person's development of recovery-based activities must meet his or her specific constellation of needs, but for individuals with StPD, there are so many challenges in daily living that recovery must be carefully designed to make success possible. To assist clients with StPD to build a recovery-supported lifestyle, the function of or the gains derived from alcohol and other drugs must be fully understood, and those needs must be met via drug-free activities and connections.

5

Cluster B

Antisocial Personality Disorder and Substance Use Disorders

Antisocial Personality Disorder Defined

Essential Features

An essential feature of antisocial personality disorder (APD) is a pervasive pattern of disregard for and the violation of the rights of others. Individuals with APD fail to conform to social norms; they are deceitful, impulsive, aggressive, and irritable. They show a reckless disregard for safety and a lack of remorse. The diagnosis of APD should not be used with anyone under the age of 18 and requires a history of conduct disorder symptoms prior to the age of 15. This pattern has been called psychopathy, sociopathy, and dyssocial personality disorder (APA, 2000).

Millon and Grossman (2007b) contend that the *Diagnostic and Statistical Manual of Mental Disorders*, IV, text revision *(DSM-IV-TR)* details criminal and socially undesirable APD behaviors but fails to delineate the personality characteristics from which such antisocial behaviors emerge. They believe that APD is best characterized by hostility, excessive self-reliance, interpersonal assertiveness, and callousness. These individuals are rebellious, socially vindictive, and contemptuous toward authority. However, they may have managed to avoid criminal involvement. Cleckley (1941; as cited in Frances et al., 1995) and Hare (1999, 2003) also emphasize the psychological traits of psychopathy including superficial charm; incapacity for love; lack of remorse, guilt, or shame; lack of insight; and a failure to learn from past experiences rather than repeated difficulty with the criminal justice system. Many individuals with APD have no history of significant criminal behavior. In fact, successful individuals with APD can be found in the rugged side of politics, law, business, and the military (Widiger & Corbit, 1995).

It is estimated that 3.6% of the general population fit the criteria for APD; it is up to three times more prevalent in men than women (Grant et al., 2004). Hare (as cited by Patrick, 2007) estimates the base rate of APD in correctional and forensic settings to be between 50% and 80%.

Self-Image

The APD self-image is one of autonomy. These individuals see themselves as unconventional and disdainful of the customs of society. They are unconstrained by personal attachments and unconfined by obligations and routines. They are comfortable with the deception and manipulation needed, in any situation, to do what is important to them, regardless of the impact on others (Millon, 1996; Millon & Grossman, 2007b).

The core APD self-image is unrealistic superiority (McWilliams, 1994). With an dazzling sense of entitlement, they see themselves as the "center of the universe" (Hare, 1999, p. 38); they believe they should be able to ignore the needs of others, do whatever they like, and seduce or bully others to avoid adverse consequences. These individuals have the fundamental features of the narcissistic personality disorder with the addition of ego-syntonic aggression, intensity, and a paranoid orientation (Kantor, 1992; Meloy, 1996; Millon, 1996).

View of Others

Millon (1996) refers to people with APD as active and independent; their independence comes from their faith in themselves and their mistrust of others. They see others as malevolent, exploitive, and inclined to dominate. They feel most secure when free of those who might harm them. Individuals with APD appear see others as motivated by the same needs and engaging in the same behaviors as they are. On the other hand, persons with APD see others who cannot control or dominate as weak, vulnerable, and available for exploitation (Beck et al., 2004; Millon, 1996).

APD is indicative of a basic failure of human attachment; others are valued for their utility only. The organizing preoccupation for these individuals is manipulating others (McWilliams, 1994) and being free of the constraints others must face. One woman with APD, in her late twenties, had to go to the Department of Motor Vehicles in a southern state to get her license reinstated after several moving traffic violations. She had resisted for months, driving without a license, but because she was on probation, getting caught could put her in jail. She was intensely angry about being forced to take care of this situation. Her therapist asked her what she was thinking when she looked around the room at all of the other people standing in line for service. Her answer: "You bunch of sheep."

Relationships

The interpersonal conduct of individuals with APD is irresponsible, untrustworthy, and unreliable; they frequently fail to meet marital, parental, employment, and financial obligations (Millon & Grossman, 2007b). They form relationships that are multiple, transient, and superficial. The more severe the APD, the more likely it is that these individuals have few feelings of loyalty, are easily provoked, and are inclined to become vindictive (Millon, 1981). Because their attachment to others is so shallow, they can be callous about the pain and suffering they cause (Sperry, 2003). They will victimize others by manipulating observed weaknesses and will, in turn, feign being a victim to absolve themselves from blame (Millon, 1981).

Individuals with APD have an unmodulated desire to control others; they use indifference and aggression to establish and maintain interpersonal dominance. Even their affection is controlling and detached. On the other hand, they are powerfully reactive to any indication that they may be controlled by others (Benjamin, 1996).

Issues with Authority

Oldham and Morris (1995) note that individuals with APD know right from wrong—they just don't care. The most distinctive characteristics of APD are an inclination to flout conventional authority, show disdain for traditional ideals (Millon & Davis, 1996), refuse to conform to social norms, and demonstrate contempt for ethics and values. They experience pleasure in transgressing social codes via deceit or illegal behavior and enjoy taking power and possessions from others. One man, living in a small town on the Ohio River, when talking about his antisocial son stealing cars, said if people didn't want their cars stolen, they should lock the car doors. Even more to the point, if they leave their keys in their cars, they obviously do not care if their cars are stolen or not. He was incensed, as was his son, that there were legal consequences to the thefts. Father and son shared an APD diagnosis and described themselves as victimized by people making it too easy to steal cars and by the police who were harassing them. Law enforcement was annoying, inconvenient, and unfair.

Behavior

The behavioral style of individuals with APD is impulsive, irritable, and aggressive. They are noted for their hostility, their forceful interpersonal behavior, and their inclination to be thrill-seeking (Sperry, 2003). Many people avoid these individuals because they are so callous, argumentative, contentious, abusive, and intimidating (Millon, 1981). Individuals with APD have been described as having a predatory stare: an expressionless, emotionless stare that prompts others to feel like potential prey. It is part of the behavioral repertoire these individuals use to manipulate and dominate (Hare, 1999).

Barratt and Stanford (1996) note that individuals with APD engage in motor impulsivity (acting without thinking), cognitive impulsivity (making up one's mind precipitously), and poor planning impulsivity (lack of thought for the future). They have low frustration tolerance and cannot delay or forgo immediate pleasure (Millon, 1996).

Affect

For individuals with APD, affect lacks subtlety, depth, and modulation. Individuals with severe APD appear to live in a presocialized emotional world; feelings are experienced in relation to self but not in relation to others. Such individuals are unable to experience emotions such as gratitude, empathy, sympathy, affection, guilt, or mutual eroticism that depend on the perception of others as whole, real, and meaningful. Dominant emotions are anger, sensitivity to shame or humiliation, envy, boredom, contempt, exhilaration, and pleasure through dominance (Meloy, 1996).

Individuals with APD are irritable. Their anger is followed easily with aggression and the intent to inflict discomfort, harm, or injury on others (Lish, Kavoussi, & Coccaro, 1996). Oldham and Morris (1995) suggest that even if the impulsivity of APD diminishes with age, the affective experience of irritability, anger, and tension does not.

Defenses

Individuals with APD use projection and acting out as regulatory mechanisms. The projection is expressed through interpretation of incidental behaviors and remarks of others as attacks. People with APD justify their outbursts as reasonable responses to the malevolence of others. When they are able to see themselves as innocent bystanders subjected to unjust persecution and hostility, they are free to counterattack and gain vindication (Millon & Grossman, 2007b).

Individuals with APD are defined by the defense of acting out; they respond to stressors with behavior rather than reflection or thought (Perry & Bond, 2005). They appear to have exploitative and resentful dispositions that discharge directly and precipitously. Although they do feel anxiety, they tend to act out so quickly to relieve the discomfort of such an unpleasant feeling that no observer has a chance to see it. There is some evidence that individuals with APD have inborn tendencies toward aggressivity (McWilliams, 1994) and have weak and ineffectual internal control on behavior or impulses. They have a low threshold for devious and irresponsible action as well as for hostile and erotic discharge (Millon & Davis, 1996).

The Self-Created World (Altered Reality) of APD

Individuals with APD create and sustain an altered reality that, although not psychotic, permits interpersonal exploitation and fosters the perception of personal superiority and control to exist at the expense of authenticity and relatedness to others. For individuals with APD, the altered reality is composed of believing that:

- I am smart, clever, and can get what I want when I want it.
- What I want is not only the most important thing, it is the only thing.
- People ask to be used and abused.
- People are too weak to stop me from getting what I want.
- No one can tell me what to do.
- People who follow the rules are stupid and weak.

Substance Use Disorders and APD

Co-Occurring Substance Use Disorders and the Impact of Drugs on APD

APD is in Cluster B, the dramatic, erratic, or impulsive cluster. Cluster B has the highest rates of alcohol and drug abuse and dependence (Nace & Tinsley, 2007) of the three *DSM-IV-TR* personality clusters. Substance misuse is so common in individuals with APD that assessment for one in the presence of the other is essential. On the other hand, there is the possibility of apparent antisocial behavior from individuals with alcoholism or addiction. Early diagnosis of APD may need to be provisional until observing these individuals after a significant period of abstinence. If, while abstinent, antisocial behaviors diminish or are discontinued, the maladaptive behaviors and attitudes are secondary to drug use. Individuals with APD engage in behaviors indicative of the personality disorder whether or not they are using alcohol or psychoactive drugs. Maladaptive thinking, ineffective or self-sabotaging defenses, and unmanageable affect may increase or intensify without the mediating effects of alcohol or other drugs. It may be possible to determine the presence of APD when there is co-occurring drug abuse or dependence if a thorough history can be obtained via other informants such as family members. A reliable and valid history is difficult to obtain from individuals with APD, and confirmation from others is crucial.

The inability of individuals with APD to connect negative consequences with behavior, contempt for authority, laws, and social norms, as well as the inclination toward impulsive action all support the use of drugs and alcohol. Richards (1993) believes that individuals with APD are specifically prone to substance abuse or dependence because of their need for a high level of stimulation. The APD inclination to demand autonomy for self and control of others within relationships often does not permit effective intervention from family, friends, or coworkers with regard to drug use. Individuals with APD will stop substance use only if they become convinced that it is in their own best interest. They see no problem with alcohol or other drugs in any other context.

Drugs of Choice for APD

Many individuals with APD engage in a polydrug pattern of use involving alcohol, marijuana, heroin, cocaine, and methamphetamine. The illegal drug culture is exciting and highly desirable to these individuals; it makes the world a fast-paced and dramatic place. Overall, however, individuals with APD tend to prefer stimulants when choice is available (Center for Substance Abuse Treatment [CSAT], 1994). Their need for stimulation can also lead to involvement with erotic violence. They may speak of verbal or physical rage as providing a high that compares to what they experience with cocaine. Cocaine and anger both enhance highly pleasurable feelings of dominance and sexuality. Benjamin (1996) proposes that working with individuals with APD is ineffective without a focus on the intensely self-reinforcing (euphoria-inducing) nature of sexual violence.

Individuals with personality disorders, due to frequent failures in self-regulation, have an increased inclination to use drugs and alcohol. For individuals with APD, the fit between what they want from life and what they can get from drugs is remarkable. Freud noted the freedom in drugs—that the pressures of reality can be evaded (Khantzian, Halliday & McAuliffe, 1990) and consequences ignored. For individuals with APD, any ability to delay gratification that may be possible when they are sober is not available when they are drunk. Poor impulse control can degrade to no impulse control when they get high. Violence becomes more likely and destructive behavior toward others routine. People around them are in greater danger when these individuals are using substances, and intervention may need to start, depending on the level of risk, with a family safety plan.

Integrated Dual Diagnosis Treatment for APD

Engaging in Treatment

Individuals with APD will probably be in treatment only as a result of legal involvement. Even self-referrals often have pending legal problems that could be ameliorated by "voluntarily" seeking treatment or rehabilitation. Family pressure to change destructive behavior may or may not carry sufficient leverage to bring individuals with APD into treatment.

Once in treatment, change may be possible for individuals with APD who are sufficiently functional to understand the utility of changing behaviors that create legal problems. For individuals with APD who can experience anxiety, depression, or attachment, the prognosis is considerably improved. If they insist, on the other hand, that their problems are a result of other peoples' behaviors or expectations, the prognosis is substantially less optimistic.

Even though entry into any type of treatment on a truly voluntary basis is rare, it does not mean that early interaction with these individuals cannot foster engagement and interest in what might be accomplished while they are receiving services. If individuals with APD have a probation officer, a court order for treatment, potential revocation of probation for noncompliance, a job on the line, a spouse or partner who has issued an ultimatum, or other consequences of their behaviors, they may become interested in developing skills that are compatible with who they are but do not repeatedly result in serious loss and significant disruption in their lives, for example, going to jail. Whereas they are likely to be disinterested in becoming good citizens, they may be interested in being more successful.

Treatment Provider Guidelines

Individuals with APD respect power and do not relate well to powerless service providers. Clinicians need to demonstrate objective neutrality and independent strength verging on indifference. If there is professional investment in helping these clients to change or improve, individuals with APD will take great delight in sabotaging treatment just to demonstrate the service providers' impotence (McWilliams, 1994). However, they are likely to complain about lack of service provider sensitivity if their attempts to manipulate or control are not successful.

If clinicians yield under pressure for special treatment or softening of program rules, or if they show the fear they may feel in response to the surging aggressivity of APD clients, they will be treated as these individuals treat anyone they see as weak—with exploitation and merciless pressure. Accordingly, the most important features of APD treatment are service provider determination, strength, and incorruptibility. Individuals with APD do not experience or understand empathy. They are not grateful to or appreciative of service providers. They use and manipulate other people and will take pleasure in any triumph over clinicians who waver from the boundaries of the treatment contract. It is at least possible to win the respect of clients with APD by being tough-minded and exacting (McWilliams, 1994).

Related to incorruptibility is the need for service providers to demonstrate uncompromising honesty, that is, being clear and straightforward, keeping promises, making good on statements of potential consequences, and persistently addressing and identifying reality. However, given the manipulative and exploitative qualities of APD behavior, it is important to note that honesty does not mean self-disclosure (McWilliams, 1994). Meloy (1996) also points out that the treatment rule for working with APD is rigorous honesty without self-disclosure. Individuals with APD are alert for and will go after any information they can get that places service providers at a disadvantage, including vulnerabilities, sensitive subjects, and fears.

Clients with APD may arouse fear or foreboding in service providers. It is important to discuss these responses with colleagues or supervisors. It is not beneficial to ignore intuitive warning signals of danger. It is possible, depending on the presence or absence of psychopathy, that these individuals could pose a risk to other clients or to their service providers. Sometimes, clinicians deny or minimize their responses so they do not look weak or timid in the eyes of their colleagues or clients. However, that intuition may be the only warning that is perceived prior to an adverse incident and should be respected by both supervisory and clinical staff.

Professional Ethics and APD

Individuals with APD assume that service providers are predatory and will use their positions for selfish purposes. Clinicians may find themselves dismayed that their identities as helpers are repudiated (McWilliams, 1994). Two possible maladaptive and erroneous behaviors become possible at that point. First, providers may over-react and relax their boundaries in an attempt to demonstrate their sincerity and willingness to be helpful. Second, they may decide that individuals with APD do not really want to be helped and probably cannot be helped, so they withdraw into disapproving distance. Both possibilities lock service providers into a stance that is reactive rather than thoughtful. Provider boundaries that are rigid are not helpful; lack of boundaries can be catastrophic. There are few types of client for whom poorly considered service provider behavior could result in more negative results. It is vital that interaction with clients with APD be considered independently of what is being invited by the observed behavior. For example, playful flirtatiousness from APD clients is an invitation to provider behavior that could range from marginally inappropriate to unethical. It is essential that clinicians consider their response and have an objective in mind before they react. Neither condemnation nor responsive flirtatiousness would be beneficial. A challenge regarding the behavior and what it is supposed to produce would likely be more to the point.

It is important to note that clinicians may find themselves positively responsive to the casual charm and spark of electricity or excitement they experience with individuals with APD. Service providers may find themselves engaged in behaviors designed to either prove that they too are exciting or that they are worthy of the attraction their clients can appear to be experiencing toward them. It is a form of seduction that can be compelling when it is going on and difficult to believe when it is over. Clinicians have been caught in this web who were later completely unable to explain why they behaved as they did in the circumstances. Meloy (1996) states that no other client population will compel service providers to face their own aggressive and destructive impulses like those with APD.

Assessment and Treatment

A diagnosis of APD requires childhood symptoms of conduct disorder prior to the age of 15 (Widiger et al., 1994). The five most indicative criteria for a prototypic APD are taking advantage of others, experiencing no remorse for harm or injury caused to others, engaging in unlawful or criminal behavior, being deceitful, and being reckless and demonstrating disregard for the rights, property, or safety of others (Shedler & Westen, 2004). It would be unusual for antisocial persons not to have committed acts for which they could have been arrested, even if they were not. Some individuals with APD have not committed aggressive crimes; they may have limited their activities to exploitative and manipulative crimes. Deceitfulness or lying, for individuals with APD, has intrinsic value or pleasure and may be engaged in for its own reward rather than for obtaining benefit or escaping consequences (Westen & Shedler, 1999; Widiger et al., 1994).

Comprehensive treatment planning for APD involves:

- Determining the severity of active psychopathic factors, with a clinical focus on the capacity to form attachments
- Determining if there is any evidence of superego disturbance
- Identifying any treatable Axis I mental or substance use disorders
- Delineating situational factors that may aggravate or worsen antisocial behaviors
- Identifying legal problems or involvement
- Engaging in treatment only if it is demonstrably safe and effective
- Paying careful attention to all countertransference reactions (Meloy, 1996)

Effective treatment includes active, direct confrontation of APD thinking patterns, attitudes, and denial or minimization of antisocial behavior. However, it is pointless to try to change the inclination these individuals have to break the law; they are unlikely to respond positively to an appeal to become a good citizen. On the other hand, reflecting on how APD behavior is disadvantageous both in the present and in the future may make a difference. If difficulty with the law, inability to hold on to a job, or failure to sustain relationships can look like a loss of autonomy, freedom, mastery, and personal choice, individuals with APD may come to accept that making changes will get them closer to what they want. In the TV series *The Shield*, police detective Vic Mackey told his attorney that he is not who he used to be (a distinctly antisocial police officer) and that he wants a second chance. When she asked him what was different, he said that he still "wanted to be a cop." When his behavior was possibly going to cost him his gun and his badge—his self-image, power, and authority—he saw the point of being straight where he had once been crooked. The essential focus in a treatment setting is related to consequences: what can be gained and what might be lost based upon behavioral choices. Self-interest is not difficult to figure out, and as long as these individuals want something positive in their lives, can feel loyalty to someone or something, or can be concerned about loss, change is possible.

It may also be effective to appeal to the narcissistic qualities in APD. Service providers can reflect that many individuals with similar personality structures are able to remain free of the criminal justice system by developing their personal strengths in ways that are meaningful and fulfilling. Oldham and Morris (1995) propose that nonpersonality disordered individuals with a similar style to that of APD are "adventurous personalities" who are nonconforming, live by their own internal code, and love the thrill of risk. They are persuasive and good at influencing others. They relish sex and have a basic wanderlust. They can take care of themselves. They are physically bold, tough, and courageous. They do not thrive in a basic 9-to-5 job; they do best when they work for themselves. They live in the present and do not feel guilty about the past or worried about the future. They are action oriented, extroverted, and do not need others to maintain their self-esteem. People who can be described in this manner, particularly men, are esteemed in this culture. They can express who they are in a manner that is not illegal and can be well rewarded by an American society that values independence, toughness, and nonconformity. The treatment challenge that can be presented to individuals with APD is whether they must be self-destructive and engage in a legal downward spiral or whether they can turn their strengths into advantages and remain free of the criminal justice system. What will not happen is that these individuals will become conforming, well-adjusted, compliant members of society. In fact, they do not need to do that to become successful and less at risk to multiple losses in their lives. If individuals with APD have felt the painful costs of their antisocial acts and are able to respond to aversive consequences, they can implement new thinking and behaving strategies (Meloy, 1996).

Treatment of individuals with APD often includes work with family members who need to establish and maintain firm boundaries and learn to set limits on APD behavior. Family members can also confirm or challenge the version of events or historical information provided by individuals with APD.

There is substantial speculation in the literature about whether time is actually the best treatment for individuals with APD. There is some possibility that APD symptoms ease as the individuals "mellow" with age. Perhaps hormones, loss of physical power, or growing pressure toward social conformity and attachment to others account for the decline in antisocial behaviors. However, Millon and Davis (1996) propose that individuals with APD do not age out; they believe that the basic personality is not altered but is expressed with less obviously flagrant behaviors.

It is important to discuss behaviors appropriate to AA or NA participation with individuals with APD. They may experience anxiety in response to the confrontation and pressure to conform to group norms involved in these groups. To manage their reactions, they may engage in exploitative behaviors such as inappropriate sexual activity with and borrowing money from more vulnerable participants (B. Carruth, personal communication, September 25, 2007).

Finally, a major consideration in offering community-based services to individuals with APD is safety for service providers, agency staff, other clients in group or milieu treatment, and the larger community. For some individuals with APD, community-based treatment is not a choice that can be made within the larger context of personal and public safety. Some individuals with APD are so damaged or dangerous that working with them is futile and naive (McWilliams, 1994). Meloy (1996) identifies five APD features that contraindicate treatment of any kind: (1) a history of sadistic and violent behavior, (2) total absence of remorse, (3) intelligence two standard deviations from the mean (in either direction), (4) no history of attachments, and (5) fear of predation by experienced service providers without overt threat from the individuals with APD.

Treatment Goals

Treatment goals for personality disorders should focus on adaptive responses to the environment; they do not necessarily include characterological restructuring (Adler, 1990). McWilliams (1994) notes that it is significant in APD treatment if these individuals use words for self-expression rather than manipulation, inhibit impulses, and experience any pride in self-control.

Beck et al. (2004) suggest the treatment goal of altering cognitive distortions of individuals with APD, which include:

- Believing that wanting something justifies any action to get it
- Believing thoughts are accurate simply because they are there
- Believing that they, as individuals, are infallible
- Thinking that if they feel right about what they do, it must be the right thing to do
- Experiencing other people as irrelevant
- Believing that negative consequences will not happen or will not matter

Bockian and Jongsma (2001) propose that treatment goals for individuals with APD should address:

- The need to be thought of as unflawed
- The determination to appear tough, indomitable, and formidable
- The inclination to be angry and defensive when status is questioned
- Irritability and aggression
- The determination to be in the dominant position in relationships
- Lack of remorse

Recovery Activities for Individuals with APD and Addiction

If these individuals are in a treatment setting, the probability of their accepting abstinence as a goal and seeking recovery is improved if they want to be free of the legal system and treatment providers. These obstacles to available choices and autonomy are annoying to persons with APD. Recovery can be conceived of as a road to freedom; such a conceptualization can make the choices involved in recovery and abstinence considerably more attractive. Personal benefit is likely to be the one motivating factor strong enough to make recovery a desirable goal. It is possible to work with their motivation and invite recovery-based activities that are in accordance with their self-image and need for stimulation. Recovery does take strength; it is a candid validation of these individuals to suggest that the strengths inherent in their personality will make recovery possible and give them what they need to achieve their goals. It is equally frank to note that their strengths, if used to pursue self-destructive ends, can lead to increasingly severe addiction and increasingly unfortunate consequences. Recovery is always a personal choice, but service providers can assist in clarifying potential outcomes based upon the choices made. It is important to go for pro-recovery behavior without worrying about whether the motivations behind the behavior has anything to do with compliance to social norms. It may be that willingness to seek recovery as a way to stay out of jail or a hospital is enough (Evans & Sullivan, 2000).

The 12-step community can be very effective for people with APD. The first step is crucial; it is important that these individuals learn to identify exactly how their drinking and drugging was out of control. It is helpful to encourage a fourth and fifth step completion with a sponsor so they can begin to confront their antisocial thinking errors and distortions that they use to justify both their substance use and their antisocial behavior. Evans and Sullivan (2000) suggest that service providers prompt these individuals with APD to encourage this step work by asking to discuss how they blame, rationalize, lie, and so on to justify their use of drugs and alcohol. What are the negative consequences they have experienced from these behaviors?

The 12-step groups present a philosophy of living that mirrors the same goals that would be most helpful for persons with personality disorders: responsibility for self, honesty in dealing with feelings, sensitivity to both the needs and the feelings of others, avoidance of impulsive actions, and the ability to tolerate stress and painful feelings (O'Malley, Kosten, & Renner, 1990). Even if these advantages do not seem particularly or inherently appealing, they are behaviors and attitudes that can make success in various endeavors more likely and personal achievement more possible.

6

Cluster B
Borderline Personality Disorder and Substance Use Disorders

Borderline Personality Disorder Defined

Essential Features

An essential feature of borderline personality disorder (BPD) is a pattern of unstable interpersonal relationships, self-image, and affect. There is marked impulsivity that begins by early adulthood (APA, 2000).

Individuals with BPD express intense, poorly modulated affect and have variable moods and irregular energy levels that appear to be only tangentially related to external events. These individuals are caught in the crosscurrents of shame for being dependent, fear of abandonment, and the longing to be assertive. They want to gain approval and affection without having to submit to others. The result is a mercurial and explosive anger that can elicit the rejection they fear (Millon & Grossman, 2007a; Preston, 2006).

Shedler and Westen (2004) identify core BPD features as emotions that spiral out of control, fear of abandonment, depression, feelings of inadequacy or inferiority, inability to self-soothe, rapid attachment to others, unstable or chaotic relationships, and an unstable self-image.

Linehan (1993) proposes diagnostic criteria for BPD that include specific patterns of dysregulation. Emotional dysregulation involves a high level of reactivity with episodic depression, anxiety, irritability, and problems with anger. Interpersonal dysregulation is demonstrated by chaotic relationships and frantic efforts to keep significant others from leaving. Behavioral dysregulation includes impulsive, self-injurious, self-mutilating, or suicidal behavior. Cognitive dysregulation involves nonpsychotic thought dysregulation including depersonalization and dissociation. Self-dysregulation is experienced as an incomplete sense of self and feelings of emptiness.

There is some question as to whether BPD is a personality disorder or an affective disorder. Millon and Davis (1996) suggest the possibility that the clinical characteristics of BPD fall into both the personality disorders and the affective spectrum disorders.

A key factor in the etiology of BPD is a genetically based temperament (Gabbard, 2005). However, other factors such as the psychosocial environment and trauma may also play a role. Multiple variables have been identified, but none appear to be either necessary or sufficient to cause BPD to develop. Instead, it appears to be a psychobiological disorder influenced by a complex interplay of genetic and environmental factors (Livesley, 2005).

Self-Image

Individuals with BPD experience an unstable self-image that oscillates between feelings of inferiority and superiority. These individuals often see themselves as defective, deficient, and victimized. On the superior side of the vacillation is a lack of humility and a core of omnipotence, conceit, and self-righteousness (Akhtar, 1995; Masterson, 1981).

Preston (2006) describes individuals with BPD as having an impaired or underdeveloped sense of self with:

- A lack of awareness of inner needs
- An inclination to abandon inner beliefs with a need to quickly placate others
- Expressions of feelings cloaked in hesitancy, apologies, or minimization
- Confusion about what is really being felt or what is really wanted
- Major life choices that are ill-defined or undirected
- An internal sense of chaos, fragmentation, and instability
- Permeable boundaries
- An inordinate reliance on others to provide reassurance
- Passivity or subjugation

View of Others

Individuals with BPD are ambivalent toward others as well as themselves. They experience rapidly fluctuating perceptions of others (Millon & Davis, 1996). For people with BPD who experienced childhood abuse, there appears to be an increased sensitivity to cues of threat, impaired processing of social information, and increased probability of responding aggressively (Spoont, 1996). They tend to attribute negative intent to others, which allows them to view the interpersonal difficulties they have as being independent of their own behavior (Layden, Newman, Freeman, & Morse, 1993). Gabbard (2005) suggests that the failure to resolve trauma appears to distinguish BPD from other personality disorders.

Individuals with BPD believe their negatively biased perceptions are absolute fact rather than viewing them as possible interpretations of events or a representation of reality based upon their internal beliefs, feelings, and past experiences. McDonald (2002) describes individuals with BPD as operating in a "believing is seeing" (p. 2) mode wherein they formulate implausible conclusions about what other people's behaviors mean and respond inappropriately, particularly when feeling threatened; they do not understand or perceive their impact on the people around them. Lost in their emotionally driven interpretations of others, they are unable to apprehend how they appear through the eyes of others (Grinfeld, 2003).

Relationships

Beck et al. (2004) note that individuals with BPD hold extreme, poorly integrated, and unrealistic expectations of interpersonal relationships. The initial position in BPD relationships is that of friendly dependency on a nurturer (which they believe is equally desired by those upon whom they depend). This becomes hostile control when, inevitably, the caregiver fails to deliver everything individuals with BPD want or need (Benjamin, 2005). The completely good, nurturing caregiver, with the most minor mistake, becomes the object of BPD hate and contempt (Oldham & Morris, 1995). Millon and Davis (1996) describe this quality of BPD behavior within relationships as paradoxical. Even though they need attention and affection, they frequently act in unpredictably contrary, manipulative, and volatile ways that elicit rejection.

Individuals with BPD experience interpersonal relationships as intensely pleasurable and intensely painful. Their relationships are based upon need gratification rather than reciprocity or the ability to recognize that others have needs of their own (Preston, 2006). Individuals with BPD are described as destroying the relationships they cannot live without (Oldham & Morris, 1995) or as loving without measure the people they will soon come to hate (Benjamin, 1996). The destructiveness within relationships has to do with unmodulated expression of feelings and a volatile rage response to perceived or potential abandonment. One individual with BPD wrote in an e-mail, "I just lost another relationship with my usual: I love you. I hate you. Don't leave me—you can't live here." Although there was some humor in her recognition of her contradictory behavior, there was also sadness that relationships were so frequently lost in her life.

Issues with Authority

Individuals with BPD are inclined to view authority figures with intensified ambivalence, fear, and rage. Those who have authority are both needed and viewed as dangerous. If the authority figures are service providers, they can be seen as replicating parental figures who had access to what was needed but were disinclined to provide it; they were potentially abusive and had to be seduced or coerced into being benign and protective. These past parental figures also seemed to have the power, skill, ability, and influence to deal with life's problems, that is, were autonomous in contrast to BPD self-experience as incompetent and powerless. The intense need individuals with BPD express toward people who are seen as powerful laced with the rage of betrayal or anticipated betrayal can be exhausting for the service providers as well as for the clients caught in the affective maelstrom of hope, hopelessness, demands, and rejections.

Behavior

Individuals with BPD evidence readily corruptible ethics, standards, and ideals. Their capacity to experience genuine guilt is weak; their only effective restraints on behavior center around shame, fear, and dread of exposure (Akhtar, 1995). They may, after interpersonal difficulties, go into a period of self-criticism and self-blame (Millon, 1996). These individuals vacillate between self-hate and rage toward others without resolution or understanding of their own part in the problems they face. Preston (2006) notes that it is remarkable how many people with BPD are unaware that their behavior is maladaptive and self-destructive. They can experience their severe acting out as necessary and helpful because it brings relief. They then engage in denial or minimization of the consequences of their behavior.

It is difficult to be comfortable with people with BPD because they so easily become sullen and hurt or obstinate and nasty. These individuals are readily provoked; they are impatient and irritable unless things go their way. Whereas BPD anguish and despair are genuine, they can also be a means of expressing hostility, frustration, and an inclination to retaliate against others. However, many individuals with BPD believe that the obstructiveness, pessimism, and immaturity that others see in them is actually a reflection of their sensitivity and the inconsiderateness that others show toward them (Millon, 1996). Unchecked, these behaviors can lead to increasing isolation and a reduction of restraint on impulsivity—factors that raise the risk of a completed suicide.

Linehan (1993) identifies six behavior patterns evidenced in BPD:

- Emotional vulnerability with severe difficulty in regulating emotions
- Unrealistically high standards and expectations for self with a tendency to invalidate or fail to recognize emotional responses, thoughts, beliefs, and behavior
- Unrelenting crises and parasuicidal behavior, that is, nonfatal, intentional self-injurious behavior that results in actual tissue damage, self-mutilation, and self-inflicted burns, with little or no intent to cause death
- Inhibited grieving
- Active passivity; these individuals often fail to engage actively in solving their own life problems while actively soliciting problem-solving from others
- Appearance of greater competence than can be demonstrated through behavior or accomplishments

Affect

Individuals with BPD have been described as "hemophiliacs of emotion" (Sperry & Carlson, 1993). Linehan (1993) suggests that BPD is primarily a dysfunction of the emotion regulation system due to affective vulnerability and intensity; the other characteristics of BPD are secondary to this dysfunction. The emotional experience of BPD is one of chronic aversive affective experiences. Failure to inhibit maladaptive, mood-dependent actions follows.

Linehan (1993) further suggests that self-mutilation has an important affect-regulating function. Although the exact mechanism is unclear, many individuals with BPD report substantial relief from anxiety and other intense negative feelings after cutting or burning themselves.

Individuals with BPD struggle with despondency, rage, fury, self-hatred, arrogance, anxiety, uncertainty, emptiness, dependency, stubbornness, and self-damaging impulses. These individuals are not able to self-comfort. They may flee into impulsive sex, food, drugs, or shopping (or shoplifting.) They are very vulnerable to substance-use disorders; use of psychoactive drugs may be initiated to manage affect.

Defenses

The BPD defensive regulatory mechanism is regression. Individuals with BPD show a tendency under stress to retreat to developmentally earlier levels of anxiety tolerance, impulse control, and social adaptation (Millon & Davis, 1996). For these individuals, the capacity to tolerate anxiety, depression, or frustration is limited. They have difficulty perceiving or accepting reality limitations. Under severe stress, they may have trouble differentiating past and present, reality and fantasy, and mature and infantile aspects of their mental life (Masterson, 1981).

Gabbard (2005) suggests that people with BPD can operate in a psychic equivalence mode; they assume that their perceptions of reality are identical to the reality itself. Therefore, when individuals with BPD are agitated and under stress, the external world looks like the internal world: chaotic, frightening, and out of control. The defenses needed to cope with such overwhelming intensity can be primitive and self-damaging.

The Self-Created World (Altered Reality) of BPD

Individuals with BPD create and sustain an altered reality that, while not psychotic, shelters their contradictory beliefs about themselves and others. This reality compromises interpersonal skills and can result in unusual perceptions and behavior. For individuals with BPD, the altered reality is composed of thinking or believing:

- I can't stand it.
- Stop the world, I want to get off.
- Harming myself is preferable to feeling so much pain.
- I can't control what I feel or what I do. People need to understand that.
- Sometimes I can't believe how much I hate the person I love or how much I need the person I can't stand.

Substance Use Disorders and BPD

Co-Occurring Substance Use Disorders and the Impact of Drugs on BPD

BPD is in Cluster B, the dramatic, erratic, or impulsive cluster; Cluster B has the highest rates of alcohol and drug abuse and dependence (Nace & Tinsley, 2007) of the three *DSM-IV-TR* personality clusters.

Individuals with BPD experience extraordinary affective discomfort. They are frequently agitated, labile, and overwhelmed. They do not define themselves as able or effective in managing their own lives. Their defenses are regressive; under stress they become much less able to adapt. Drugs and alcohol can offer these individuals a way of coping; drugs can block out sensations of pain, discomfort, and negative affect. The appeal of drugs and other compulsive behavior in soothing, distracting, and escaping is apparent and powerful. About 50% to 70% of individuals with BPD also have a substance use disorder (Gregory, 2006).

Stone (1993) suggests that a complicated reciprocal relationship exists between BPD and illicit drugs. Use of alcohol and certain drugs, for example, amphetamines, can intensify the symptomotology of BPD by making impulsivity worse. Benzodiazepines can reduce inhibition and release borderline behavioral aggression. Excessive alcohol can reduce cognitive skills, disinhibit affective expression, and permit despair. Yet real-world interaction triggers overwhelming negative affect, and psychoactive drugs seem to block the pain and sooth the turmoil while actually making maladaptive behaviors worse (Millon, 1996). In other words, drugs can make BPD symptoms worse while apparently offering relief from BPD symptoms.

Drugs of Choice for BPD

Individuals with BPD often use alcohol and other drugs in a chaotic and unpredictable pattern. They will use almost any drug or route of administration to their own worst advantage. They often abuse prescribed benzodiazepines or other sedative–hypnotics and may hoard these medications for suicide attempts (Richards, 1993).

Another issue regarding drug of choice for individuals with BPD has to do with their intolerance for being alone and the intensity of their relationships. These individuals often use drugs and alcohol as part of their contact with needed others. The drug of choice is then incidental to that used by their social contacts or significant others. Recovery in these situations is dependent upon linking addicted individuals with BPD to a strong support network that fosters abstinence and upon engaging significant others in the treatment process.

Integrated Dual Diagnosis Treatment for BPD

Engaging in Treatment

Individuals with BPD may enter treatment in either mental health or substance abuse facilities. They may self-refer or be referred via the criminal justice system. If self-referred, these individuals may have an extensive history with mental health treatment. They may have significant difficulty in benefiting from treatment due to affective lability and severe ambivalence. Individuals with BPD and co-occurring substance use disorders may be drug-seeking and volatile when displeased with either the treatment or the service providers.

Whatever the challenges brought to the treatment setting, individuals with BPD need to feel understood, welcomed, and hopeful to be able to engage in the treatment process. It is an unfortunate result of ineffective treatment techniques that service providers may feel ineffective and helpless when working with clients with BPD and may communicate, overtly or covertly, that they are not pleased to initiate services with "another one." Researchers Gallop, Lancee, and Garfinkel (1989) found that stereotyped perceptions play a crucial role in how clinicians interpret and respond to behavior of clients with BPD (as cited by Potter, 2006). The researchers concluded that the label *BPD* alone is sufficient to diminish service provider empathy. This attitude is destructive and introduces hopelessness into the treatment process.

Treatment Provider Guidelines

Basic treatment principles in working with individuals with BPD include:

- Identify, confront, and treat comorbid substance abuse disorders and depression.
- Identify and confront self-defeating behaviors.
- Maintain a stable treatment environment.
- Learn to differentiate nonlethal self-harm from true suicidal intent.
- Stress that treatment is a collaborative enterprise; service providers are neither omnipotent nor omniscient.
- Manage transference.
- Manage countertransference.
- Do not provide services in professional isolation (Gunderson & Links, 1996; Sperry, 2003).

Linehan (1993) suggests basic assumptions needed by service providers regarding individuals with BPD:

- They are doing the best they can.
- They want to improve.
- They need to do better, try harder, and be more motivated to change.
- They did not cause all of their problems, but they have to solve them anyway.
- The lives of individuals with BPD who are suicidal are unbearable as they are currently being lived.
- Individuals with BPD must learn new behaviors that are not mood-dependent.
- Services providers working with these individuals need support.

It is important to remember that BPD self-mutilation, which can evoke service provider feelings of anxiety and anger at feeling manipulated, is dangerous behavior. The behavior is reinforced by the relief from internal pressure it provides through de-focusing from affective pain. Individuals with BPD are often able to dissociate from the physical pain and cannot modulate the behavior via an aversive reaction to that pain. Crisis management and a direct treatment focus on self-damage is essential.

Professional Ethics and BPD

One of the most demanding tasks for service providers is maintaining their own equilibrium when faced with strong emotional pressures from clients with BPD. It is a challenge to be aware of and empathic with BPD emotional pain without minimizing or denying it, blaming the victim, or reacting by becoming numb. Clinicians must recognize the inevitability of their own strong emotional reactions that come with this work; they must develop the professional support structure and the skills to manage their feelings without becoming ineffective or punitive. Each provider must be realistic about his or her capacity and willingness to tolerate the "white heat" of BPD interaction (Pilkonis, 1997, p. 10).

Potential treatment provider responses to individuals with BPD range from over-involvement and excessive emotional investment to detachment with excessive self-protective distancing. The over-involved position manifests in service provider certainty of being able to rescue individuals with BPD from their psychological problems. The self-protective responses show up in the service provider's eagerness to limit or terminate the therapeutic relationship in response to outbursts and irrational demands. There is a mid-range on this continuum that is characterized by sedate caring, interest, supportiveness, and objective understanding. It is important to remember that the therapeutic relationship with individuals with BPD can be so unstable that service providers bounce back and forth between the excessively distant and excessively involved extremes—mirroring the BPD pathology (Layden et al., 1993).

In the worst of circumstances, Gabbard and Wilkinson (1994) believe that service provider reactions to clients with BPD can lead to unethical boundary violations. Clinicians may come to believe that they are responsible for clients with BPD and that love or friendship within the therapeutic relationship will be healing. Clinicians may respond to the demands of clients with BPD to be treated as exceptions to usual treatment and program procedures. To ward off anger at being denied special consideration, treatment providers may extend sessions, engage in inappropriate self-disclosure, defer payment, not charge any fee, or engage in sexual behavior.

Another difficulty in working with borderline pathology is the active coercion of nurturing until the service providers burn out. Whether there is or is not any progress in treatment, clients with BPD are likely to eventually feel abandoned and engage in rageful and self-destructive behavior. Service providers can feel an escalating loss of control and engage in hostile dominance as a means to contain the tactics of abuse that individuals with BPD have learned and are willing to use (Benjamin, 2005).

In productive therapeutic relationships, service providers maintain benign objectivity, show genuine concern for the well-being of clients with BPD, are consistently positive and supportive, maintain a firm grounding in reality, an even temperament, and an unthreatened willingness to address acting out and distortions from clients with BPD. Willingness to consult with colleagues is also essential for a healthy approach to working with these individuals (Layden et al., 1993). It is imperative that service providers working in private practice develop a peer consultation or supervision structure that mitigates against professional isolation. They need to have access to other professionals who can provide a more objective set of eyes and ears and be in a position to challenge service providers' reactions, plans, or clinical decisions.

Assessment and Treatment

Individuals with BPD typically come to treatment with an erratic and unpredictable pattern of problems including unstable relationships, labile mood, impulsivity, and identity confusion. Variability is the hallmark of BPD; no single feature or pattern is invariably present (Beck et al., 2004).

Assessment of individuals with BPD should include:

- A history of self-harm as well as unsafe or suicidal behaviors

- A list of potential means for self-harm
- A history of previous treatment
- A history of dissociative experiences (identify what is lost: behavior, affect sensation, or knowledge)
- A psychosocial history and history of sexual abuse
- Evaluation for the presence of psychotic thinking (CSAT, 1994)

It is imperative that the assessment addresses substance use and compulsive behaviors. Because it is possible to see borderline-like behaviors that are secondary to or a product of the substance use and not indicative of a personality disorder, McGlynn (2003) suggests that the following behaviors be excluded as symptoms of personality disorders:

- Behaviors when intoxicated or when withdrawing
- Behaviors only engaged in when seeking, concealing, or using substances
- Behaviors that began after substance use onset and are inconsistent with prior personality
- Behaviors that cease after a significant period of abstinence

In treatment for borderline personality disorder, Linehan (1993) suggests that impulsive and suicidal behaviors be seen as maladaptive solution behaviors to the problem of overwhelming, uncontrollable, intensely painful negative affect. Linehan's dialectical behavior therapy (DBT) approach uses supportive acceptance balanced with confrontation and change strategies. For example, individuals with BPD can learn some basic skills for effective emotional modulation. They need to reduce maladaptive mood-dependent behaviors. They must learn to trust and validate themselves as well as their emotions, thoughts, and activities. Four major emotional modulation abilities are (1) inhibiting inappropriate behavior related to strong negative or positive affect, (2) self-regulating physiological arousal associated with emotions, (3) refocusing attention in the presence of strong emotions, and (4) organizing self for action in the service of an external, non–mood-dependent goal. DBT includes active education about emotional regulation, interpersonal effectiveness, distress tolerance, core mindfulness, and self-management skills. Mindfulness is a skill that helps individuals with BPD learn to observe themselves without judging; they can begin to develop a benign sense of self, learn to distance themselves from their emotional experience, and practice living in the here and now (Lynch & Robins, 1997).

In addressing BPD aggression, it is important to identify motives that exist in the here and now and to make the accompanying inappropriate behavior visible and dystonic. Aggression in individuals with BPD can be understood in terms of an immature self full of rage at caregivers who failed to provide for survival and developmental needs—and who may have been directly involved in abuse (Gunderson & Links, 1996). However, current aggression elicits counteraggression and must be managed. Individuals with BPD must learn to recognize their own inclination toward and skills in being abusive toward others.

They must take responsibility for their behavior and stop abusing others in the present for the abuse they experienced in the past. If they do not take responsibility for and change their querulousness and irritability, they face increasingly negative interpersonal consequences. A positive prognosis in treatment appears to be significantly dependent on the management of hostility (Stone, 1993) and achieving abstinence from psychoactive drugs (Preston, 2006; Zanarini, Frankenburg, Hennen, Reich, & Silk, 2004).

Individuals with BPD are particularly vulnerable to the escape offered by psychoactive drugs and alcohol. A key modification of DBT for individuals with BPD and substance use disorders is called dialectical abstinence or DBT-SUD (DBT–Substance Use Disorders). Dialectical abstinence contains elements of both abstinence and harm reduction; there is a focus on abstinence and a planned approach to relapse that is designed to mitigate harm and resume abstinence. It balances an insistence on total abstinence with a policy of total provider acceptance upon relapse. DBT-SUD focuses on temperamental emotional vulnerability, the history or presence of an invalidating environment, and problems with emotional dysregulation. As a behavioral treatment, DBT-SUD relentlessly pursues changing maladaptive behaviors, and as an acceptance-based treatment, it provides unwavering validation and coping skills. Distress tolerance skills assist managing the ordinary pain of life without engaging in harmful behaviors such as using drugs. Another important skill is that of alternate rebellion. DBT-SUD treatment providers recognize that rebellion itself is not a problem but emphasize the importance of determining a way to rebel that has no lasting negative consequences.

DBT-SUD treats drug use as a method of coping. It does not assert that going off drugs will make everything all right; it is acknowledged that it will not. However, it is proposed that problem behaviors occur in specific contexts and are misguided attempts to solve problems; in effect, the chosen solution becomes the problem. Understanding the relevant context in which drug use occurs can make it possible to better predict using or getting high and permit seeking nondestructive, alternative behaviors. Service providers using DBT-SUD engage in a number of interventions that are geared toward increasing client attachment to treatment. Attachment strategies include discussing nonattached behaviors, for example, arriving late, use of validation techniques, increased contact, and increasing or decreasing length of sessions as needed. There is recognition in DBT-SUD that individuals with BPD need to find a new peer support group that supports abstinence and protects them from feeling lonely or abandoned (Lynch & Robins, 1997; McGlynn, 2003; Rosenthal, 2006).

The issue of prescribed medication for clients with BPD is complex and difficult. These individuals often demand medication for anxiety and become quite angry when denied. They can be noncompliant with medication—either using too much or too little. The intensity of their discomfort can make the prescribing of medication with addictive potential seem more reasonable than it should. They are quite frequently successful in obtaining the medication they seek from at least one doctor from whom they receive services. Then it becomes difficult to withdraw a drug to which they may have already developed physical tolerance and psychological dependence. Triebwasser and Siever (2006) note that polypharmacy for individuals with BPD often seems to be a cumulative process. Medications with unclear benefits continue to be prescribed due to provider fear of inducing a clinical deterioration in worrisome clients while more and more medications are added because of persistent symptomatology. This type of polypharmacy has little empirical support and may result in exposing a vulnerable population to dangerous iatrogenic complications.

Treatment Goals

Treatment goals for individuals with BPD must include management of unsafe behaviors, affect management, and reduction of psychoactive substance use. Linehan (1993) suggests that a central BPD treatment goal is management of self-mutilating behavior. The rate of completed suicides for individuals with BPD who cut or burn themselves is twice that of those who do not. This behavior can also damage the body irrevocably and presents the possibility of accidental death. The effectiveness of treatment will be based, at least in part, on the development of an intent in these individuals to help rather than harm themselves.

According to Zanarini et al. (2004) and Preston (2006), the strongest indicator of a poor prognosis for BPD is ongoing problematic substance use. Conversely, the strongest predictor of BPD remission is the absence of a substance use disorder. Lifetime risk of suicide in individuals with BPD is 10%. However, with untreated alcoholism, dually diagnosed individuals with BPD have substantially greater risk (Gunderson & Links, 1996). It is clear that use of alcohol and other drugs must be given a significant and persistent focus in treatment if a positive outcome is to be facilitated.

Recovery Activities for Individuals with BPD and Addiction

When individuals with BPD are able to achieve abstinence from their drug or drugs of choice, they are vulnerable to alternative compulsive behaviors such as eating, shopping, impulsive and unsafe sexual behavior, and gambling. Recovery activities need to address the full range of self-destructive behaviors as these individuals are seeking skills in managing strong affect without harming themselves. Many people with BPD have histories of physical and sexual abuse. There may be concerns regarding compulsive sexual behavior that can be addressed in both treatment and in support groups for individuals with similar experiences.

While many recovery activities can be done alone, recovery is not something most people can do without help, mutual support, and a sense of connection with a recovering community. This is particularly important for individuals with BPD. They are very much in need of meaningful contact with others who can help them achieve and sustain an emotional balance while they undertake an extensive and sometimes bewildering range of changes in recovery from the personality disorder and from addiction.

Participation in 12-step groups may be more successful for individuals with BPD if they have pre–12-step practice sessions. These individuals should be helped to organize their thoughts and to practice saying "pass" when feeling unsafe. Heterosexual individuals with

BPD should be encouraged to join same-sex groups and have same sex sponsors as needed; homosexual individuals with BPD also need to select sponsors that are not likely to be potential sexual partners.

Individuals with BPD and addiction are likely to benefit from the Wellness Recovery Action Plan (WRAP) as developed by Mary Ann Copeland (2000). In WRAP groups, these individuals can develop lists or tools to support them in their recovery, for example, what they need to do on a daily or weekly basis to maintain their equilibrium, what they need to do when they start to feel vulnerable or have stronger than usual cravings, and what they need to do in a crisis. This type of plan can include all of the skills learned in DBT or other types of treatment, in AA or NA or other peer support groups, and from others developing their own WRAP plan. Having a well-defined "toolkit" for recovery can support individuals with BPD through some of the very real challenges they face managing their affective responses and working toward abstinence.

7

Cluster B

Histrionic Personality Disorder and
Substance Use Disorders

Histrionic Personality Disorder Defined

Essential Features

The essential feature of histrionic personality disorder (HPD) is a pervasive and excessive pattern of emotionality and attention-seeking behavior. These individuals are lively, dramatic, enthusiastic, and flirtatious. They may be inappropriately sexually provocative, express strong emotions with an impressionistic style, and be easily influenced by others (APA, 2000).

Frances et al. (1995) describe individuals with HPD as manipulative, vain, and demanding. However, in addition to the focus on physical appeal, the authors note that there may also be a genetic association between HPD and somatization disorder. Benjamin (2005) believes that HPD falls into two subtypes: (1) those who are flirtatious and focused on physical attractiveness and (2) those who are concerned with somatic symptoms. Whereas the *DSM-IV-TR* (APA, 2000) emphasizes the flirtatious version, individuals with HPD vary in the degree to which they are sexually seductive or concerned about physical symptoms. Some, for reasons of age or physical unattractiveness, may receive such a negative reaction to their seductive behavior that they must rely more heavily on somatic concerns. It is possible for some individuals with HPD to tyrannize their families with their physical symptoms.

Individuals with HPD demonstrate what American society tends to foster and admire: to be well liked, popular, extroverted, attractive, and sociable (Millon & Davis, 1996). In fact, Widiger et al. (1994) describe HPD as an extreme variant of extroversion. In a nonpathological form, extroversion is being high-spirited, buoyant, and optimistic. These factors coalesce into a personality disorder only when the needs behind the behavior are pathologically inflexible, repetitious, and persistent (Millon & Grossman, 2007b). It is then that the manipulativeness and disinhibited exploitation of others become factors and the personality-disordered version of extroversion becomes apparent.

The 2001–2002 National Epidemiologic Survey noted that there are no risk differentials observed for gender in HPD (Grant et al., 2004); it is as likely for men as women. Individuals with HPD may decompensate in later adult years due to the lack of maturation and frequent failure of intimate relationships. The consequences of these factors grow more severe with age. The usual course of untreated HPD is precarious as life opportunities are missed or destroyed (Kernberg, 1992).

Self-Image

Individuals with HPD view themselves as gregarious, sociable, friendly, and agreeable. They consider themselves to be charming, stimulating, and well liked even when others do not hold a similar view. They value their capacity to attract people via their physical appearance and by appearing to be interesting and lively people. For individuals with HPD, indications of internal distress, weakness, depression, or hostility are denied or suppressed and are not included in their view of themselves (Millon & Grossman, 2007b).

For individuals with HPD, vanity and seductiveness function to bolster and maintain self-esteem; they often become overinvested in how they look and dread the impact of aging (McWilliams, 1994). Growing old is threatening to their need to see themselves as glamorous and attractive people who are desired and admired by others. A core HPD response to aging is to deny that it is happening. One female with HPD, who was both alcohol and drug dependent, wore tight, sexy shorts and tight t-shirts during the summers; she would call attention to her body with statements like "I need to exercise more, look at my belly." She was extremely slender, and the belly state-ment was designed to elicit both attention and exclamations that she had a very firm and well-shaped abdomen indeed. This woman was 62 years old, with false teeth and the severe signs of physical aging that can accompany poor health and years of addiction. Although her youthful flirtatiousness was embarrassing to the people around her, they were rarely willing to challenge her behavior.

Individuals with HPD are consumed with attention to superfici-alities and spend little time or attention on their internal life. They often do not know who they are apart from their identification with others. These individuals regularly alter and recompose themselves to create a socially attractive but changing facade. A scientist once told his histrionic personality-disordered brother-in-law that "he was a man of strong and changing opinions." While he captured the man's behavior well, he could have added that the strong opinions belonged to whomever his brother-in-law was associating with at that moment. On his own, his strong opinions were limited to those activities that gave him pleasure or were aversive to him; he did not inform himself in either current events or intellectual pursuits, and he formed virtually no adherence to any particular point of view or belief system.

Individuals with HPD also fail to attend to the details and specif-ics of their experiences. They have, accordingly, memories that are diffuse and general, with a tremendous lack of detail (Will, 1995) and, as a result, a poorly developed sense of self.

If individuals with HPD are made aware of their behavior and the displeasure of others in response, they will feel shame and guilt until they can convince themselves it is not true or push the issue aside, distance themselves from the people causing this discomfort, and return to their view of themselves as charming and agreeable.

View of Others

Individuals with HPD experience others as strong and capable (McWilliams, 1994). They view themselves as less powerful; from that weaker position, they absolve themselves from adult responsibilities. They then engage in manipulative behavior with people they see as potential sources of attention and care-taking. They will behave in a seductive and enticing manner unless they are denied what they are seeking. They can then become rageful. Their own needs are paramount, and other people are expected to meet those needs.

The attention individuals with HPD give to others does not help them learn to be empathic. Their intense observation skills are dedicated to determining what behaviors, attitudes, or feelings are most likely to result in winning the admiration and approval of others. Essentially, these individuals watch other people watch them. Their actual focus is on how they are doing and how they are being received. As a result of this focus on self, they are not effective in understanding other people.

Relationships

The HPD failure to view others realistically is reflected by their difficulties in developing and sustaining satisfactory relationships. Individuals with HPD tend to have stormy relationships that seem to start out as ideal but end up as disasters (Beck et al., 2004). Their relationships are characterized by demandingness, manipulation, dependency, and helplessness (Millon & Grossman, 2007b).

These individuals are unable to tolerate isolation; when alone, they feel desperate and are unable to wait for new relationships to develop gradually (Horowitz, 1991). They are inclined to define relationships with or connections to others as closer or more significant than they really are. They do not see when they are being humored or placated by people who may have lost patience with their relentless need for attention and their failure to relate in a genuine way. Others may eventually withhold their own efforts to relate to individuals with HPD once they come to accept that there is little reciprocity and the connection is not authentic; rather there is only a continuing HPD demand to be attended to and admired.

On the surface, HPD relationships reflect warmth, energy, and responsiveness. Covertly, there is a disrespectful determination to force nurturance (Benjamin, 1996). Individuals with HPD long to be loved and taken care of by someone who is both powerful and able to be controlled through the use of charm and seductiveness (McWilliams, 1994). Individuals with HPD marry responsible and parental partners who will pay the bills, get the car fixed, take the children to their doctor appointments, and worry about the future. These same partners are then vulnerable to feeling like they are boring, invisible, and uninteresting, frequently without understanding that those feelings are the result of the role they have accepted in a relationship dominated by the needs and behaviors of their partner with HPD. When relationships begin to fail, individuals with HPD resort to crying, coercion, temper tantrums, assaultive behavior, and suicidal gestures to avoid rejection and abandonment (Beck et al., 2004).

Even though individuals with HPD attempt to bind others to them, they are often dissatisfied with single attachments. They tend to be lacking in fidelity, loyalty, and commitment (Millon & Grossman, 2007b). Partners can be deeply wounded when the person who seems to need them also betrays them—often repeatedly. The betrayal can be sexual infidelity, but it can also be an emotional alliance with someone whom the individual finds attractive.

If their inclination to be psychologically and emotionally exploitive is severe, individuals with HPD can be destructive to members of their families. When everyone in the household must attend to the needs of the parent with HPD, children are pressed into becoming caretakers, and the significant other or partner must function as the only adult in the household. Under these circumstances, histrionic parental behaviors can range from unfortunate to dangerous. One mother with severe HPD turned the care of her small children over to a man just released from jail after serving time for pedophilia. She wanted to work in a restaurant and bar and was away from home from early evening to early in the morning. The man quickly re-offended. When the mother was challenged about her choice, she said that this man had paid his debt to society and she had been sure he was fine. The children were removed from her care.

Additionally, individuals with HPD, with ideas about their own youthfulness, can be attracted to underage youth in a disinhibited and sexual manner.

Issues with Authority

Individuals with HPD will engage in illegal behavior with little internal moral restraint. They are often able to evade negative consequences through the appeal of their interpersonal behavior. They are not inclined to be argumentative or aggressive with authority figures. They are engaging, responsive, and enthusiastic. They frequently tell people in authority how wonderful, effective, and competent they are. For individuals with HPD, misinformation in the service of making others feel good is fine; that is, they are quite at ease with evasion and dishonesty. Individuals with HPD have been known to evade traffic tickets because they approach police officers with a combination of submissiveness, seductivity, and a breathless appreciation for the courage officers of the law must have in their difficult but vital jobs.

Behavior

Individuals with HPD are overreactive, volatile, and provocative. They may engage in outrageously inappropriate seductive behavior. They have a penchant for momentary excitements, fleeting adventures, and ill-advised hedonism (Donat, 1995). The HPD behavioral style is dramatic, demanding, self-indulgent, and inconsiderate (Sperry, 2003). These individuals tend to be capricious, easily excited, and intolerant of disappointment. The words and feelings they express appear shallow and simulated (Millon & Grossman, 2007b).

Individuals with HPD can be quite effective in situations where a first impression is important and vague expression of ideas is preferred over precision. They are less successful where performance is evaluated by objective measures of competence, diligence, and depth. Acting, marketing, politics, and the arts are fields where individuals with HPD do well and manage competition effectively (Richards, 1993).

HPD cognition is global, diffuse, and impressionistic; these individuals are distractible and suggestible. They are attentive to fleeting and superficial events but integrate their experience poorly. They are not inclined toward sustained intellectual concentration and avoid introspective thought. (Beck et al., 2004). They lack genuine curiosity and have habits of superficiality and dilettantism.

Affect

Individuals with HPD express their emotions intensely yet remain unconvincing. Their feelings have an infantile quality, are changeable, and lack depth and genuineness (Beck et al., 2004). They experience recurrent flooding of affect, and sudden enraged, despairing, or fearful states may occur. These individuals describe themselves as trying to control outbursts of temper. Partners of individuals with HPD describe themselves as targets of rage, acting out, and even violence if they do not acquiesce to demands. Patience is rare, and these individuals may use alcohol or other drugs to quickly alter states of negative feeling (Horowitz, 1991).

Defenses

HPD defenses include dissociative mechanisms. These individuals are attuned to external rather than internal events and avoid potentially disruptive urges by dissociating from thoughts and feelings that threaten their view of themselves or the world. They dissociate entire segments of memory that prompt discomfort. In particular, they must keep away from awareness of their pervasive emptiness (Millon & Davis, 1996).

Repression is another HPD defense; frequent splitting off from conscious awareness of self results in an intrapsychic impoverishment. Psychological growth is precluded, and these individuals remain immature.

In the service of both defenses, these individuals engage in self-distracting activities to avoid being aware of or seeing the connection between their emotions and their behavior. Accordingly, they claim innocence when their conduct results in interpersonal conflict and allege that others have misunderstood their intentions (Kubacki & Smith, 1995).

The Self-Created World (Altered Reality) of HPD

Individuals with HPD create an altered reality that, although not psychotic, allows incongruent self-perceptions and compromises understanding of others. This blurred reality keeps the world at a distance and interferes with personal authenticity and the ability to genuinely connect to others. For individuals with HPD, the altered reality is composed of believing or hoping that:

- I hate being alone; besides isn't there a song about people who need people?
- I have so many close friends.

- I can always get people to smile, even if they are angry.
- Of course I flirt; people love it.
- I am absolutely devastated if I can't get to the gym to work out every day.
- I love clothes. People can't help themselves; they love to look at me.
- Let's face it, I'm an intuitive, sensitive, and expressive person.
- My own children worry about me and fuss over me.

Substance Use Disorders and HPD

Co-Occurring Substance Use Disorders and the Impact of Drugs on HPD

HPD is in Cluster B, the dramatic, erratic, or impulsive cluster; Cluster B has the highest rates of alcohol or drug abuse and dependence (Nace & Tinsley, 2007) of the three *DSM-IV-TR* personality clusters. The incidence of co-occurring substance use disorders is so high for individuals with HPD that it is imperative to assess drug and alcohol use when they enter mental health treatment.

Richards (1993) believes that individuals with personality disorders have an increased inclination to use psychoactive drugs and alcohol as alternative solutions to life problems. For individuals with HPD, shallowness and absence of internal integration leave them with little ability to understand and integrate emotional experiences across situations. Alcohol and other drugs serve as alternatives to personality resilience and maturity. This is particularly effective for individuals with HPD because drug use facilitates dissociative behavior.

Kearney (1996) defines denial as a form of self-protection; it is a failure to acknowledge problems and take effective steps to change behavior. He believes denial can be detected in most human misery and involves a conflict between knowing and not knowing. HPD is a disorder in which denial is a core feature. It is a style of being that refuses to see or know what is unpleasant or unwanted. The denial of the personality intertwines with the denial of addiction; both sustain immaturity and foster poor integration of reality. Addiction to substances fits people with HPD; the behaviors may make no sense to others, but the internal logic is so strong that it is an extraordinarily difficult behavior to interrupt (Hoskins, 1989; Peele, 1989).

Millon & Davis (1996) state that individuals with HPD may become involved in drug or alcohol use because the substances can free them to act out in ways that are congenial with their inclination to be stimulus seeking. Through psychoactive drugs, these individuals are able to transform themselves; they gain feelings of well-being, bolster a flagging sense of self-worth, and perhaps even come to feel powerful. Drugs and alcohol can disinhibit controlled HPD impulses so that there need be no assumption of personal responsibility or guilt for behavior.

Drugs of Choice for HPD

Drugs of choice for individuals with HPD include antianxiety agents and stimulants, but often they use what is fashionable within their social context. Not only are they influenced by others concerning drug of choice, but they are likely to follow others in their choice of places and circumstances to use substances, route of administration, and even which treatment centers to attend. These individuals use drugs and alcohol as part of their interpersonal, sexual, and romantic behavior (Richards, 1993). For people with HPD, an intense and relentless need for relationships may prove to be the most dominant and enduring feature in their lives. Their behavior, including substance use and drug of choice, is controlled by their interactions with others. They have little ability or inclination to be self-directed. Overall, even abstinence can be the direction these individuals take when it is supported by the social network within which they find themselves. If the powerful psychological need is for relationships rather than the psychoactive drugs they use, it is possible that these individuals could be less at risk for substance dependence than may have seemed to be the case. Integration into an abstinence-based social context may be quite effective in facilitating long-term recovery.

For individuals with HPD, it is also important to watch for emerging compulsive sexual behavior when abstinence from drugs and alcohol is achieved. This alternative addictive behavior may become apparent in the context of 12-step groups and subvert recovery. It is also possible that a shift to disinhibited sexual behavior will prompt the partners of individuals with HPD to reintroduce alcohol or other drugs into their lives to stop the unfaithfulness.

Integrated Dual Diagnosis Treatment for HPD

Engaging in Treatment

Individuals with HPD may enter treatment via the criminal justice system or through self-referral. Because of their interpersonal skills and inclination to seek approval through pleasing others, they may initially look like "dream clients." However, they are usually seeking relief from a crisis in their lives, either emotional or criminal, and the accompanying fear and depression. Once the depressed mood is lifted or the legal charges are taken care of, motivation for change is eliminated or greatly reduced. Turkat (1990) is pessimistic about achieving fundamental change in the histrionic personality structure because once the external motivation for change is gone, so are HPD individuals from the treatment setting. The greatest potential for long-term change for clients with HPD and substance use disorders comes from integration into an abstinence-based social structure that provides ongoing support and fosters less destructive choices. Treatment can serve as a bridge from crisis to an altered social context that teaches greater maturity and provides the opportunity for less destructive relationships.

Treatment Provider Guidelines

The style of histrionic clients can be very appealing; dramatic renditions of experience can be quite absorbing and amusing (Beck et al., 2004). It is often easy to form what appears to be a therapeutic relationship. Even though HPD attachment is shallow, treatment providers are seen as valued sources of admiration, attention, and support (McCann, 1995); clinicians must be able to confront demands these clients make for socializing, sexually and interpersonally provocative behavior, and continuous avoidance of relevant issues.

Clients with HPD often communicate early in treatment that their service providers have helped them make large and significant strides in treatment in a short amount of time (McCann, 1995). Although it may be enticing to believe this rendition of the clinicians' therapeutic effectiveness, it is important to determine if there is genuine treatment progress. It is disconcerting to discover that both HPD clients and their flattered service providers were caught in the same web of "let's pretend." Then, with the embarrassment of being exposed and their own needs unfortunately highlighted, these same service providers could become angry and punishing.

Clear treatment goals, focusing, and limit-setting are important for clients with HPD (McCann, 1995). It is imperative that service providers treat individuals with HPD as adults capable of making their own decisions and being responsible for themselves.

Individuals with HPD often fear losing an exciting lifestyle. They have or try to have a sense of never-ending youthfulness; they evade the more difficult issues of adulthood. In a sense, individuals with HPD attempt to live their lives as though they were in an American-made movie; that is, they will have a happily-ever-after ending no matter how severe the adversity, how formidable the obstacles, or how wide-ranging the negative consequences of their behavior. As a result, working with HPD clients can feel like being Scrooge just before his Christmas conversion; the reflection of life's negative consequences and inevitable pain are almost unseemly in the face of HPD compulsive optimism, denial, dissociation, and evasion. Even so, it is important for service providers to actively foster behaviors that are mature, responsible, and based in reality if these individuals are to emerge from their position of childlike powerlessness, irresponsibility, and the growing negative impact of their vocational, interpersonal, marital, and parental failures.

Professional Ethics and HPD

It is possible to be drawn into the enjoyment generated by clients with HPD and their extravagantly expressed admiration of service providers. They are likely to attempt to ensure good care by dressing attractively and being entertaining. They often attempt to form a "special" bond and suggest social contact outside of the treatment relationship. For clinicians who are staid and undramatic, individuals with HPD can be so emotionally and sexually exciting that they find themselves thinking and fantasizing about their clients in ways that compromise their capacity to maintain professional boundaries (Kubacki & Smith, 1995). Service providers must be aware of and able to manage either their own responsiveness to seductive behavior or their own need to be seen as attractive by clients with HPD. These clients can be particularly challenging when clinicians are going through a difficult time in their own lives, for example, a divorce, grief, or depression. Personal need for comfort or reassurance is easily recognized by HPD clients, and their skills at providing what is needed, at least on the surface, can result in astonishingly inappropriate behavior from service providers. These professionals, if they find themselves before a licensure board or in a courtroom as a consequence, are often unable to explain either the choices they made or their behavior.

If their attempt to engage service providers in inappropriate behavior is refused, clients with HPD may respond with intense anger, accusations, or impulsive acting out. Unfortunately, individuals with HPD are so inclined to describe relationships as warm, close, and special, that their partners may become reactive to the possibility of intimacy between their HPD significant others and the services providers. Accordingly, boundaries and professionalism are imperative conditions to a therapeutic experience for clients with HPD. There is a temptation to blame individuals with HPD for the situation, but it is the responsibility of the service providers, not the clients, to establish and sustain ethics and professionalism in treatment relationships.

On the other hand, individuals with HPD can interact in a way that actually robs others of their self-esteem. This happens via the continuous pressure to view these individuals as attractive and appealing—to show continuous approval. This moves others, including treatment providers, into the admiring observer position. By definition, the anonymous people in the audience are less interesting or exciting than the beautiful people holding forth on center stage. The impact is both subtle and cumulative, leaving the people interacting with individuals with HPD inexplicably unsure of themselves. Service providers need to be aware of the potential for esteem-devaluation, or their own defenses will be triggered. They may begin to engage in distancing and infantilization. They may begin to ridicule the HPD self-dramatization and fail to respond appropriately to what appears to be pseudoaffect (McWilliams, 1994).

Assessment and Treatment

Assessment of individuals who may have HPD should include the following questions:

- Have other people told you that you seem to need to be the center of attention?
- Do people misinterpret your friendliness as a romantic or sexual invitation?
- Do your emotions change quickly?
- Has anyone ever commented that your emotions do not seem real or sincere? When people have commented that your emotions are not genuine or are insincere, what do you do or say? What do you think?
- Are you disappointed if people don't notice how you look?
- Note during the assessment whether these individuals relate concrete examples with appropriate detail about significant events. Are they impressionistic and vague rather than specific and detailed? Ask follow-up questions that seek descriptive details.
- Do you think you would make a good actor or actress? What specifically would make you a good actor or actress?
- Do your opinions change depending on whom you are with? If someone says he or she has a headache or upset stomach, do you find you feel the same thing?
- Do you ever feel a close personal relationship with a boss or a professional you have not known very long (Zimmerman, 1994; Peter Pociluyko, personal communication, August, 2007)?

Assessment of individuals who may have HPD must include exploration of substance use issues. These individuals are prone to alcoholism and drug addiction and are quite adept at denying the related behaviors and negative consequences. They seek easy escape from pain and fail to observe or accept responsibility for the impact of their behavior on others. These factors foster both entry into and maintenance of addiction. One husband with HPD engaged in mutual alcoholic behavior with his wife until he wanted out of the marriage. He then hospitalized his wife for alcoholism after she received a speeding ticket during a black-out. He continued to deny his own severe drinking problem. His physician confronted him about smelling alcohol on his breath at an 8:30 a.m. medical appointment; he denied drinking and said it was mouthwash. Because his alcoholism was expressed in maintenance drinking and did not involve black-outs, he was able to maintain his conviction that his wife had a problem and he did not. He successfully got a divorce and soon thereafter married for the fourth time.

Co-occurring disorders treatment for individuals with HPD must address:

- Self-definition as helpless
- Stimulus-seeking behavior
- Denial, escapism, and dissociation
- Self-definition as childlike and weak versus the power in others
- Addiction-sustaining social network
- Benefits and consequences of a reality-focused consciousness and, conversely, consequences and perceived benefits of evading reality and seeking fantasies
- Function of the drug(s) of choice
- The power of AA or NA in their lives, not only for recovery, but to learn a more self-responsible and principled way of life

Treatment Goals

Treatment goals for all individuals with personality disorders should include developing adaptive skills and reducing self-defeating defenses. The goal is not to "rub the spots off the leopard"; characterological restructuring is unlikely. Instead, these individuals need to work toward becoming more genuine, less self-absorbed, and less interpersonally manipulative and controlling.

HPD treatment must involve pressure to delay gratification and to achieve greater maturity. These clients may have little interest in learning to think clearly and hold steady under pressure if they fear that maturation will result in no one wanting to take care of them any more (Benjamin, 2005). Addressing these fears with a positive frame means developing treatment goals that include integration of gentleness with strength, moderating emotional expression, and encouraging warmth, genuineness, and empathy (Sperry, 2003).

Further, treatment goals must help clients with HPD focus attention on topics that are usually avoided and unresolved (Horowitz, 1996). They need to learn to live with reality on its terms rather than on their terms, see reality as it is, cope with reality as they find it, and increase self-reliance, self-confidence, and courage (Sperry & Carlson, 1993).

While abstinence can be a goal, the possibility of achieving that goal corresponds directly with the success individuals with HPD have in establishing a rewarding social environment that supports recovery. There is little chance of success if they remain in relationships with people who are drinking and drugging. Also, if psychoactive drugs are shoring up flagging self-esteem, giving them up will

result in psychological pain; individuals with HPD have low tolerance for discomfort and yield to the desire to get high to feel better.
Loss of drugs could force reality on individuals with HPD. They usually have little experience in recognizing and tolerating the pain in
life. They do not define reality as a positive force; they are much more
inclined to prefer the fantasies they have about both themselves and
others. Loss of relationships, low self-esteem, and unpleasant reality
are very difficult for individuals with HPD to withstand. Managing
all of these issues must be simultaneous with achieving abstinence,
or they may relapse or substitute equally destructive addictive behaviors such as compulsive shopping or compulsive sexual behavior.

Recovery Activities for Individuals with HPD and Addiction

Dually diagnosed individuals with HPD have many personality
characteristics that are valued in American society. They are outgoing, gregarious, eager to please, and engaging. If these strengths
can be used without excessive interpersonal exploitation, recovery
activities will be substantially facilitated. The 2001–2002 National
Epidemiologic Survey on Alcohol and Related Conditions (Grant et
al., 2004) noted that individuals with HPD have strengths that can
enhance recovery.

In mental health recovery, activities that help individuals with
HPD gain maturity, develop a personal sense of efficacy and resolve,
and learn to relate to others without manipulative efforts to control
not only allow greater adaptivity but assist in substance use recovery
as well.

In recovery from substance use disorders, individuals with HPD
need to become involved in AA, NA, or other peer support groups to
the point that they support and sustain their abstinence via the relationships they make and the people who come to count on them for
support. The energy and emotional need of individuals with HPD
can be expressed in a positive way through intense involvement in
the 12-step community both locally and nationally. Their interpersonal skills will stand them in good stead as they learn to connect to
and flourish in an abstinence-based social structure.

8

Cluster B
*Narcissistic Personality Disorder
and Substance Use Disorders*

Narcissistic Personality Disorder Defined

Essential Features

An essential feature of narcissistic personality disorder (NPD) is a pervasive pattern of grandiosity, need for admiration, and lack of empathy (APA, 2000). Kantor (1992) further describes the clinical characteristics of NPD as inordinate self-pride, self-concern, ideas of perfection, a reluctance to accept blame or criticism, and an absence of altruism, although gestures may be made for the sake of appearances.

Individuals with NPD presume their own superiority, overstate their accomplishments, and feel entitled to privileges that they may neither earn nor deserve (Yudofsky, 2005). Bernstein (2001) suggests that they intend to live out their fantasies of being the smartest, the best, and the most talented of all people. As it is possible that individuals with NPD show little real ability, they may only be exceptional in their imagination. They can bewilder coworkers when their confidence in themselves far exceeds any demonstrated skill or talent. With enough exposure, people may come to feel disdainful of the self-aggrandizement and self-congratulatory behavior of people with NPD. In response, these individuals become deeply offended and withdraw into angry inaccessibility (Benjamin, 1996). The fragile maintenance of their exaggerated self-concept can lead to irrational behavior and flight from job settings when serious mistakes or lack of ability may be revealed.

Individuals with NPD have a particularly difficult time with the limitations inherent in aging; NPD has been associated with deterioration in midlife with the realization of mortality and loss of physical vitality (Wink, 1995). One individual with severe NPD faced, at the age of 54, a career in ruins, no money, no job prospects, and yet another failed relationship. When all of his fantasies of a bright future collapsed under his age, his work and marital history, and his dismal finances, he hung himself. Once he was in his fifties, his dream of becoming a highly paid executive with a lovely wife, beautiful children, an expensive home, and influence in a large corporation could no longer be sustained. Reality presented him with, in his opinion, a life that was not worth living. On the other hand, when individuals with NPD are talented and successful enough to be admired and emulated by others (McWilliams, 1994), they can be nearly symptom-free and well-functioning.

NPD traits are common in adolescents and do not necessarily lead to NPD in adulthood. Whereas the *DSM-IV-TR* (APA, 2000) states that individuals who are diagnosed with NPD are 50–75% male, Levy, Reynoso, Wasserman, and Clarkin (2007) cite several studies that found no gender differences in the prevalence of NPD. Gunderson, Ronningstam, and Smith (1995) note that the NPD grandiosity may be overt and involve arrogant and haughty behavior or it may be more covert and less easily recognized.

Self-Image

A belief in personal superiority forms the core of the NPD self-image; the presumption of superiority is, for these individuals, sufficient proof of its existence. Their sense of security and contentment rests upon thinking highly of themselves. Negative aspects of self are denied or rationalized (Richards, 1993). However, maintenance of self-importance, often without commensurate success, can create a painful disparity between genuine and illusory competence. McWilliams (1994) believes that individuals with NPD have some sense of their psychological fragility. They can experience a grandiose self-state or a depleted, shamed self-state. With external affirmation, they tend to feel self-righteous, contemptuous of others, self-sufficient, and vain. With the loss of external validation, they can feel a sense of falseness, envy, ugliness, and inferiority. As a consequence, the

NPD superiority is accompanied by fragile self-esteem and hypersensitivity to criticism. Anything short of absolute positive regard from others is unacceptable (Dowson & Grounds, 1995). Individuals with NPD seem surprised when they do not receive the praise they expect (APA, 2000) and appear to have little awareness that their behavior may be seen as objectionable or irrational to others (Millon & Grossman, 2007b).

View of Others

Individuals with NPD have trouble cooperating with other people because their attention is on themselves (Kantor, 1992). They have difficulty recognizing the experience, feelings, and reality of others. They consider vulnerability in other people to be a sign of weakness that can be exploited; when given the opportunity, individuals with NPD become dominant, arrogant, demanding, and coercive (Birtchnell, 1995; Oldham & Morris, 1995). Because they believe that (1) wanting something is reason enough for them to have it, (2) others are as consumed by concern for those with NPD as the individuals themselves are, and (3) other people will submerge their desires or interests in favor of the pleasure, comfort, and welfare of those with NPD, they expect that whatever they want will be given to them through the effort and sacrifices made by others. Narcissistic individuals take advantage of people and value them only for what they can provide. Unfortunately, they rarely recognize, acknowledge, or appreciate what is done for them. Individuals with NPD are often envious and begrudge others their possessions or successes even while they assume others are envious of them.

Relationships

NPD relationships are impaired because of entitlement and disregard for others; these individuals expect special consideration without reciprocal responsibilities (Millon & Grossman, 2007b). Their capacity to feel love is marginal (McWilliams, 1994), and their relationships must have potential for advancing their purposes. A woman with NPD and a career in business came into therapy because her fiancé had just terminated their engagement, at least in part due to her cocaine use. She expressed only limited feelings of loss, but she was furious that he "broke up" a couple that was as striking as they were when they went anywhere together. He was tall, brunette, handsome, and imposing. She was tall, blond, attractive, and compelling. Together they attracted a great deal of attention from others. With his departure, she was going to have to find another partner who set off her good looks as well as her fiancé had done. She wanted to be half of a perfect couple, with a perfect career, living in a perfect home, taking delightful and perfect vacations. She minimized her cocaine use and believed her fiancé had no reason to leave her.

In spite of the apparent self-sufficiency of individuals with NPD, their intense need to feel and to be treated as special leads them to overburden their relationships with demands for self-esteem–enhancing interaction (McWilliams, 1994); they are likely to contribute little or nothing in return for the gratifications they seek. This limits individuals with NPD to relationships with people who will not leave such an unequal bargain. Partners of individuals with NPD have often had an NPD parent who indoctrinated them to interpret exploitation as love (Golomb, 1992).

Individuals with NPD have illusory and changing versions of relationships. It can be a bewildering experience to be with people who so effortlessly create a fictional world in which they dismiss conflict, deny failure, and do not question the correctness of their own beliefs. Past experiences are rewritten so that these individuals consistently come out as the most essential, important, and admirable people in any scenario (Millon & Davis, 1996). Individuals caught up in relationships with people with NPD can be genuinely stunned that they believed in and acted in accordance with the NPD fiction until some event broke the spell.

A grave concern regarding individuals with severe NPD has to do with their cold seductiveness and promiscuity, their limited capacity for love, and their inability to either genuinely comprehend or accept the incest taboo (Akhtar, 1992). If they do not see their children as separate individuals but as sources of need gratification, sexual behavior may be possible.

Issues with Authority

Competent individuals with NPD are often in positions of authority. In dealing with other authority figures they are nondeferential, condescending, and presumptive of special treatment. They do not reveal any information derogatory to themselves and behave with self-righteous indignation when questioned. Lying is not difficult; concealment is routine. These individuals are unwilling to accept that society's limitations apply to them.

As managers or employers, individuals with NPD can be destructive toward subordinates and the organizations in which they work. Yudofsky (2005) describes the characteristics of narcissistic personality-disordered managers as including:

- Valuing loyalty in subordinates over competence or productivity
- Overestimating their knowledge and overstating their accomplishments
- Not appreciating the important contributions of others
- Taking personal credit for the accomplishments of others
- Being competitive with and threatened by peers
- Insisting on making all the decisions
- Never admitting mistakes
- Distrusting and intimidating subordinates who make independent decisions
- Surrounding themselves with subordinates who never disagree with them
- Failing to mentor or advance the careers of subordinates
- Pursuing highly visible short-term successes
- Misappropriating resources for their personal benefit
- Devaluing and underestimating the achievements of competitors
- Responding to constructive criticism with anger and thoughts of retribution
- Prioritizing their own ambitions over the needs of the organization

Behavior

NPD behavior is usually haughty. These individuals behave in an arrogant, supercilious, pompous, and disdainful manner. They have a careless disregard for their own personal integrity and a self-important indifference to the rights or needs of others (Millon & Davis, 1996). Yet they can also show assertiveness, social poise, and assurance (Wink, 1995). Their ambition and confidence may lead to success, but their performance can also be impaired by their intolerance of criticism (APA, 2000) and their inclination to feel mistreated (Golomb, 1992). It can become problematic for individuals with NPD to stay in long-term employment where responsibility for error or failure gets harder and harder to obscure (Richards, 1992; Wink, 1995).

Individuals with NPD tend to be abrasive. When others fail to give them what they want, they may engage in temper tantrums, verbal harangues, and emotional or physical abuse. They are particularly apt to become resentful and contemptuous of anyone who holds them accountable for their exploitative, self-centered behavior (Beck et al., 2004). Individuals with NPD lie to others and deceive themselves; they will do whatever is needed to reinforce their self-ascribed superior status (Akhtar, 1992).

Affect

NPD affect is generally characterized by feigned tranquility. This changes when individuals with NPD experience a loss of confidence. They then become irritable, annoyed, and subject to repeated bouts of depression (Millon & Grossman, 2007b).

Individuals with NPD frequently experience rage, indignation, fear, envy, and frustrated entitlement (Beck et al., 2004; Richards, 1993). Kernberg (1992) suggests that the rage experienced by these individuals served, early in life, to eliminate pain but became useful, later in life, to eliminate obstacles to gratification. Many NPD parents, supervisors, or lovers can use their temper, and the fear others have of their rage, to control the behavior and limit the spontaneity of those around them. The intensity of NPD affect should not be underestimated. Depression, rage, envy, and hatred are potentially powerful behavioral drivers; violence or sudden unexpected assault can be the outcome of external derogation or humiliation of individuals with NPD.

Defenses

McWilliams (1994) suggests that individuals with NPD have unrealistic ideals for themselves; then they either convince themselves that they have attained these ideals (the grandiose posture) or feel inherently flawed and that they are failures (the depressive posture). When there is no significant external pressure, these individuals simply live as though the reality they prefer is the reality they have. If rationalizations and self-deception fail, these individuals have little recourse other than fantasy. They have an uninhibited imagination and engage in self-glorifying fantasies. What is unmanageable through fantasy is repressed and kept from awareness. The fragility of this stance is demonstrated when the environment strongly and convincingly contradicts the fantasies of individuals with NPD. Their defenses break down, and their response can be anxiety, depression, rage, or suicidal behavior.

The Self-Created World (Altered Reality) of NPD

Individuals with NPD create an altered reality that, while not psychotic, sustains their beliefs about themselves and others. The characteristic difficulties of individuals with NPD almost all stem from their lack of solid contact with reality (Millon & Davis, 1996).

The narcissistic personality disorder world includes the beliefs that:

- Others are fortunate to be near me.
- I am special, talented, intelligent, and beautiful.
- Others naturally and understandably like to do things for me.
- I was meant to be great.
- I should "have it all."
- I was meant to have people around me who are worthy of me.

Substance Use Disorders and NPD

Co-Occurring Substance Use Disorders and the Impact of Drugs on NPD

NPD is in Cluster B, the dramatic, erratic, or impulsive cluster; Cluster B has the highest rates of alcohol or drug abuse and dependence (Nace & Tinsley, 2007) of the three *DSM-IV-TR* personality clusters.

Freud said that drugs can give immediate pleasure and provide a greatly desired degree of independence from the external world and the pressures of reality (Khantzian et al., 1990). Individuals with NPD value both the escape from reality and the management of feelings without the requirement of attitudinal or behavioral change offered by the use of psychoactive drugs.

Individuals with NPD are vulnerable to substance misuse:

- For the feelings of dominance and well-being they provide (Benjamin, 1996)
- For the experience of wholeness and vitality (Rodin & Izenberg, 1997)
- As a mistaken and erroneous way to achieve significance and avoid a painful clash with reality (Sperry & Carlson, 1993)
- As part of the overall narcissistic pattern of self-involvement and self-indulgence (Beck et al., 2004)
- Because of their need for a high level of stimulation (Richards, 1993)
- To provide immediate relief from discomfort and a sense of self-importance and power (Beck et al., 2004).

The belief that they are unique and special insulates individuals with NPD from the recognition that they have developed a reliance on drugs. It also allows them to believe that they can escape the negative effects of addiction and that they can easily quit (Beck et al., 2004). They maintain the grandiose conviction, sometimes in extraordinary circumstances, that they are in charge of their addiction (Richards, 1993) and that they are exempt from both the consequences of their behavior and the laws of nature (Salzman, 1981).

Another factor in the NPD attraction to illicit drugs is the consummate skill required for and the power coming from dealing drugs. It is possible that these activities may be more rewarding to individuals with NPD than the drug use itself (Richards, 1993).

Drugs of Choice for NPD

For individuals with NPD, there are drugs that support an inflated sense of self and drugs that interrupt or moderate feelings of depression and low self-esteem. Most of these individuals will use drugs that enhance their feelings of vigor, power, or euphoria, for example, cocaine or methamphetamine. Individuals with NPD, to ward off unwanted intrusions of unpleasant reality, may isolate and use alcohol or other sedative–hypnotics. Some individuals with NPD prefer the autistic stimulation of psychedelics (Richards, 1993).

Integrated Dual Diagnosis Treatment for NPD

Engaging in Treatment

Individuals with NPD may engage mental health services for depression or anxiety if they are experiencing environmental pressure such as loss of a job or divorce. They usually see their difficulties as caused by others and as being independent of their own behavior. These individuals do not tolerate discomfort well; they become depressed in response to a crisis that punctures narcissistic grandiosity and reflects the discrepancy between NPD expectations or fantasies and reality (Beck et al., 2004). They may enter treatment believing that they have a unique problem and that they are entitled to its complete resolution; therefore, anything less than the unlimited efforts of service providers is unacceptable (Dowson & Grounds, 1995). If they enter treatment because of drug-related legal problems, they will see the problem as being anywhere but in their own use of substances.

These individuals may have trouble accepting treatment. Their view of themselves, their past, their current situation, and what they need from treatment will all be distorted by their need for self-aggrandizement. They will resist reality-based feedback, whether about personality-disordered behavior or substance use concerns, and may flee the treatment setting if they are not sufficiently affirmed and comforted. It is necessary to join with these individuals in an empathic and sustaining manner to develop a therapeutic relationship. However, the return to comfort for individuals with NPD may be all that they are seeking, and they could leave treatment. It becomes an assessment and treatment challenge to connect well enough with these individuals to allow for realistic feedback and the development of abstinence and adaptive behaviors.

Treatment Provider Guidelines

According to Kantor (1992), personality disorders are composed mostly of abrasive and maladaptive traits that are favored over more adaptive traits (although there are adaptive traits within all personality disorders). Service providers must be able to validate clients, suggest adaptive change, and affirm adaptive behaviors without

becoming overly responsive to the annoying qualities that character-
ize the personality disorder.

Working with individuals with NPD sometimes involves managing unreasonable demands, expectations, or criticism. They become
angry if they believe service providers have failed to be sufficiently
responsive to their needs; over time, it is nearly impossible to avoid
disappointing these clients. If service providers respond negatively
to the NPD self-aggrandizing or arrogance, even nonverbally, these
individuals pick up the criticism and experience rejection (Rodin &
Izenberg, 1997).

For individuals with NPD, validation of their thinking and emotional experience is crucial to the growth of more adaptive skills
(Rodin & Izenberg, 1997). They may seem to have an invulnerable
armor of grandiosity, self-centeredness, and arrogance. Even the
depression beneath the arrogance is made up of narcissistic outrage
and feelings of humiliation (Masterson, 1981). Yet the psychological
frailty is real, as is the vulnerability to disillusionment (Rodin & Izenberg, 1997). They must discover that their behavior has consequences
and their use of alcohol and other drugs is a concern. Service providers must confront clients with NPD with the aspects of reality they
are denying or avoiding. Still, it is important to remember that even
though these individuals persist in blaming others for their problems, adopt a position of superiority over treatment providers, and
perceive constructive confrontation as humiliating criticism (Millon
& Davis, 1996), service provider impatience, indignation, or counter-
arrogance is nonproductive and will result in treatment failure.

The need for tact and caution has to do with the tenuous quality of
professional relationships with clients with NPD. These individuals
will flee any situation in which they experience their self-concept as
diminished. One very astute alcohol counselor, in conducting an initial assessment, asked a well-dressed businessman (who brought his
brief case, cell phone, and other implements of his busy professional
life to the interview) about his most recent DUI. The man, who also
had NPD, engaged in a description of getting lost on the way to a
party. He acknowledged that he had been drinking. He pulled into a
convenience store parking lot and spotted a uniformed police officer
coming out of the store, who, of course, observed that he was driving. He approached the officer and asked for directions. The officer
smelled the alcohol, saw the unsteady gait, and made the arrest. The
service provider initially said nothing. Later in the interview, after

making a stronger connection with the client, the counselor said, "Isn't it interesting how stupid alcohol can make the smartest people?" At that point, seeing the stupidity of his actions blamed upon the alcohol, the client could acknowledge that his behavior, not the overzealous behavior of the law officer, had resulted in his arrest.

Clients with NPD do not see or accept their own defects. Learning to tolerate one's own faults must be modeled by service providers (Benjamin, 2005) via their apparent nonjudgmental, accepting, and realistic attitudes toward their own human imperfection (McWilliams, 1994). Confrontation with individuals with NPD must be embedded in strong support (Benjamin, 1996). It also needs to be clear, direct, repetitive, and firm to breach the defenses used by clients with NPD.

Service providers new to the field often need close supervision to manage their interventions with clients with NPD. Some individuals are vulnerable to the demeaning behavior of these individuals and respond with anxious and excessive attempts to prove that they are capable, trained, and effective. Others respond with anger and engage in behavior that indicates that their own narcissism has been challenged.

Professional Ethics and NPD

An ethical issue presented by individuals with NPD emanates from their apparent approval, or promised approval, if service providers will breach program rules and sidestep various restrictions because these clients are "special." It can feel like a "you and me against the world" alliance. If, at a later point, NPD individuals become angry with their service providers, they can "blow the whistle" on the previous bending of the rules and failed boundaries. They would be right, at that point, to indicate that the ethical breach can only be the responsibility of the service providers—not the recipients of service. The allure of an illicit alliance may be most enticing to novice service providers; however, the feeling of being special that seems to come from such an alliance can capture seasoned clinicians if their sense of balance, life problems, or other issues have left them feeling unsteady, unsure, or in greater emotional need than usual.

Another potential pitfall with individuals with NPD comes from growing service provider boredom, frustration, or anger at the client's demands to be treated as both special and immune from confrontation. Because these individuals are inclined to demand a great deal and give very little, working with them can result in feeling dismissed and ignored. Service provider attitudes and behavior can become destructive, moralistic, and negatively parental. Again, should clinicians' behavior become either marginally or blatantly counterproductive, the responsibility does not lie with the clients. If service providers begin to feel the pull toward the "dark side" of their own emotions, they must seek assistance through supervision or consultation to be able to continue working with these individuals. Should rebalancing prove to be unattainable, clients with NPD must be transferred from service providers who may have become angry, defensive, and punishing. It is important to remember that personality-disordered behavior tends to elicit the worst in the people around them—including service providers. Self-monitoring is essential to avoid the chagrined realization that the clinician's behavior became as indicative of narcissism as the behavior of the NPD client.

Assessment and Treatment

Bernstein (2001) proposes a checklist for indicators of narcissism:

- They are firmly convinced that they are better, smarter, or more talented than others.
- They love competition but are poor losers.
- They have fantasies of doing something great or being famous, and they want to be treated as though this were already true.
- They have little interest in what other people are thinking or feeling.
- They believe it is very important to live in the right place and associate with the right people.
- They take advantage of others.
- They feel unique.
- They feel "put upon" when asked to take care of their responsibilities.
- They regularly disregard rules because they are special.
- They become irritated when others do not automatically do what they want.
- They believe criticism is motivated by jealousy or envy.
- They do not recognize their own mistakes.

What to focus on in the treatment process for individuals with NPD may be easier to identify than how to address it. Service providers need to carefully reflect the consequences of NPD behavior and suggest that achieving greater interpersonal effectiveness is a benefit of behavior change. The powerful thrust individuals with NPD have toward achieving perfection can be harnessed in the pursuit of less self-destructive or self-defeating behaviors. Such an approach is much more effective when presented as capitalizing on apparent strengths rather than eliminating deficiencies.

It is also important to remember that a narcissistic view of self can be harnessed in the treatment process. For individuals with NPD, the idea of servitude to drugs and the self-image of weakness can be shaped into motivation to achieve abstinence. They may embrace the idea of abstinence as symbolic of their personal strength, and although this concept does not counter the personality pathology, it can be used to encourage acceptance of recovery from either substance abuse or substance dependence as a benefit in their lives. In early recovery in particular, this can be a source of motivation for change.

In treatment, individuals with NPD may feel sorry for the other people in a treatment group who cannot handle alcohol or other drugs. They may believe they have a special power of will and the strength to control the substances they use. It is more effective to go with this self-view than attempt to dispute it. Congratulating these individuals on their strengths can compel them to demonstrate the very strength they believe they have. It can then be suggested that others who have found addiction to be a much stronger opponent than they had anticipated were able to achieve abstinence by engaging in positive behaviors and accepting of the help of others.

Medication for individuals with NPD usually addresses symptoms of co-occurring Axis I disorders such as depression. This is important if reality has intruded enough for these individuals to believe that they would rather die than live in a world that does not support their view of themselves. They can be vulnerable to completed suicide if they have sustained a significant blow to their narcissism.

Individuals with NPD are particularly prone to relapse. They are inclined to believe that they can reengage in controlled use because of what they have learned about addiction. Once in relapse, individuals with NPD have significant trouble returning to abstinence, seeking treatment, or reengaging in recovery activities because of the shame and humiliation (Richards, 1993).

Treatment Goals

Cognitive treatment for individuals with NPD addresses their dys-functional beliefs about the self, the world, and the future; focus is on three basic components of NPD: grandiosity, hypersensitivity to criticism, and empathic deficits (Beck et al., 2004). Interpersonal therapy addresses recognizing and blocking the patterns of entitle-ment and envy of the success of others (Sperry, 2003). Masterson (1981) suggests that the NPD idea that perfection provides protec-tion and life must be trouble-free and perfect should be addressed in the treatment process.

Treatment goals address the most adaptive expression of a person-ality style by enhancing the strengths and positive potential found in individuals with NPD. The goals address being more effective and less symptomatic within the confines of the personality disorder. Changes in behavior, definitions of self and others, and learning tolerance for reality could, over time, provide sufficient corrective experiences for individuals with NPD that the severity of the person-ality disorder diminishes and negative consequences abate.

Recovery Activities for Individuals with NPD and Addiction

Individuals with NPD have very strong motivation to be seen as suc-cessful, strong, and capable. This can be a positive force in recovery as well as treatment. Their determination to attend to their image, both with self and others, can be used to make positive choices. It is very painful for them to be seen as weak or to be pitied for their problems. Much as nuclear power can be used to destroy or to create much-needed energy, the NPD need to be superior can permit these individuals to enter the 12-step community, achieve abstinence, and take on a leadership role in the groups they attend. As long as this is not a cover for secretive addictive behavior, it can provide a positive push toward recovery.

Once involved in peer support groups such as AA or NA, individ-uals with NPD have the opportunity to hear and to learn about gen-uine humility, self-acceptance that is not inflated, and humor about being human. They may come to better understand and respond to the needs of others. What is learned in peer support groups is ben-eficial for both substance use disorders and personality disorders.

The impact can be so important that it is well worth the effort to persuade these individuals to get past their initial rejection of "all those addicts" in AA that are "nothing like" the individuals with NPD. They can benefit significantly from the AA confrontation of entitlement with humor and the gentle pressure to confront problems rather than deny or attempt to escape them through the use of alcohol or other drugs or by any other means (Benjamin, 1996).

Part of recovery is gaining respect for the power of addiction without feeling that power is indicative of their own personal weakness. In learning about and accepting their need for the help of others to sustain their recovery, they are again the recipients of dual benefit for both their substance use disorder and their personality disorder. As in treatment, harnessing the motivation to look strong can lead to acceptance of recovery activities, including those associated with managing relapse, when framed as indicative of their strength rather than an exposure of their weakness.

9

Cluster C
*Avoidant Personality Disorder and
Substance Use Disorders*

Avoidant Personality Disorder Defined

Essential Features

An essential feature of avoidant personality disorder (AvPD) is a pervasive pattern of social inhibition, feelings of inadequacy, and hypersensitivity to negative evaluation (APA, 2000). Millon and Davis (1996) call AvPD the withdrawn pattern. These individuals are oversensitive and hyperreactive to the moods and feelings of others. Individuals with AvPD experience affective disharmony, cognitive interference, and interpersonal distrust. This pattern has been described as being preoccupied with security and strained when associating with people.

Everly (1995) states that the most severe AvPD pathology is in the area of self-image. The core personality fails to adapt in a competent manner to interpersonal adversity—both past and present. Stone (1993) sees the key traits of AvPD as social reticence and avoidance of interpersonal activities. These individuals are easily hurt by criticism; they fear showing their anxiety in public. They would like to be close to others and to live up to their potential but are afraid of being hurt, rejected, and unsuccessful (Beck et al., 2004).

There is an overlap between AvPD and social phobia, generalized type (APA, 2000). The essential feature of social phobia (social anxiety disorder) is a marked and persistent fear of social or performance situations that may provoke embarrassment. Most often, the social or performance situation is avoided, though it may be endured with dread. Sutherland & Frances (1996) suggest that AvPD and social phobia are constructs that differ only in the severity of dysfunction. Frances et al. (1995) propose the possibility that they are two different constructs for the same condition. The *DSM-IV-TR* (APA, 2000) states that AvPD may be a more severe variant of generalized social phobia, although it is not qualitatively distinct. Benjamin (1996) notes that the interpersonal patterns for generalized social phobia are very similar to AvPD; both groups avoid social contact and restrain themselves because of fear of humiliation or rejection. She proposes that social phobia is diagnosed if symptoms of pervasive anxiety or panic are present. Millon and Martinez (1995) believe that the avoidant personality is essentially a problem of relating to people, whereas social phobia is largely a problem of performing in situations.

Frances et al. (1995) note the considerable overlap between AvPD and dependent personality disorder (DPD). These two constructs share interpersonal insecurity, low self-esteem, and a strong desire for interpersonal relationships. However, Benjamin (1996) describes the desperate attempts to avoid being alone that may be seen in DPD as an exclusionary indicator for AvPD.

Whereas the *DSM-IV-TR* states that the risk of AvPD appears to be equal for men and for women, Grant et al. (2004), in the 2002 National Epidemiologic Survey on Alcohol and Related Conditions, found that the risk for AvPD is significantly greater for women.

Self-Image

Individuals with AvPD are preoccupied with their unpleasant self-definition of being socially inept, unlikable, and inadequate. This self-image usually results from childhood rejection or ridicule by significant others such as parents, siblings, or peers. These individuals are often unable to recognize positive qualities that make them both likable and desirable (Will, 1995). They experience themselves as lonely, sad, and unwanted. They are self-conscious and blame themselves for their social undesirability (Millon & Grossman, 2007a).

The deflated self-image of individuals with AvPD references their entire being. Nothing about them escapes their self-derision and contempt (Millon & Grossman, 2007a). Their self-criticism can become paralyzing in the presence of people to whom they are attracted.

Individuals with AvPD wear a psychological "hair shirt." Centuries ago, a hair shirt, made of rough, abrasive fiber, was worn against the skin for penance; the shirt made every move agonizing. Individuals with AvPD wear their coarse, abrasive, and painful self-image so that it abrades their confidence, their sense of hope, and their belief in themselves.

Individuals with AvPD are certain that they are unattractive and unappealing. They are vulnerable to shame about how they look and may engage in compulsive shopping for items that improve, or promise to improve, appearance such as clothing, make-up, and jewelry. One individual with AvPD said that she became convinced by the time she was an early adolescent that she was "abnormally ugly" unless she was wearing full make-up and carefully selected clothing. Another individual with AvPD said she came to believe, from childhood on, that she was "too ugly to live." Neither of these women was unusual in their appearance in any way.

View of Others

Individuals with AvPD see people as critical, uninterested, and demeaning (Beck et al., 2004) and the world as unfriendly, cold, and humiliating. As a result, individuals with AvPD experience significant social anxiety and are awkward and uncomfortable with other people (Millon & Grossman, 2007a). However, they are caught in an intense approach–avoidance conflict; they believe close relationships could be rewarding but are so anxious around people that their only solace or comfort comes in avoiding most interpersonal contact (Donat, 1995).

Individuals with AvPD tend to respond to low-level criticism with intense hurt. To make matters worse, they become so socially apprehensive that they may interpret neutral events as evidence of disdain or ridicule by others (Donat, 1995). They assume that no matter what they say or do, others will find fault with them (APA, 2000). As a result, these individuals experience unremitting self-contempt and anger toward others.

One woman with AvPD, in her early fifties, remembered her sorrow and envy in fifth grade because she realized that it would never be easy for her to make friends; she saw herself as awkward and not very pretty. She understood that her only friend, who was not always particularly kind, could and would have as many friends as she liked because the other kids wanted to be around her, but that the client would often be alone because she could not attract others. Long before she became aware of herself as a sexual being, she came to believe that she was unable to attract others to her; she saw the disinterest in their eyes and was hurt very deeply by their indifference. These memories, and many others, remained with her throughout adulthood without amelioration or reduction in intensity. She knew that love came to others. Marriage was possible for others. She would have to learn to live her life alone. Interestingly enough, she actually married twice but could never shake the self-view of having to be alone and on her own. Even married, she assumed that each of her husbands would leave her and she would meet her ultimate destiny of abandonment and loneliness. She left her first husband and had been married to her second husband for over twenty years. Facts often lose in the struggle with impaired self-confidence and a damaged view of self.

As in the example above, even memories for individuals with AvPD are composed of intense, conflict-ridden, problematic early relationships. So, at the same time they are avoiding the external distress of contact with others, they must also avoid the wounds inside them. The external environment brings no peace or comfort, and their painful thoughts do not allow them to find solace within themselves (Millon & Grossman, 2007a). As will be discussed later, if people with AvPD find no relief from others and are their own worst enemy, alcohol and other drugs can often do for them what they cannot do for themselves: make them feel better.

Relationships

Individuals with AvPD are "lonely loners." They would like to be involved in relationships but cannot tolerate the feelings they experience around other people. Because they retreat from others in anticipation of rejection, they lead socially impoverished lives. They have immature and unrealistic expectations of relationships; they believe that to be loved, they must have no imperfections (Oldham & Morris, 1995).

Individuals with AvPD develop intimacy with people who are experienced as safe, but they may seriously damage their relationships via the attitudes, feelings, and behaviors that are reflective of their avoidant style. They are inclined to be so self-protective that they:

- Will, if given the opportunity, foster secret relationships away from their partners so they feel less vulnerable and will, at least theoretically, not have to be lonely or distraught if primary relationships fail.
- Protect themselves through interpersonal distance so that they feel less vulnerable, leaving their partners bewildered about the lack of intimacy and closeness in the relationships.
- Maintain intermittent or ongoing relationship fantasies in which they are confident, clever, deeply and unconditionally loved, admired, and desired; the lack of risk in fantasy relationships diminishes the sense of risk in the real relationships but also creates another undisclosed source of distance from real people.
- Are disinclined to take risks within relationships; this can lead to all, or virtually all, risks falling to their partners, for example, initiating all emotional and sexual contact, attempting to talk about the relationships, and sharing loving feelings.
- May feel ashamed of their partners in a larger social context; they fear others will mock them because they are not attractive enough to be with a desirable companion.

Both adult partners and the children of individuals with AvPD may find that they have to assume or hope that they are valued because expression of warmth, need, commitment, involvement, and caring can all be absorbed into avoidant self-protectiveness.

Issues with Authority

Individuals with AvPD are unlikely to provoke or resist authority. They are inclined to be compliant and cooperative. However, whether the authority figures are service providers or law enforcement officers, people with AvPD are not forthcoming and resist self-disclosure. Exposure may mean ridicule, shame, and censure. They do not willingly give away the information they believe will result in such a painful experience.

Behavior

Individuals with AvPD behave in a fretful, restive manner. They overreact to innocuous experiences but maintain control over their physical behaviors and expression of emotions. Their speech is constrained (Millon & Grossman, 2007a). They can be seen as good listeners because they assume that other people would become quickly bored with anything they might have to say, so they encourage others to talk about themselves.

Kantor (1992) notes that individuals with AvPD, as with all of the personality disorders, have a tendency to live in the past or in fantasy; they receive too little input from the here and now. This diminished ability to pay attention results in mild memory disturbances and a characteristic immaturity. These individuals are hyperalert to potential criticism but are distracted by their own extraordinary sensitivity to subtleties of tone and feeling, so much so that, overall, they may appear inattentive (Millon & Davis, 1996).

Individuals with AvPD behave in a stiff, shy, and apprehensive manner that is disquieting to others. The very rejection they fear may be the direct result of other people becoming impatient and uncomfortable with their unremitting tension and inability to accept that they can be a part of an interaction without special guarantees of safety. In fact, people with AvPD, overtly or covertly, seek others to assume most of the responsibility in any interaction; they are not able to be responsible for their own well-being socially and become a burden on the nurturing and care-taking capacity of those around them. For those who experience severe avoidant symptoms, no amount of protectiveness or gentleness from others can ease their fear; they withdraw without explanation and leave behind a general bewilderment about what went wrong. One man with AvPD, in his thirties, described himself as "easy to get rid of"; he would withdraw from relationships in response to any sign that there might be a problem. Unfortunately, it took very little for him to decide that he was not wanted. He would abruptly terminate relationships without a word.

Affect

Shame is one of the central AvPD affective experiences. The shame that comes from even trivial embarrassments is intolerable.

Individuals with AvPD feel exposed and filled with dread; they anticipate ridicule. Their vulnerability to shame leads to anguish. They describe a constant and confusing undercurrent of tension, sadness, and anger. Sometimes this relentless pain results in a general state of numbness. They possess few social skills or personal strengths that can bring them to the pleasures and comforts of life. They attempt to avoid pain, to need nothing, to depend on no one, and to deny desire (Millon & Davis, 1996). Their sorrow is made up of needing the people they know will not love or care about them.

Individuals with AvPD are vulnerable to both anxiety and depression. If they do not currently feel despair, they anticipate feeling it in the future. They are inclined toward pessimism, have an extraordinary sensitivity to psychological pain, and can be preoccupied with the certainty that their life will most assuredly get worse and hopelessness will overtake them. Occasionally, these individuals lose control and explode with rage (Benjamin, 1996; Millon & Grossman, 2007a).

Defenses

The paramount goal for individuals with AvPD is to protect themselves from psychic pain. They have few internal strengths available to them to manage tension or stress; the energy they have is directed toward avoidance rather than adaptation. They use fantasy and escape to interrupt their painful thoughts, diffuse their emotions, and reduce the sharp anguish of being themselves. These individuals depend on fantasies for needs gratification and longed-for but unavailable relationships (Dorr, 1995; Kubacki & Smith, 1995; Millon & Grossman, 2007a).

AvPD social avoidance, the result of anticipated rejection, is readily apparent. What is less obvious is the concurrent cognitive and emotional avoidance (Beck et al., 2004). AvPD dysphoria is so agonizing that these individuals use activities and addictions to distract themselves from negative thoughts and feelings. These patterns of cognitive, emotional, and behavioral avoidance are reinforced by a reduction in current sadness and become automatic. They also result in memory difficulties, failure to learn adaptive methods of coping with anxiety, and a diffused, almost dreamy, quality. It is important to consider the impact of released pain and loss of ability to manage sorrow when working with these individuals to reduce maladaptive defenses and to achieve abstinence.

The Self-Created World (Altered Reality) of AvPD

Individuals with AvPD create and sustain an altered reality that, although not psychotic, permits fantasy, fear, and defenses to seem externally validated rather than internally generated. This reality keeps the world at a distance and allows a perception of predictability to exist at the expense of genuine interpersonal connection. For individuals with AvPD, the altered reality is composed of believing or hoping that:

- Maybe someday someone will love me enough that I will stop hating myself.
- Other people are stronger, more self-confident, and acceptable than I am; it is all just plain easier for them than it is for me.
- I am lonely, and I can't do anything about it. I have to face it—I'll probably live my life alone.
- I wish I could stop caring so much.
- If I took a chance, approached someone, and they rejected me, I just couldn't stand it.

Substance Use Disorders and AvPD

Co-Occurring Substance Use Disorders and the Impact of Drugs on AvPD

Individuals with personality disorders are particularly susceptible to the impact drugs have on their lives. Their failure to self-regulate and manage life stressors and the general loss of maturation to the characteristics of their personality disorder leave these individuals vulnerable to the seduction of drugs and alcohol for solace, courage, augmented positive feelings, diminished pain, and escape from the demands of reality. Individuals with AvPD are very likely to overvalue the one reliable source of self-comfort they can find in psychoactive drugs. To work effectively with co-occurring AvPD and substance use disorders, the importance of drugs for self-soothing and giving courage to socialize must not be understated or overlooked.

Consider the remarkable fit between what drugs offer and what these individuals need. They cannot be at peace when they are alone and are often anguished when with others. They are easily hurt by criticism and are their own most vicious critics. They long for love and fear they must be perfect to get it. They feel the pain of their loneliness without the remedy of social confidence to connect to others. Alcohol and drugs can modify troubled feelings without influencing their cause, augment confidence by blurring reality and reducing sensitivity, and silence the inner voice of self-contempt, or at least make it nearly inaudible. Drugs and alcohol allow entrance into a social context where use of substances is an instant and inauthentic connection and create a world of possibilities that these individuals, when clean and sober, cannot access.

AvPD addiction may seem to be a magical solution to the pain of life (Peele, 1985). The dependence can be quite advanced—with significant negative consequences in place—before these individuals can begin to consider parting with the only "real friend" they ever had. The key that opened the doorway to excess for preaddicted individuals with AvPD was the good feeling they learned to create, and repeatedly recreate, through drug-using activity (Milkman & Sunderwirth, 1987). Abstinence will increase pain. There must be other means of managing the stress of an avoidant lifestyle if drugs are to be given up.

Drugs of Choice for AvPD

For individuals with AvPD, alcohol and other drugs, as noted above, assist in modulating hyperarousal and self-deprecatory thoughts. They may prefer mild hallucinogens over other drugs, perhaps because they facilitate fantasy. However, sedatives and antianxiety agents are the drugs of choice for most clients with AvPD (Richards, 1993). Whereas sedative–hypnotics calm anxiety, stimulants or PCP can provide a sense of strength or reduced vulnerability. The drug of choice for these individuals will be whatever gives them a sense of efficacy or allows them to believe they can be attractive and effective interpersonally.

Many individuals with AvPD also develop compulsive behaviors that relate to appearance enhancement, fantasy, and self-comfort. They may enter treatment with compulsive shopping, compulsive sexual behaviors, and eating disorders in place as well as alcohol or drug addiction. Abstinence, to be effective, needs to address all self-destructive behaviors as well as the use of substances.

Integrated Dual Diagnosis Treatment for AvPD

Engaging in Treatment

Individuals with AvPD may enter treatment via the criminal justice system or through self-referral. If they come in on their own, they are likely to be so apprehensive that any difficulty in the intake process will precipitate withdrawal. They respond to kindness and positive regard, but any indication of irritability or annoyance on the part of reception or intake personnel may prove intolerable.

Treatment Provider Guidelines

For individuals with AvPD, developing trust in service providers is both essential and difficult. They are hypersensitive and prone to feeling judged and injured by interpretation and confrontation in the treatment process (McCann, 1995). They may hide the shame they feel while remaining superficially compliant with treatment. They are inclined to engage in testing behavior to see if they will be accepted and supported (Kubacki & Smith, 1995). Accordingly, service providers must be patient, nonthreatening, and sympathetic in order to establish rapport with avoidant clients. These individuals will be less likely to flee treatment if they can be assisted to feel safe, supported, and accepted (Donat, 1995).

Clinicians need to recognize that individuals with AvPD tend to withhold or understate information that is relevant and be alert to the AvPD infectious helplessness, lack of attentiveness, and firmly held negative beliefs (Sperry, 2003). Individuals with AvPD may initially elicit service provider overprotectiveness. They must be encouraged to take risks. On the other hand, if they cannot tolerate making necessary changes, the diminished quality of their lives may be the best they can manage. Service providers cannot take on client responsibilities (Donat, 1995) or attempt to push them further than they are willing or able to go.

It is a balancing act not unlike that faced by a Little League coach with a frightened eight-year-old boy who does not want to play but is being forced to participate by his parents. Should the coach teach the boy about life by shouting, "Be a man! You're eight!" Should the coach be empathic and protective and say, "Don't worry about it. You just sit right there on the bench until you are ready to play. No problem." Or should the coach devise a series of slowly escalating experiences, for example, individualized (away from the game) batting practice, in which the child can have small successes that can lead to willingness to play in the game? It is imperative that clients with co-occurring AvPD and addiction take on small challenges that can be mastered and will not overwhelm them with anxiety. These individuals know how to fail. They expect to disappoint others. Services providers who allow treatment plans to be developed that are overly ambitious set up another situation wherein these individuals, once again, cannot do what is expected of them because of their psychological vulnerability and paralyzing anxiety. They already know that if they were different, that is, stronger or more confident, they could succeed. They need to learn that they can succeed even as who they are: anxious and self-rejecting.

Professional Ethics and AvPD

It is important that service providers remain aware of their own reactions to the hypersensitivity and psychological fragility of individuals with AvPD. Service providers can become frustrated with the slow pace of discernible progress for these individuals. Yet the belief that gradual change is both possible and beneficial must often come from the clinicians. Clients with AvPD need someone else to believe in them while they begin the long process toward self-confidence and a sense of self-efficacy. Clinical impatience would be easily perceived by these individuals and could prompt treatment failure.

On the other hand, it may be appealing to service providers to be the trusted, admired, and depended upon "good parent" that these individuals never had. The treatment relationship can become "interpersonal methadone" (Benjamin, 1996, p. 302); clinicians can become a safe haven and actually reduce AvPD need for interpersonal connection within their social environment. Part of the efficacy of group treatment is the opportunity for individuals with AvPD to develop trust in others and in themselves without seeing service providers as their only safety in a perilous world. To become frustrated and impatient or to become overinvested in soothing AvPD pain would be a failure in therapeutic boundaries, and the AvPD clients would pay the price.

Assessment and Treatment

When assessing individuals for AvPD, the following questions have been suggested (Zimmerman, 1994; Peter Pociluyko, personal communication, August 2007):

- Do you try to avoid work that involves contact with many people?
- Are you afraid people will criticize or reject you? What do you most fear people will say about you?
- Have you ever turned down a promotion or a job because it would have required increased contact with people?
- Do you avoid getting to know people because you are worried they may not like you? Has this affected the number of friends you have?
- Even in a close relationship, do you sometimes not share your thoughts or feelings because you are afraid the other person might put you down?
- If you are criticized, do you think about it for hours, or even days? How does it affect your behavior?
- Do you feel inadequate in social situations?
- Do you feel like you are not as interesting or fun as other people? Compared to other people, how would you describe yourself in terms of being interesting or fun?
- Would you describe yourself as someone who is willing to take risks or take on new activities or would you prefer to remain with the familiar?
- When you have been successful in interacting with others, what did you do that was different?

Several approaches and modalities have been suggested for effective AvPD treatment. Behavioral treatment interventions such as graduated exposure, social skills training, and systematic desensitization (Sutherland & Frances, 1996) focus on recognition of situations being avoided and on negative, deprecatory self-statements. In addition, anxiety management training, socialization experiences, development of communication skills, drug refusal skills, and basic assertiveness training can be quite helpful (Donat, 1995).

Cognitive interventions address AvPD distortions regarding competency and self-worth. If the AvPD internal self-talk has become savage in its self-deprecatory intent, little progress in treatment for either the personality disorder or the addiction can be achieved without interrupting this pattern. The negative self-statements must be clearly identified; clients should be asked specifically what they call themselves when feeling inept, inadequate, or unacceptable. The words can be startling in their intensity and viciousness. These must be countered in the treatment process with constructive, realistic, and self-accepting statements of encouragement and affirmations directed toward self-efficacy.

The confidence individuals with AvPD can gain through supported social exposure is vital for significant change. Even though these clients believe themselves unable to tolerate the anxiety of the group process, they still long for relationships and need the skills that make developing and maintaining relationships possible. Group therapy is a powerful intervention; individuals with AvPD find out that they can be accepted and supported by others, that they are not alone in their struggle, and that they can make a difference in the lives of others through their own willingness to be helpful. Because entry into a group can be particularly difficult for clients with AvPD, they need to be prepared and supported through the initial sessions. It may be helpful to have them meet individually with a trusted service provider concurrent with the initial group sessions.

Integrated treatment for co-occurring AvPD and addiction must address the impact of drug use on how these individuals manage their lives. Although they are disinclined to directly argue with requirements that they become abstinent, they may be determined to return to the drug use they see as essential as soon as they are free of legal consequences. They are accustomed to being more vulnerable socially, interpersonally, and psychologically than other people around them. They may believe that no one could possibly understand how strong their need is, and therefore, they will risk more severe addiction and repeated illegal behavior without necessarily saying why. Salzman (1981) believes that the inner forces that initiate and sustain addiction are immaturity and escapism. New ways must be learned for dealing with feelings of unattractiveness and helplessness other than compulsivity. A nonaddicted lifestyle for individuals with AvPD includes the awareness that negative feelings, unsolvable problems, and a sense of inadequate rewards will never disappear entirely. To move beyond addiction, they must be willing to tolerate the uncertainly of life (Peele, 1985).

Generally, medication for individuals with personality disorders addresses target symptoms rather than the personality disorder itself. AvPD usually involves dysphoria accompanied by mood instability, low energy, leaden fatigue, and depression. Many dysphoric individuals respond to standard antidepressant medications (Ellison & Adler, 1990).

Anti-anxiety medication can be very appealing to individuals with AvPD. It is possible that sedative–hypnotics are the clients' drug of choice and tolerance is already in place. These individuals must develop nonchemical courage and the strength they need to manage interpersonal anxiety. Even if they are not already involved with minor tranquilizers, they are likely to overvalue their effects. Iatrogenic addiction is a significant concern.

Treatment Goals

For individuals with co-occurring AvPD and addiction, the goals of treatment are abstinence, increased self-esteem, increased confidence in interpersonal relationships, and a desensitized reaction to criticism (Sperry, 2003). Treatment should be directed toward reinforcing a self-concept of competency, tolerance for failure, and a balance between caution and action (Dorr, 1995).

No treatment goal for any personality disorder should be an attempt for clients to become their own personality and temperament opposite. Whereas individuals with AvPD may fantasize about becoming outgoing, confident extroverts, the development of a more functional version of their basic personality traits can lead to a substantial improvement in the quality of their lives. Oldham and Morris (1995) suggest that the more functional expression of the avoidant personality disorder is the "sensitive personality style" (p. 180). These individuals are comfortable with the familiar, stay close to family and a limited number of friends, care what others think about them, are cautious and deliberate in dealing with others, and maintain a courteous, polite, interpersonal reserve. There is no need to be extroverted to avoid isolation, and greater involvement with others can be a significant support to abstinence and recovery from addiction.

Recovery Activities for Individuals with AvPD and Addiction

In an east coast MSW graduate program, the students who took an elective course on substance abuse were required to attend four open

12-step groups and write a paper about their experience by the end of the semester. Every class started with a brief discussion on a student's group attendance the prior week. On the day the assigned paper was due, a final discussion was held about peer support groups. One student who was bright, capable, involved, and enthusiastic said, "Once I realized I would not die of fear, going to the groups became fun." Service providers need to understand that if a graduate student with many strengths and no personality disorder could experience such strong anxiety, how much more difficult would it be for individuals with AvPD to overcome their fear and attend AA or NA? Any assistance is well worth the effort. Perhaps AA members could attend the first meetings with these individuals. Other treatment group members could go with them. They could be encouraged to arrive late and leave early for one or two meetings so they would not need to interact or feel bad because they could not bring themselves to talk with people at the meetings. Monitoring and following up with clients with co-occurring AvPD and substance dependence in their attendance and experiences with the meetings can provide both support and assistance. Continued participation is more likely if these individuals can interpret events as benign and safe rather than anxiety-inducing and negative. The impact of the 12-step or other peer support groups may be powerful enough to allow individuals with AvPD to seek their strength through the recovery community rather than through drug use.

10

Cluster C
Dependent Personality Disorder and Substance Use Disorders

Dependent Personality Disorder Defined

Essential Features

An essential feature of dependent personality disorder (DPD) is a pervasive and excessive need to be taken care of that results in submissive and clinging behavior. Individuals with DPD are often pessimistic. They are characterized by self-doubt and are inclined to belittle their abilities and assets. They respond to the criticism and disapproval of others as proof of their worthlessness. They seek others to dominate and protect them. Occupational functioning may be impaired if independent initiative is required; these individuals avoid positions of responsibility (APA, 2000).

Individuals with DPD are not fully adults. There is a deficit in maturation because they look to others to take responsibility for fulfilling their needs and managing their lives. This results in an underdeveloped capacity to adapt adequately and difficulty in functioning independently (Dorr, 1995).

Individuals with DPD are characterized by an overt and nondiscriminate dependency; a transparent, intense, and unremitting need to be loved; the determination to maintain stable long-term relationships that change very little over time; and a reluctance to compete (Kantor, 1992). They subjugate their personal needs to those of others, tolerate mistreatment, and fail to be appropriately self-assertive.

They often live with someone who is controlling, domineering, over-protective, and infantilizing (Frances et al., 1995).

According to the *DSM-IV-TR* (APA, 2000), there are similar DPD prevalence rates for men and women. However, the National Epidemiologic Survey on Alcohol and Related Conditions (Grant et al., 2004) found that the risk for DPD was significantly greater for women. Men with DPD tend to appear more autocratic and capable; women appear more noticeably submissive (Sperry & Carlson, 1993). Men with DPD appear to be demanding because they are intolerant of being alone and dislike separation from those upon whom they depend. Their partners may hear statements such as, "Where are you going?" "When will you be back?" "Where have you been?" "Do you really have to go?"

It has been suggested that genetic factors account for a relatively small portion of the variability in dependency levels. Parent–child relationships appears to be the major causal factor. Either authoritarian or overprotective parenting may lead to high levels of dependency and the belief that functioning is not possible without the guidance and protection of others. These individuals come to accept that relationships are maintained by acquiescing to requests, expectations, and demands (Bornstein, 1996).

Self-Image

Individuals with DPD see themselves as inadequate and helpless; they believe they are in a cold and dangerous world and unable to cope on their own. The solution to being powerless in a frightening world is to find capable people who will nurture and support. These individuals can then abdicate self-responsibility and turn their fate over to others. Within protective relationships, people with DPD deny their individuality and subordinate their desires, thoughts, opinions, and values to those held by significant others. They then can imagine themselves to be one with those who protect them from anxiety and dread (Beck et al., 2004; Millon & Grossman, 2007b).

However, to be comfortable with themselves and their inordinate helplessness, individuals with DPD must deny the feelings they experience and the deceptive strategies they employ. They limit their awareness of both themselves and others. Their restricted perceptiveness allows them to be naive, uncritical, considerate, thoughtful, cooperative, and modest (Millon & Grossman, 2007b). However, their limited tolerance for negative feelings, perceptions, and interactions results in the interpersonal and logistical ineptness that they already believe to be true about themselves.

View of Others

Individuals with DPD see other people as more capable of shouldering life's responsibilities, navigating a complex world, and dealing with the competitiveness of life (Millon, 1981). Others should provide a sense of security, take over responsibility, and offer continuous support (Richards, 1993).

DPD judgment of others is distorted by the inclination to see others as they wish they were rather than as they are (Kantor, 1992). These individuals retain unsophisticated ideas and childlike views of people (Millon & Davis, 1996). Dependent individuals play the inferior role very effectively; they communicate how sympathetic, strong, and competent they believe the dominant people in their lives are (Millon, 1981). With these methods, individuals with DPD are often able to get along with unpredictable, isolated, or unpleasant people (Kantor).

Relationships

Individuals with DPD see relationships as necessary for survival. To establish and maintain these life-sustaining relationships, people with DPD avoid expressing anger. They are more than docile; they are admiring, unquestioning, and willing to give their all. They are loyal and affectionate (Millon, 1981).

To sustain relationships at all costs, individuals with DPD approach both their own and others' failures and shortcomings with a saccharine attitude and indulgent tolerance (Millon, 1981). They engage in a mawkish minimization, denial, or distortion of both their own and others' negative, self-defeating, or destructive behaviors in order to sustain an idealized, and sometimes fictional, story of the relationships upon which they depend. They ask for little beyond acceptance and support (Millon & Davis, 1996). This self-protection at the cost of acknowledging what is real allows individuals with DPD to remain with an alcoholic or addicted partner at the expense of their children. One woman with DPD has consistently, throughout her marriage, denied that her husband has a problem with alcohol. When their three adult children speak of their father's addiction, she is annoyed and impatient. The father has late-stage alcoholism with clear organic damage and a career brought to ruin by his drinking and damaged cognitive functions. The adult children complain that they have to call their father before 8:30 a.m. (when the mother is already at work; the father has not been able to earn a living for many years) because if they wait until later, he is already too drunk to talk with them. Mother's response: "No, he's not." This mother, like many others who cling to alcoholic spouses, will lie for her husband and to her husband. She will lie to her children. Their reality was and continues to be retold through the lens of a dependent woman who refuses to acknowledge her family's situation or her husband's increasingly self-destructive addiction. She has not yielded her denial even into old age as her husband has become seriously incoherent and paranoid in his thinking. Her children are convinced that she will go to her grave with a fictional story of her marriage, her family, and her own life. She will never acknowledge the damage that she and her husband have done to their children or the ruined relationships with other family members because of the toxic behaviors of a severe alcoholic and a spouse in supportive denial.

It is important to note that individuals with DPD, in spite of the intensity of their need for others, are able to redirect their dependency and unmodulated attachment to other powerful figures if they cannot prevent the loss of a relationship. It is the strength of the dependency needs that is being addressed; attachment figures are more important for the security and safety they provide than any specific individual characteristics. Attachment to others is a self-referenced and, at times, haphazard process of securing the protection of the most readily available person willing to provide nurturance and care. Yet, if the DPD is severe enough, these individuals can be dangerous to significant others who are trying to leave them. Sometimes, the best way to safely detach from partners with DPD is to encourage and even assist them to attach to someone else.

Issues with Authority

Individuals with DPD do not engage in provocative or rebellious behavior toward authority figures. They are likely to elicit protective behavior from uniformed authority because of their conciliatory, anxious eagerness to please. Because of their need for support and care, they are disinclined to question authority or dispute orders from others. If they do get into trouble with law enforcement personnel, it is usually in the company of others who are taking the lead in illegal behavior.

Individuals with DPD can function well in families or workplaces where rewards are based on compliance. They do best where interpersonal and supportive contact is available (Richards, 1993). There can be difficulty on the job if there is a need for or expectation of either individual initiative or tolerance for conflict. Supervisors with DPD have significant difficulty confronting negative or unacceptable behaviors in subordinates. They are also so loath to displease their supervisors that they may actually withhold vital information that they believe would be upsetting.

Behavior

The lack of self-confidence in individuals with DPD is apparent in their posture, voice, and mannerisms. They are cooperative, passive, and yielding. They may be viewed by others as thoughtful, apologetic and acquiescent. They appear humble, gracious, and gentle (Millon, 1981).

The DPD inclination to avoid or deny harsh realities, restrict thoughts and feelings that may elicit displeasure, minimize difficulties, and fail to see problems may appear as mildly diminished cognitive capability. They rely on feelings and empathic attunement with others rather than on thinking and problem solving. They are adept at sensing what others will reject and in identifying any threat to their support system. These individuals show remarkable patience and persistence in preserving what they have. They use cajolery, bribery, moral censure, promises to change (rarely kept), and even threats of self-harm to keep relationships upon which they depend. They put their efforts into avoiding failure (Kantor, 1992; Richards, 1993).

Affect

The underlying characterological pessimism of DPD lends itself to a chronic, mild depression or dysthymia. When faced with abandonment, rejection, or loss, these individuals may experience major depression. Critical to the tendency to avoid risks in relationships is the threat of depression brought on by interpersonal rejection and accompanied by loss of self-esteem and self-confidence (Millon, 1996).

Individuals with DPD can be plagued by fatigue, lethargy, and diffuse anxieties; these individuals are often unable to feel much joy in living. Because they feel they must appear satisfied and content around those upon whom they depend, they suffer in silence. When asked, they describe themselves as pessimistic, discouraged, and dejected (Millon, 1981). They mitigate their depression with a defensively sustained belief that everything will turn out all right (Kantor, 1992). This is a fragile management of encroaching sorrow and may mean the situation will elevate to a crisis when reality, for example, a partner leaving, forces itself into DPD awareness.

Defenses

The primary defense mechanism for people with DPD is introjection. These individuals go beyond identification to seek internalization of the more powerful other; they long for an inseparable interpersonal bond. Denial is another defense used to smooth over uncomfortable interpersonal events or hostile impulses. These individuals soften the edges of interpersonal strain with a syrupy sweetness and a tendency to cover up or gloss over troublesome events. They characteristically limit their awareness of themselves and others to a narrow, comfortable sphere. They are minimally introspective and inclined to see only the good in situations, including the pleasant side of disquieting events (Kubacki & Smith, 1995; Millon, 1981).

The Self-Created World (Altered Reality) of DPD

Individuals with DPD create and sustain an altered reality that, although not psychotic, permits self-defeating behaviors to continue and compromises maturation. This reality keeps the world at a distance and allows a perception of safety and security to exist at the expense of personal growth and authenticity. For individuals with DPD, the altered reality is composed of believing or hoping that:

- Being "really good" is the equivalent of being "really safe"
- Being in a loving relationship is the only real way to be happy
- Being kind, understanding, and helpful will smooth over many difficulties
- Focusing on the unpleasant is unnecessary
- People really mean well, even when they do things we don't understand
- Someone who loves me won't mind taking care of me and making my decisions

Substance Use Disorders and DPD

Co-Occurring Substance Use Disorders and the Impact of Drugs on DPD

Individuals with personality disorders, due to their frequent failures in self-regulation, have an increased inclination to use drugs and alcohol as alternative solutions to life problems (Khantzian et al., 1990). Both using drugs and having a personality disorder involve behaviors that provide distance from unwanted reality. For individuals with DPD, alcohol and other drugs offer an easy, passive way to deal with or escape from problems (Beck et al., 2004). Alcohol and other drugs can make it possible for individuals with DPD to:

- Reduce anxiety
- Express emotions that are denied due to fear of losing security and support
- Ease the pain of unmet interpersonal and emotional needs
- Manage separation fears when a partner comes and goes during routine daily activities or is not particularly supportive
- Escape competency demands

There may be some protection from addiction if significant others are disapproving of these individuals' drug use. However, the disapproval may be responded to by secretive use and greater anxiety, depression, and self-loathing (Richards, 1993). Individuals with DPD may, in a setting where alcohol or drug use is unacceptable, hide their bottles or drugs all over the house in an attempt to disguise their involvement. This works best if those with DPD are actually home alone a good portion of the time or spend time in a workshop or with other hobbies that can serve as a cover for substance use.

Drugs of Choice for DPD

Individuals with DPD are rarely inclined, on their own, to obtain illegal drugs. If laws are broken in the process of getting money for or actually obtaining illegal drugs, it is likely that someone with a stronger personality made the choices and planned the actions that would result in trouble with law enforcement. Left to their own devices, they are likely to obtain alcohol and prescription drugs because they are legal. Individuals with DPD are so appealing as patients that they are able to win over various health providers to prescribe sedatives, narcotics, or stimulants, depending upon whether they say they need to calm down, reduce pain, or lose weight. They may then:

- Attempt to alternate the use of various area pharmacies to disguise multiple prescriptions
- Fail to share with any one health provider how many other family physicians, dentists, or psychiatrists they are seeing
- Lie to significant others about how many types of drugs for which they have prescriptions
- Be very creative about hiding bottles
- Mix and match prescription drugs with alcohol to augment the impact of any one of the substances

All of this activity may be done in a cloud of dread and guilt, but individuals with DPD may be certain they will "fall apart" if deprived of the drugs they use to manage or disguise their emotions.

If, on the other hand, individuals with DPD are close to or live with individuals who drink and use drugs, they will use the same drugs at the same time in the same amount via the same route of administration as their significant others. They will be so enmeshed in the relationship that abstinence is not an option. For these individuals with DPD, no alcohol and drug treatment has any possibility of being effective unless the using relationship is altered or terminated.

Integrated Dual Diagnosis Treatment for DPD

Engaging in Treatment

Individuals with DPD are frequently found in outpatient mental health clinics. Sharoff (2002) suggests that one of the most common presenting problems in therapy involves individuals with DPD in stable, unsatisfactory relationships that they are angry about and too fearful to leave. These individuals may engage in fantasies of magical refueling with the help of powerful, benevolent service providers (Van Denburg, 1995). Clients with DPD rarely come in for treatment saying they are too dependent, nor do they identify decision making as the critical problem. In fact, these individuals usually know they are dependent and do not particularly see it as a problem (Kantor, 1992). Instead, they complain of anxiety, tension, or depression (Turkat, 1990). Although individuals with DPD often experience a positive treatment outcome (Sperry, 2003), it remains a serious challenge for these people to leave abusive relationships.

If individuals with DPD enter drug and alcohol treatment it is usually in response to legal problems or a significant other who is demanding that they stop drinking or using drugs. Their dependence on external support, whether on relationships or drugs, is central to their maladaptive personality-disordered defenses. They may be able to achieve abstinence in treatment but relapse immediately afterward. They are also capable of being completely cooperative in a treatment program during the day and getting high at home in the evening if they are in a using relationship. Their personality difficulties are intrinsic to their drug and alcohol problems, and treatment can rarely be successful without addressing both.

Treatment Provider Guidelines

Individuals with DPD can seem easy to treat initially; they are attentive, cooperative, and appreciative. They engage easily in the treatment process and agree with nearly everything their service providers say. They are extremely compliant and openly idealize the treatment providers. Then, after a period of time, it becomes apparent that these same clients are clinging to treatment and resisting any attempt to enhance autonomy (Beck et al., 2004). Clients with

DPD express their discomfort or disagreement indirectly and may fail to carry out suggestions given to them in treatment (Kubacki & Smith, 1995).

These individuals are likely to develop a strong dependence on service providers while continuing to devalue their own ability to make use of the treatment. All progress is attributed to the service providers and not to the self (McCann, 1995). It is important that service providers do not reestablish the dominance–submission pattern that characterizes other relationships for these individuals (Millon, 1981). It needs to be determined if apparent gains in treatment are merely reflective of temporary compliance with strong, demanding treatment providers (Dorr, 1995).

Professional Ethics and DPD

The willingness that individuals with DPD have to submit to more powerful others makes it imperative that professional boundaries and limits are established and adhered to closely. Clients with DPD may repeatedly attempt to have service providers take responsibility for decisions they should make for themselves. Should service providers accept this role, they could become external substitutes for these clients' own will. It may actually be easier and more efficient to make the decisions, and service providers may yield to the temptation out of exasperation, disdain, contempt (Sperry, 2003), or a personal wish to assume an idealized role as a wise and all-knowing benevolent presence. If treatment providers dominate clients with DPD, they may find themselves, after a period of time, entangled in a complex web of dependency and anger with individuals who will eventually feel betrayed and damaged.

Another concern with these clients is that they make many demands on service providers for advice, succor, or concrete help that often cannot or should not be met. Their level of need may elicit service provider withdrawal, annoyance, and a wish that these clients would leave treatment (Perry, 1996; Richards, 1993). Treatment providers vary in their tolerance for adult clients who are needy and clinging. It is imperative that annoyance be neither denied nor justified. Some service providers know they should not work with passive–dependent clients because their tolerance is so limited and their inclination toward anger too difficult to contain, but everyone has a limit to the amount of dependency he or she can withstand and remain productive. Although clients with DPD may seem easier to work with than individuals with more provocative personality disorders, there is still a need to carefully self-monitor so that service provider extremes of domination or rejection can be avoided.

Another problem is that clients with DPD may be in unsatisfying, abusive relationships. Their repeated stories about mistreatment may evoke the service providers' desire to control DPD self-defeating behaviors. They may prematurely challenge DPD clients to leave abusive relationships and overlook the right these individuals have to make their own choices. They could also place these clients into the difficult bind of having to choose between a demanding service provider and an abusive partner—while having difficulty telling the difference between the two powerful others in their lives.

Assessment and Treatment

Zimmerman (1994) suggests the following questions when assessing individuals for DPD:

- Some people enjoy making decisions. Others prefer to have someone they trust to guide them. Which do you prefer?
- Is it hard for you to express a different opinion with someone you are close to? What do you think might happen if you did?
- Do you often pretend to agree with others even if you do not? Why?
- Do you often need help to get started on a project?
- Do you ever volunteer to do unpleasant things for others?
- Are you uncomfortable when you are alone?
- Have you found that you are desperate to get into another relationship right away when a relationship ends?
- Do you worry about important people in your life leaving you?

A critical element in the assessment of DPD is behavior within relationships. When a dominant caretaker is available to individuals with DPD, they have the assurance they need and may not seek treatment. The discomfort and distress occur when they are alone and frightened. When individuals with DPD do enter treatment, they usually describe a history of molding their personalities to dominant figures with whom they are or have been involved.

Often, clients with DPD seek treatment to make their unsuccessful, symbiotic relationships more fulfilling; they would be content to stay dependent on their primary caretakers if these stronger individuals would just be supportive, encouraging, and loving (Sharoff, 2002). Service providers should gradually increase the level of expectations for autonomous decision making, action, and socially effective responses. This includes self-management of crises and self-soothing under stress. Sharoff suggests several cognitive techniques that include skill-building, increasing rejection tolerance, and fostering sufficient self-esteem so that clients with DPD can come to believe they have a right to values, beliefs, ambition, and independence. He also stresses acceptance of reality, that is, seeing people and relationships as they are. Clients should not deny reality or turn away from it. Defining situations as they actually are permits different courses of action to be considered.

In treatment, service providers must empathize with the feelings of inadequacy experienced by clients with DPD but should also point out behaviors that demonstrate their self-efficacy, autonomy, and competence (McCann, 1995). Cognitive–behavioral approaches focus on accurate self-appraisal and independent decision making. Initial dependent behavior is accepted but addressed and reflected upon in the treatment process. When there is resistance to change, service providers should help these clients think through their ambivalence about changing and substitute constructive behavior for old dependent habits (Perry, 1996).

Individuals with DPD often do well in inpatient treatment and in early phases of recovery from substance use disorders because the stabilizing and supportive aspects of the treatment process meet their basic dependency needs. However, these individuals may resist significant progress; they are inclined to remain in the attached, secure, weak, and dependent position of early treatment. The greater independence involved in later phases of treatment provokes anxiety and depression. They then become quite vulnerable to relapse as drugs and alcohol modulate feelings of abandonment. Relapse potential, particularly in relation to personality issues, needs to be addressed directly and clearly. It is important that these individuals see the impact of their dependency on the choices they make in regard to drugs and alcohol as well as other areas of their lives.

Group involvement can also be effective in confronting individuals with DPD about their self-absolution from responsibility for themselves. It is important to remember that, for individuals with DPD, self-destructive behavior in the service of relationship maintenance looks like a reasonable trade-off to them, no matter what it looks like to others. Group members can be effective in pointing out the impact of abusive or self-destructive relationships.

Of concern, particularly in the treatment of addicted individuals with severe DPD, is their potential for disinhibition and violence if they feel seriously threatened. These clients usually have low activity levels and barely discernible aggression. However, they can become threatened, guarded, wary, and even violent if their basic dependency is threatened. When they feel endangered and are intoxicated, individuals with severe DPD have made mortal attacks on their families. Also, because of their avoidance of adult activities, immaturity, and self-identity as children, sexual offenses against children have been made, particularly during times of intoxication and abandonment by other adults (Richards, 1993).

There is little evidence to suggest that the use of medication will result in long-term benefits in the personality functioning of individuals with DPD (Perry, 1996). Stone (1993) believes that DPD is not amenable to pharmacological measures; treatment relies upon verbal therapies. It is recommended that target symptoms rather than specific personality disorders be medicated. One of these target symptoms is dysphoria—marked by low energy, leaden fatigue, and depression. Some individuals with DPD respond well to antidepressant medications (Ellison & Adler, 1990).

Unfortunately, individuals with DPD tend to be appealing clients. They are not inclined to be demanding and provocative. This can be precisely why they are given benzodiazepines for anxiety by psychiatrists who may feel both benevolent and protective. Their inclination to use denial and escape to manage their lives makes the use of sedative–hypnotics familiar and pleasant. Iatrogenic addiction is a serious concern.

Treatment Goals

Adler (1990) suggests that treatment goals for all personality disorders include preventing further deterioration, regaining an adaptive equilibrium, alleviating symptoms, and fostering improved adaptive capacity. Treatment interventions teach more adaptive methods of managing distress, improving interpersonal effectiveness, and building skills for affect regulation.

Even though DPD treatment progress is made evident through increased independent functioning, this cannot be an initial therapeutic goal. Early in the treatment process, accommodation needs to be made so that some of the dependency needs evidenced by these clients can be gratified via appropriate support and encouragement from service providers and enough security can be developed to allow change to be pursued (Van Denburg, 1995).

Sperry (2003) suggests that the basic goal for DPD treatment is self-efficacy. Individuals with DPD must recognize their dependent patterns and the high price they pay to maintain those patterns. The long-range goal is to increase DPD individuals' sense of independence and ability to function. Clients with DPD must build strength rather than foster neediness (Benjamin, 1996).

Although clients with DPD must eventually become more active and self-reliant, such a change will trigger fantasies and fears regarding the consequences of being independent or may be an accurate expectation of rejection by significant others who prefer submission. Should they become more autonomous, most individuals with DPD fear being abandoned. It may be reassuring if the goal of treatment is autonomy: the capacity for independence and the ability to develop intimate relationships (Beck et al., 2004).

Progress in abstinence or recovery from addiction is consistently confounded by the debilitating immaturity of DPD. DPD is exacerbated by substance abuse or dependence. On the other hand, progress in one disorder augments or amplifies recovery in the other.

Recovery Activities for Individuals with DPD and Addiction

Because individuals with DPD follow the lead of those around them, it is particularly important to assess their social environment to locate areas of peer pressure or the social function of their drug use. NA or AA contacts are easy for these individuals, but there is no assurance that they will seek out and attach to the healthier and more sincere members of their groups. They can often be prey for more aggressive or narcissistic people in any system. Specific guidance and reinforcement of preferred interpersonal attachments are often crucial to addicted individuals with DPD (Richards, 1993).

Peer group involvement can be essential to individuals with DPD. It can be particularly beneficial for them to attend same-sex 12-step meetings. Women can encourage, model, and support independent behaviors and adult decision making in ways that are sustaining and convincing. Men can, in a supportive mixed-sex group, challenge dependent behaviors and either describe or model alternative behaviors. In either group, changes are often celebrated, and individuals with DPD can be assisted with their fears that greater personal strength will result in abandonment.

In any case, connection to the recovery community, whether in mental health, substance abuse, or dual diagnosis, allows these individuals to feel less alone and frightened. They are likely to make progress in both personality and substance use disorders as long as they can be assisted in forming positive relationships in which they are fully participating adults.

11

Cluster C
Obsessive–Compulsive Personality Disorder and Substance Use Disorders

Obsessive–Compulsive Personality Disorder Defined

Essential Features

An essential feature of obsessive–compulsive personality disorder (OCPD) is a preoccupation with orderliness, perfectionism, and control at the expense of flexibility, openness, and efficiency. Individuals with OCPD are conscientious, scrupulous, and inflexible about morality, ethics, and values. They may force themselves and others to follow rigid moral principles and very high standards of performance. They are inclined to be severely self-critical. These individuals are deferential to authority and rules. They insist on literal compliance, regardless of circumstances (APA, 2000).

Frances et al. (1995) describe individuals with OCPD as:

- Perfectionistic, constricted, and excessively disciplined
- Behaviorally rigid, formal, cool, distant, intellectualized, and detailed
- Driven by a chronic sense of time pressure and an inability to relax
- Controlling of themselves, others, and situations
- Indirect in their expression of anger
- Often inclined to hoard money and other possessions
- Preoccupied with neatness and cleanliness
- Inflexible and stubborn in relationships

Individuals with OCPD have an ongoing conflict between obedience and defiance. Behaviorally, they are compliant; inwardly, they possess a strong desire to assert themselves and defy the regulations imposed upon them. Individuals with OCPD incorporate the values of others and submerge their own individuality, yet the more they adapt, the more they feel anger and resentment (Millon, 1981; Millon & Grossman, 2007b).

OCPD and obsessive–compulsive disorder (OCD) are currently defined as separate and distinct disorders (McCullough & Maltsberger, 1996). Most individuals with OCD do not meet the criteria for OCPD. Approximately 50% of individuals meeting the criteria for OCD also meet the criteria for one or more personality disorders; it is most frequently comorbid with avoidant personality and dependent personality disorder (Pfohl & Blum, 1995). OCPD is described as ego syntonic. In fact, these individuals are so sure they are right that they insist those around them do things their way. On the other hand, the obsessive thoughts and compulsions of OCD are recognized by the individual as intrusive and unusual; these internal experiences and behaviors are ego dystonic and are often hidden from others. According to the *DSM-IV-TR* (APA, 2000), OCPD is diagnosed about twice as often in males as females, yet the National Epidemiologic Survey on Alcohol and Related Conditions (Grant et al., 2004) found no sex difference in the risk of OCPD.

Self-Image

Individuals with OCPD see themselves as responsible people. They are as harsh in their judgments of themselves as they are with others; they are angry at themselves for being imperfect and expect themselves to be dependable, loyal, prudent, and conscientious (Millon & Grossman, 2007b). Individuals with OCPD do not allow themselves many vices. They are inclined to eat properly, exercise, take vitamins, and drink moderately, all in an attempt to ward off or avoid the consequences of illness, accident, or injury. The comedian Redd Foxx seemed to have had individuals with OCPD in mind when he said that all these people who eat right, don't smoke, and don't drink are going to feel really stupid some day, lying in a hospital, dying of nothing. His humor underscores the futility of hoping that very good behavior can keep anyone safe forever.

Individuals with OCPD are inclined to feel self-doubt and guilt if they do not live up to their ideals, but they do not recognize their own ambivalence about achieving aspirations and meeting expectations (Millon, 1981).

View of Others

Individuals with OCPD see others as irresponsible, self-indulgent, and incompetent (Beck et al., 2004). They are contemptuous of those who are frivolous and impulsive. They consider emotionally driven behavior to be immature and foolish. They do not usually recognize that they judge others in accord with rules that they themselves unconsciously detest (Millon, 1981).

Some individuals with OCPD become aware of their impact on others, but they do not seem to understand it; others with OCPD appear oblivious to the negative emotions they elicit when they insist upon doing things exactly as they "should" be done. In fact, if confronted, individuals with OCPD are inclined to believe that people have no right to be angry (Turkat, 1990). In a large suburban office, a ladies restroom had holders for three rolls of toilet paper. A staff member at the company (well–known for her obsessive–compulsive behaviors) was so incensed by the illogical and messy way women used the three rolls of paper that she posted a sign saying: "Please do not begin using a new roll of toilet paper until the previous roll—from left to right—has been completely finished." Needless to say, not one woman in the office followed this posted rule, and the three rolls were consistently in varying degrees of depletion. The woman who made the sign became an object of ridicule. These individuals are often surprised that others feel controlled and invaded by such behavior.

Relationships

McWilliams (1994) suggests that a central issue in the OCPD family of origin is control. Whether or not that is the case, control is a major factor in current OCPD relationships. The behavior of individuals with OCPD with significant others is likely to be disrespectful and domineering. They are not necessarily attempting to behave negatively, but they appear to be orchestrating the entire family to a pattern of orderliness, discipline, and safety. Whereas their organized behavior may or may not be effective in various work settings, it sets the stage for individuals with OCPD to engage in ongoing and unpleasant power struggles with members of their families. For example, one man with OCPD insisted that members of his family fold their dirty laundry before placing garments in the dirty clothes hamper. Although that may have served him well in the military, his wife and children were exasperated with this control of their behavior. He had trouble understanding why when he was only trying to do things the right way.

Issues with Authority

Individuals with OCPD relate to others in terms of rank or status, with an authoritarian rather than egalitarian style. They are deferential, ingratiating, and obsequious with individuals of greater rank, power, or position but are autocratic, condemnatory, and self-righteous with people they perceive as having less power than themselves. They justify their aggressive approach to controlling others by referring to rules or to authorities higher than themselves, whether that higher power is a boss, a police officer, or God. By allying themselves with those in power, individuals with OCPD gain considerable strength and authority for themselves and evade the potential negative impact of taking a stand of their own (Millon & Grossman, 2007b). Even if, as suggested by Pollack (1995), individuals with OCPD do resist authority through furtive, withholding behavior, their inclination to disown their own responsibility through attribution of decision-making authority to others can make them dangerous to people in subordinate positions. They are likely to follow a "bad" order and become punishing toward subordinates who resist.

Behavior

Individuals with OCPD may fail to give direction to their lives. They dread making mistakes and can become indecisive, restrained, and immobilized under stress. The conflict between being socially compliant and the desire to rebel and be assertive can result in passivity and failure to achieve. They cannot rebel because they remain trapped by their fear of being punished. They experience severe physical tension and use rigid psychological controls to inhibit their impulses and adhere to the expectations of others. They can only partially resolve this ambivalence by suppressing resentment and engaging in overconforming behavior. The powerful anger lurking behind their front of propriety and restraint occasionally breaks through. For the most part, these individuals not only follow the rules; they defend them. As a consequence, they can be seen by others as moralistic and self-righteous (Millon & Grossman, 2007b).

People with OCPD are excessively devoted to work and productivity. Oldham and Morris (1995) note that these individuals invest all of their energy in work, and then become tense, strained, anxious, and overwhelmed by the amount of work they have. People with OCPD maintain control of their occupational demands through attention to regulations, details, procedures, and schedules. They are extremely careful and prone to repetition. They may allocate time poorly, with major tasks being left to the last moment. They may become so involved in making everything perfect that they are unable to complete projects at all. Some individuals with OCPD have failed to file and pay their income taxes for years because they never seemed to have quite enough information to ensure that the paperwork was completely accurate (B. Carruth, personal communication, September 25, 2007). However, they are reluctant to delegate tasks and stubbornly insist that things be done their way. They may reject help, even when needed, because they believe no one else can do it right. They often refuse to compromise, even when they recognize that it is in their own best interests—because of the principle of the thing (APA, 2000).

Individuals with OCPD are inclined to be pack rats. These individuals hoard and protect their belongings against all intrusions, even if significant others complain about the space taken up by what they have accumulated. The wife of a man with OCPD complained that he would pull over to the side of the road to pick up something that had been dropped or discarded by others. He responded that one never knows when these items might come in handy. His wife said, "*One* glove?"

Feeling deprived of so many wishes and desires in childhood, individuals with OCPD protect what they have achieved as adults. This can result in miserly, ungenerous behavior. They may live below their means so that spending can be controlled to provide for mis-chance or future need (APA, 2000).

Affect

Despite their elaborate defenses, individuals with OCPD tend to have troublesome psychiatric symptoms. They are plagued by both their own exacting standards and the high expectations they perceive others hold for them. As a result, they are susceptible to a full range of affective disorders (Millon, 1996; Millon & Grossman, 2007b).

Individuals with OCPD are vulnerable to distress in situations in which they are unable to maintain control over their physical or interpersonal environment (APA, 2000). A man with OCPD set a personal goal for himself of climbing every mountain in Colorado over 14,000 feet; he had, at one point, successfully climbed all but four of them. He was anxious, though, because the climbing season was over; he ruminated that his health might not hold out over the intervening winter months and he would be unable to complete his goal. He could neither experience nor express satisfaction or pleasure with what he had done to date. His health was fine. He was concerned about the unknown that might interfere with his ability to meet his goal, and it depleted his capacity for pride in his accomplishments. Although uncertainty is a factor in everyone's life, if it is allowed to dampen hope and create distress where satisfaction is due, then the risk of pessimism and dejection substantially increases.

McWilliams (1994) believes that the basic affective conflict in OCPD is rage and fear: rage at being controlled and fear of being punished. Sperry (2003) describes the OCPD emotional style as grim, angry, frustrated, and irritable. Individuals with OCPD are prone to depression, especially as they get older (Frances et al., 1995). These individuals, who are conscientious, hardworking, and well-integrated into society, are vulnerable to loss; they are sharply aware of their declining abilities and decreasing productivity as they age. They respond to these changes with self-punitive and self-denigrating thoughts. As they face the final years of their careers or approach retirement, they are confronted by the realization that they will not attain all of their life goals or meet their own standards of excellence. Another potential issue in the late onset of depression for individuals with OCPD is the barrenness of their existence after giving up so much of themselves to their rigid conformity. Major depression in individuals with OCPD tends to have an agitated and apprehensive quality (Millon, 1996).

Individuals with OCPD are also quite vulnerable to anxiety. They fear making mistakes and being less than perfect. Benjamin (2005) suggests that OCPD developmental history may have included relentless coercion to perform correctly and follow the rules, regardless of the personal cost. As children, individuals with OCPD were punished for failure and were given few, if any, rewards for success. The most they could hope for was to avoid criticism or punishment. It was an environment of little warmth; the emphasis was on control. As adults, these individuals have learned to reduce their level of anxiety by incorporating this control. They restrict their activities and adhere carefully to rules so that they do not engage in unacceptable behavior (Millon & Grossman, 2007b). Part of the reason that unstructured activities or situations are so anxiety-provoking for individuals with OCPD is the lack of safety involved in not knowing the rules of conduct.

Defenses

OCPD defenses are intellectualization, isolation of affect, undoing, reaction formation, displacement, and regression. These defenses control anxiety but extract a heavy price in terms of personal constriction (McCullough & Maltsberger, 1996). When these defenses work, individuals with OCPD can appear deliberate and calm. However, they must still manage the internal turmoil of their unresolved struggle between obedience and defiance that threatens to upset the balance they have so carefully developed.

Individuals with OCPD must control against both external eruption of their anger and the internal disruption of emotions and impulses:

- The external expression of hostility and aggression can be managed by finding and allying with punitive authority figures.
- If hostility breaks through, these individuals use undoing or actions that have an unconscious meaning of atonement or magical protection (McWilliams, 1994). The undoing expiates them

from unacceptable behavior and returns them to the goodwill of those in authority.

- Internal impulses are controlled through the use of sublimation. Sublimation allows unacceptable hostility to be expressed in socially acceptable ways.
- Keeping hostile impulses in check can also be accomplished with the use of reaction formation and isolation. Ingratiating and obsequious OCPD behavior may be traced to a reaction formation of their own rebellious urges. They bind their defiance and anger so tightly that the opposite behavior emerges. These individuals also compartmentalize or isolate their emotional response to situations. They block or neutralize responses that would embarrass them or elicit disapproval from others (Millon, 1981; Millon & Grossman, 2007b).

One man with OCPD, in his fifties, had cancer. It was treatable, and he was doing well physically. However, as he had known himself to be a very angry man, he decided that his anger was the cause of his cancer. His treatment regimen, therefore, included a refusal to get angry over anything at all. He began to equate anger with illness, vulnerability, and death. He decided that a cheerful and happy demeanor was the path to good health. The results were unnerving high spirits expressed with an inauthentic joviality. He dissociated from his anger without any resolution of years of rage and resentment. The overall effect was one of a very bad actor attempting to portray youthful exuberance and optimism. One relative who had not seen him for several years described himself as "shocked" by the enormity of the change and the absolute failure of authenticity or personal genuineness. The man developed an agitated, anxious depression without any reduction in his chronic level of anger. His whole approach to the problem was the hope that punishment could be avoided if only he were "good"; he feared that his anger was bad and made him vulnerable to the punishment of illness.

The Self-Created World (Altered Reality) of OCPD

Individuals with OCPD create and sustain an altered reality that, although not psychotic, allows rigid adherence to security-enhancing behaviors at the expense of authenticity, spontaneity, and relatedness to others. For individuals with OCPD, the altered reality is composed of believing or hoping that:

- Being "really good" is the equivalent of being "really safe."
- Being in control is a means to manage an unsafe future.
- You can't be too organized.
- Everyone should follow the rules.
- People should do things my way—the right way.
- Tension is just the byproduct of being responsible.

Substance Use Disorders and OCPD

Co-Occurring Substance Use Disorders and the Impact of Drugs on OCPD

Individuals with OCPD are so intent upon being in control that they may be intolerant of the disruptive feelings accompanying intoxication from, dependence on, and withdrawal from drug and alcohol use. And, even though they are disinclined to engage in illegal activities and the high-risk behaviors that are inherent in the use of street drugs, there are still three factors that can make alcohol and other drugs, as well as compulsive behaviors, enticing for these individuals.

First, OCPD anxiety is bound into behavior meant to please and pacify powerful others, but tension and pressure take their toll anyway; drugs that sooth, calm, and reduce anxiety can become increasingly important. Both addictive and compulsive behaviors may be an attempt to manage internal discomfort and negative feelings while continuing to adhere to rigid patterns of coping.

Second, these individuals demand of themselves a level of work-related effort that is exhausting. They are extremely reactive to any loss of productivity with age or illness and are vulnerable to severe distress if not able to work at a level that protects them from depression and anxiety. Initial attempts to manage fatigue and endurance might be limited to legal drugs, for example, caffeine. If they have access, through a cooperative physician, to stronger drugs, they will be attracted to the central nervous system stimulants that allow them to manipulate their energy and ability to focus.

Third, if the use of stimulants is successful in bolstering productivity and sustaining energy, then the need to sleep at night becomes an equal target for chemical management. Central nervous system depressants, for example, wine or antihistamines, become the means to sleep so these individuals can sustain their intensely demanding schedules without being defeated by exhaustion. Again, a cooperative physician may provide sedatives with addictive potential to facilitate sleep.

Individuals with OCPD are disinclined to allow their drug use or compulsive behaviors to be known by others. They usually engage in secretive use and hidden behaviors. However, drugs and alcohol can easily become an accelerating problem for these individuals because they acquire ingrained habits with little effort.

Individuals with OCPD are vulnerable to compulsive behaviors related to money and sexual behaviors, for example, compulsive hoarding or compulsive use of phone sex.

Drugs of Choice for OCPD

It is important to note that no one or two drugs are invariably the choice of a specific personality disorder. The drug of choice is related to accessibility, experience, and physiological response. However, Milkman and Sunderwirth (1987) propose that the drug of choice is also a pharmacological defense mechanism; it is chosen because of how well it fits with an individual's usual style of coping and how effectively it bolsters already established patterns for managing psychological threat. As noted above, individuals with OCPD are attracted to drugs that enhance work performance. One professional with OCPD, upon learning that caffeinated water was on the market, commented, "Oh, we can make our coffee with that!" Her coworkers began to suggest, after that remark, that she should create a mobile intravenous caffeine device that would allow her to have a constant drip of the stimulant directly into her bloodstream throughout the day. Individuals with OCPD are vulnerable to overvaluing the ability of stimulants to boost productivity and then sedatives to relax when they need to rest. They may feel a combination of guilt and defiant anger as they attempt to manage their energy levels via chemicals.

Integrated Dual Diagnosis Treatment for OCPD

Engaging in Treatment

Individuals with OCPD often enter treatment for depression because their productivity is slipping. They appear to be particularly sensitive to natural changes in cognitive skills due to normal aging (Turkat, 1990). They also come in for treatment because they frequently experience psychosomatic disorders due to the problems they have with discharging tension. They may also experience severe anxiety, immobilization, and excessive fatigue (Millon, 1981). These individuals also come in for treatment as a result of someone else's concern about their behavior. Interpersonal difficulties for people with OCPD are related to their failure to grasp the impact of their behavior. They are inept at reading other peoples' emotions and at experiencing and understanding their own. They usually deny they are having problems with others either on the job or at home (Turkat, 1990) and are not certain why their families or supervisors insist that they seek treatment.

Initially, clients with OCPD appear to be cooperative. They are polite, rational, and detail oriented (Turkat, 1990). These individuals want to defer to their service providers and be perfect clients (Benjamin, 2005). They are serious, conscientious, honest, motivated, and hard-working. Over time, however, it becomes apparent that they are inclined to be consciously compliant and unconsciously oppositional (McWilliams, 1994). They are as likely to replicate their conflicts with obedience and defiance within the treatment setting as in other areas of their lives.

Treatment Provider Guidelines

According to McWilliams (1994), the first rule of treatment for service providers working with clients with OCPD is ordinary kindness. These individuals are accustomed to being exasperating to others without fully comprehending why. Working with them can be tedious. They are likely to engage in long monologues of self-justification, lofty goals and ambitions, and reasons why family members, intimate others, and subordinates at work need to be rigidly controlled (Stone, 1993). The strained, affect-controlled, and detail-oriented speech of individuals with OCPD must be met with patience, tolerance, and the ability to listen without drifting off into personal reveries. It is not beneficial to brush aside, no matter how gently, material that these individuals see as important in an effort to get on with affective issues. Pressure to prematurely focus on and experience emotions is both alien and alienating. Service providers need to be careful that they do not overvalue communications regarding feelings and imply that clients with OCPD are not "doing treatment right" when their attempts to communicate are basically intellectual.

Treatment providers also need to be watchful of these individuals' becoming over-conscientious; they are inclined to approach treatment as a task that must be carefully managed with hard work and careful adherence to the ground rules of honest discourse. They answer questions fully, often with exhausting detail. They follow assignments, for example, write a lifeline, the same way. It is important that their attempts to be fully compliant are not met with impatience, amusement, or even a covert implication that they are doing something wrong. Instead, service providers must be aware of how these individuals will respond and develop their questions and assignments accordingly. Clients with OCPD who bring their dogged persistence and task-orientedness to treatment are often able to stay with the treatment process, develop a good therapeutic alliance, and enjoy a favorable outcome (Stone, 1993).

Clients do not owe it to service providers to be interesting, charming, or entertaining. It is the responsibility of service providers to be interested in the well-being of these clients and to manage their own responses of anger, impatience, or withdrawal if they feel "tortured" by the painstaking details provided in sessions with clients with OCPD.

The success of treatment with these individuals is a matter of managing their inhibitory defenses, utilizing their strengths, supporting their conscientious intentions, and accepting them in spite of their interpersonally problematic behavior. Individuals with OCPD do not generally inspire warmth in the people around them, including service providers. Their argumentative and self-justifying behavior can make them seem to be stronger or tougher than they really are. It is important to remember that their defensive structure covers vulnerability to shame, humiliation, and dread.

Professional Ethics and OCPD

Individuals with OCPD react badly to service providers who appear to be irresponsible or inclined to bend the rules. Although it is unlikely that clients with OCPD would file complaints or bring lawsuits with only minimal provocation, they might do so if they believe they will not get what they need from service providers who appear indifferent or unresponsive. They may be particularly reactive to someone who is not listening to them or does not seem interested in hearing what they have to say. These individuals do know how to reach out to a higher authority with their complaints. They can do this in a work setting and would certainly be able to translate that behavior to any services they may be receiving. If this type of behavior is triggered, these individuals will be as thorough and doggedly determined in making a complaint as they are in any other parts of their lives.

Because clients with OCPD can be challenging to work with, particularly if they have covert oppositional traits, they can evoke the following responses in service providers:

- Adopting a routinized, uncreative way of relating
- Accepting and mirroring the client's own stereotyped self-presentation
- Exasperation, irritation, boredom, and fatigue
- Frustration and feeling tormented by these individuals' tendencies to repeat topics

These reactions can lead to service provider–induced treatment failure and must be addressed directly through supervision or consultation (Beck et al., 2004; Kantor, 1992; Richards, 1993; Stone, 1993).

Assessment and Treatment

Zimmerman (1994) suggests the following questions in the assessment of individuals with OCPD:

- Have you ever been told that you spend too much time making lists and schedules? Do you think you do?
- When you have something that needs to be done, do you spend so much time getting organized that you have trouble getting it finished on time?

- Would you describe yourself as perfectionistic? Would others?
- Would you call yourself a workaholic? Would others? Do you spend so much time working that you have little time for family, friends, or entertainment?
- Do you have difficulty taking time off from work?
- Do you have a strong sense of moral and ethical values?
- Do you worry that you have done something immoral or unethical?
- Has anyone ever complained about all the things you save?
- Do you do jobs yourself because no one else will do them to your satisfaction?
- Do you take on other peoples' responsibilities to make sure things are done right?
- How is it for you to spend money on yourself? On others?
- Do you save as much as you can for future problems?
- Do people describe you as stubborn?

Caution is needed in monitoring individuals with OCPD for relapse. They are vulnerable to shame and can be quite secretive about a relapse both in treatment and the self-help community, particularly if they had been doing well for some time. They need ongoing encouragement to see themselves realistically and to work on recovery as a process rather than an event. However, if a relapse is successfully managed and they are able to reengage in recovery activities having learned skills to manage craving and other triggers, their self-confidence in managing other aspects of their lives will be enhanced as well.

Treatment Goals

Treatment for clients with OCPD has to address the issue of control. For significant change, these individuals must develop tolerance for:

- Their own emotional vulnerability
- Their lack of control over people and situations
- The presence of chance, uncertainty, and impermanence in their lives

These sources of anxiety cannot be controlled away, defended against, or dissolved in the drug of choice.

Treatment goals must allow for acceptance of the basic personality style and temperament of clients with OCPD. Although personality can be modified in treatment, it is rarely transformed. Nevertheless, autonomy, realistic self-esteem, self-acceptance, and tolerance for uncertainty can be expanded even if obsessive–compulsive conflicts and defenses remain in place (McWilliams, 1994).

Recovery Activities for Individuals with OCPD and Addiction

Dually diagnosed individuals with OCPD, once engaged in treatment, are inclined to pursue whatever activities are recommended for recovery. This tendency to work on assigned tasks permits these individuals to accomplish a great deal.

In mental health recovery, individuals with OCPD would likely be quite adept at the written activities in the Wellness Recovery Action Plan (Copeland, 2000). They can benefit from developing lists of activities that support wellness, things that need to be done each day to support recovery, and what to do when discomfort arises or symptoms begin to worsen. These individuals are likely to make comprehensive lists and keep those lists where they can find them. The greatest challenge to service providers in this process is not to inadvertently encourage an obsessive–compulsive zeal to create the best, most complete, and most helpful lists that have ever been written.

In recovery from addiction, these individuals can benefit significantly from 12-step or other peer support groups. They can be exposed to the gentle humor, self-acceptance, self-responsibility, and humility of these groups. These attitudes, particularly self-responsibility in the context of self-acceptance and self-esteem, could have a strong healing impact on the fierce self-denigration and self-blame individuals with OCPD are prone to experience. Caution is needed concerning which groups these individuals join. If they are exposed to groups that are not positive and in harmony with recovery, they will feel at home in the context of negativity and blame themselves if they are uncomfortable with others in the meetings. This could result in withdrawal or actual reinforcement for the negative aspects of their personality disorder. They need to find a sponsor or sponsors who can be patient and reinforce positive behaviors.

12

Depressive Personality Disorder and Substance Use Disorders
Appendix B in the DSM-IV-TR

Depressive Personality Disorder Defined

Essential Features

The *DSM-IV-TR* (APA, 2000) describes the depressive personality disorder (DpPD) as a pervasive pattern of depressive thinking and behavior that begins in early adulthood and is present in a variety of contexts. The disorder does not occur exclusively during episodes of major depression and is not better accounted for by dysthymia. Individuals with DpPD are described as:

- Persistently dejected, gloomy, cheerless, and excessively serious
- Having little capacity to relax
- Lacking a sense of humor
- Feeling undeserving
- Preoccupied and brooding
- Harshly self-judging
- Having low self-esteem
- Sensitive and easily wounded
- Judgmental toward and critical of others (APA, 2000; Klein & Miller, 1993; Millon & Davis, 1996)

Akiskal's (1983; as noted in Phillips, Hirschfeld, Shea, & Gunderson, 1995) additional criteria for the depressive personality include:

- Indeterminate early onset

- Psychomotor inertia
- Passivity and indecisiveness
- Skepticism and an inclination to complain
- Conscientiousness or self-discipline

Millon and Davis (1996) refer to DpPD as the "giving-up pattern." These individuals see the future as dark and dangerous; in fact, they view the future as negatively as they view the present. They believe that anticipating the worst is just being realistic. They overestimate all difficulties, doubt that anything will improve, and underestimate themselves (Klein & Miller, 1993).

Westen and Shedler (1999) suggest that, other than in Appendix B, the *DSM-IV-TR* (APA, 2000) fails to recognize a large category of individuals best characterized as having a dysphoric or depressive personality. They believe their data support the inclusion of a depressive or dysphoric personality disorder diagnosis in the *DSM-V*. They describe the dysphoric personality disorder, in part, as:

- Feeling inadequate, inferior, or like a failure
- Feeling unhappy, depressed, or despondent
- Feeling ashamed or embarrassed
- Blaming self or feeling responsible for bad things that happen
- Feeling guilty
- Fearing rejection or abandonment
- Feeling helpless, powerless, or at the mercy of forces beyond one's control
- Feeling needy or dependent

DpPD was introduced in 1994 in the *DSM-IV*, Appendix B. The utility of the category is under review, and there continues to be an unresolved debate about whether chronic, mild depression is a personality disorder or a mood disorder (Skodol, 2005).

Klein and Miller (1993) suggest that although the *DSM-III-R* (APA, 1987) subsumed the depressive personality under the broader rubric of dysthymia, there are distinct differences between the two constructs. A diagnosis of dysthymia requires a chronic mood disturbance, whereas a depressed mood is not a core feature of the depressive personality. These authors propose that dysthymia is a more severe condition than is implied by the depressive personality. Thus, DpPD can be conceptualized as the characterological variant in a spectrum of affective conditions in which dysthymia and major depression are the more severe disorders (Kwon et al., 2000). Millon and Davis (1996) acknowledge that DpPD is difficult to differentiate from dysthymic disorder. They suggest that the essential distinction is that DpPD should be evident in childhood or adolescence. However, because the *DSM-IV-TR* (APA, 2000) recognizes an early onset dysthymia (prior to the age of 21), it is not clear that the differentiation regarding age is particularly helpful.

Although a depressive personality disorder could be a milder form of dysthymic disorder (Silverstein, 2007), it has also been suggested that it represents a form of premorbid vulnerability that can predispose people to major depression and other mood disorders.

Phillips et al. (1998) argue that, in their research, 63% of individuals with DpPD did not have co-occurring dysthymia, 60% did not have a co-occurring major depression, and 40% did not have another co-occurring personality disorder. Laptook, Klein, and Dougherty (2006) note recent studies indicating that fewer than 50% of individuals with DpPD meet the criteria for dysthymia, and fewer than 50% of individuals with dysthymia meet the criteria for DpPD. These researchers all propose that DpPD and dysthymia are overlapping diagnostic categories but are not the same diagnosis. Phillips, Gunderson, Hirschfeld, and Smith (1990) suggest that DpPD is characterized by cognitive psychopathology, and dysthymia is characterized by affective and somatic psychopathology. DpPD should also be more stable, durable, and resistant to change across both situations and time than is dysthymia.

The *DSM-IV-TR* (APA, 2000) description of dysthymic disorder does not clearly exclude cognitive symptoms and focus only on affective and somatic symptoms. Dysthymia includes a pattern of low self-esteem, a view of self as uninteresting and incapable, and hopelessness. It also involves the somatic symptoms of poor appetite or overeating, insomnia or hypersomnia, low energy or fatigue, and poor concentration or difficulty making decisions. Overall, the most common symptoms of dysthymic disorder are described as feelings of inadequacy, social withdrawal, feelings of guilt or brooding about the past, irritability, loss of interest or pleasure, and decreased activity, effectiveness, or productivity. It is further stated in the *DSM-IV-TR* that vegetative symptoms are less common in dysthymia than in major depression. Finally, dysthymic disorder is described as having a chronic course with an early and insidious onset.

In other words, the distinctions drawn in the research are not as well reflected in the *DSM-IV-TR* (APA, 2000) criteria sets as they might be for diagnostic clarity. It is probably most reasonable, in clinical settings, to be less concerned about diagnosis than an accurate understanding of the person experiencing mild chronic depression with dysphoric attitudes, beliefs, and behaviors. Anyone experiencing distress and impairment with this clinical picture should be considered for a medication evaluation to determine if antidepressant medication might help. The vulnerability to co-occurring substance use disorders is very similar and the therapeutic interventions that are effective for one will likely be effective for the other regardless of which diagnosis is used.

Self-Image

Individuals with DpPD see themselves as fundamentally different from others and focus on their inadequacies. They feel guilty for possessing few if any valuable traits and see friendship as something they are unlikely to deserve or attain. They consider the loneliness they experience as no more than they deserve (Millon et al., 2004). They have a clear sense of self; it is just a painfully negative one (McWilliams, 1994). Benign remarks from others can be misunderstood and set off obsessive brooding. Adverse experiences precipitate the conviction that they were caused by personal deficiencies (Millon et al.).

One individual with DpPD made both professional and personal decisions based upon her beliefs about her own limited potential, in spite of indicators that she was capable and able to be effective. She was hyperalert to any criticism from others and experienced intense and painful emotional reactions to any possibility that others did not respect or like her. She did not attend to the successes she had achieved or the strong positive feedback she received. She approached the future with dread because she was sure that new circumstances would reveal her inadequacies and deficiencies. Transitions, such as graduation from college, promotions, marriage, divorce, and even retirement, ignited fear, dread, and a despondent certainty that whatever she had achieved to date would be completely lost in the new challenges that would, in all probability, result in failure, loss, and despair.

View of Others

Individuals with DpPD are nearly as critical of others as they are of themselves (Bockian & Jongsma, 2001). It is likely that some of the guilt these individuals experience has its roots in the unpleasant and uncharitable thoughts they have toward other people.

In spite of their need or longing for connection to others, they see themselves as so unworthy or unattractive that they are very fearful of the judgment of others. It is as though these individuals are caught in a web of criticism they feel toward both themselves and others as well as the criticism they fear from others to the point that people become almost too dangerous to tolerate. Yet they cannot withdraw into the solitude that they dread, so they remain perpetually drawn toward and needing to escape from other people. For individuals with DpPD, the world is a threatening, lonely, and disappointing place. Life may seem to be genuinely worthwhile only for others; these individuals know they are living a diminished existence (Millon et al., 2004).

Relationships

McWilliams (1994) notes that depressive people are likely to blame themselves for failed relationships while remembering the other person fondly. They believe they drive away people they care about with their own undesirable qualities. They feel vulnerable and unshielded with others, fear abandonment, and seek nurturance and protection. Even though these individuals crave love and support from others, they fail to reciprocate in ways that are gratifying or reinforcing for others. Their cloying need for reassurance, self-preoccupation, and ongoing self-denigration can become annoying or exasperating (Millon & Grossman, 2007a). They may precipitate the rejection they dread and experience confirmation that their needs drain and exhaust others. They may accept that they are inherently destructive within relationships (McWilliams. 1994).

A man in his fifties, with DpPD, stayed with his wife after she was unfaithful and had spent a great deal of the couple's money on her lover because he blamed himself for her unhappiness and because he was certain that no one else would ever love him. The future he saw was filled with a horrifying loneliness in spite of the very real loneliness he felt living with a woman who made it clear she did not love him. He continued to cling to the relationship well beyond the time his wife told him she was finished with him and wanted a divorce.

Issues with Authority

Individuals with DpPD are not particularly inclined to seek positions of authority in their work. They are too unsure of themselves and too sensitive to criticism. The more authority and responsibility people have on the job, the more vulnerable they are to being the target of other peoples' issues with authority. If people with DpPD feel the full force of their subordinates' anger, grievances, or dissatisfaction, no matter how unfounded they may be, they are inclined to blame themselves and feel intense antagonism toward the people who are treating them so badly. One individual with DpPD was promoted to the position of foreman in an electronics factory. He was so uncomfortable with the visibility he had, so unsure that he could handle the responsibility, and so sensitive to the rather rough-edged remarks he received from the men he supervised that he asked for a voluntary demotion and went back on the line. Although this reaction cost his family a great deal of money over the years and put advancement permanently out of his reach, the emotional comfort of escaping the authority spotlight made the retreat seem worthwhile. Unfortunately, it also confirmed this man's view of himself as hopelessly inadequate and life as consisting of nothing more than tedium and loss.

Individuals with DpPD are inclined to follow orders and work hard for people in positions of authority. They fear criticism and are anxious to please authority figures. They are likely to inhibit expressions of critical, hostile, or aggressive thoughts or feelings and to blame themselves rather than others when things go wrong (Phillips et al., 1995).

Behavior

Individuals with DpPD tend toward behavioral constriction and constraint (Phillips et al., 1995). They may be quiet, introverted, and unassertive (APA, 2000). People with this personality disorder appear disconsolate, forlorn, and somber. They sound dispirited and discouraged. They show little initiative and are inclined to be fatalistic. They engage in acts of self-denial and even self-punishment. They may be so harshly self-judging that they engage in self-destructive behavior (Millon et al., 2004).

Somatic concerns are common, and they may experience loss of interest in sexual activity. They can appear slowed down. The impact of these DpPD responses on relationships can range from disheartening to destructive.

Affect

Individuals with DpPD feel sad and guilty; they seem to be in an endless dejected and gloomy mood. They feel a pervasive pessimism and anticipate the worst. They expect life itself to go wrong and spend their days brooding and worrying (Millon et al., 2004). They are inclined to accept the unhappiness and the despondency pervading their lives as inevitable and unavoidable. Millon and Grossman (2007a) suggest that they have such significant inner depletion and self-abdication that they appear to be "playing dead as a means of staying alive" (p. 131). McWilliams (1994) notes that these individuals seldom feel spontaneous or unconflicted anger on their own behalf; instead, they feel guilt. Westen and Shedler (1999) suggest that individuals with DpPD are best described as unhappy, ashamed, anxious, and embarrassed.

Defenses

Millon and Grossman (2007a) describe DpPD as showing a diminished capacity to initiate action or to regulate feelings, impulses, or conflict. Individuals with DpPD struggle to keep their distressing feelings at bay and to minimize intrapsychic pain. They engage in self-denial, self-punishment, and self-torment. They diminish positive memories and are so punitive toward themselves that they allow themselves to experience very little pleasure. The depressive personality shares with the avoidant personality a deficiency in the ability to experience pleasure and an overreactivity to pain (Millon et al., 2004).

With an aversive reaction to negative feelings and little capacity for enthusiasm, individuals with DpPD are at risk of draining the color, excitement, and meaning out of their lives. They may actually be more accurate observers of the realities of life than people whose optimism endorses a breezy denial of the harder facts of existence. Their somber view of the vicissitudes of living may be repeatedly confirmed by experience (Ratey & Johnson, 1997). If the depressive view becomes more severe, loss of hope and suicidal thinking or behavior can become a risk. With depleted defenses, safety can become a concern.

The Self-Created World (Altered Reality) of DpPD

Two quasi-humorous sayings seem to fit individuals with DpPD: "There is no point in being pessimistic—it wouldn't work anyway." and "The good thing about pessimism is that you are never disappointed." They reflect this personality's adherence to the dark side of perception and a refusal to turn from the shadows. This view of reality can trigger a vulnerability to drug and alcohol use, result in a life permeated with sadness, and compromise the ability to form and sustain relationships with others. For individuals with DpPD, their reality is composed of thinking or believing:

- Life is loss; get used to it.
- People say I am pessimistic; really, I am just realistic.
- I am prepared for the worst.
- You should never expect too much from life.
- If I could have one wish, I would wish for the emotional hide of an elephant so things would not get to me so easily.
- Some say the glass is half empty; some say the glass is half full; I say the glass is irrelevant to the pointlessness of life.

Substance Use Disorders and DpPD

Co-Occurring Substance Use Disorders and the Impact of Drugs on DpPD

As with many of the personality disorders, the dynamics of DpPD lead to a level of unmet need, a sensitivity to the emotional pain of living, and an inability to self-soothe that make alcohol and other drugs, as well as compulsive behaviors, important, compelling, and so rewarding that abuse or dependence are serious risks. McWilliams (1994) suggests that individuals with DpPD can use drugs or compulsive behaviors such as gambling to manage or ignore painful emotions. DiClemente (2003) suggests that there is an interactive process among personal characteristics, expectations, environment, and other risk factors that compose the influence of personality on addiction. Individuals with depressive personality disorder have fewer protective resources for self-regulation to offset the strongly reinforcing effects of drugs and alcohol. These individuals can find a level of comfort in drugs or compulsive behaviors that is simply unavailable any other way. It is possible that a medication evaluation for SSRIs or other antidepressants might mitigate the somatic components of the depression and reduce the need for alcohol or other drugs. If, however, addiction is already in place, substance use disorder treatment will be vital in addition to the potential help available through psychotropic and therapeutic intervention.

Drugs of Choice for DpPD

There is no evidence of a single drug of choice for any specific personality disorder. For everyone, choice comes from an interplay of social, psychological, and biological factors. For individuals with depressive personality disorder, any drug that eases the anguish of living or can induce euphoria would have compelling addictive potential. Drugs can also mitigate against fear, guilt, remorse, and self-hate by blurring the impact of feelings. On the other hand, as they say in AA, "There is no problem that alcohol can't make worse." Substance misuse eventually adds to the pain of living for these individuals if negative consequences become apparent.

Integrated Dual Diagnosis Treatment for DpPD

Engaging in Treatment

To engage individuals with DpPD, service providers must be able to join with them in their serious and somber stance. To be determinedly upbeat or excessively optimistic would give the appearance of being trivial, shallow, or oblivious to real life. Individuals with DpPD need to be understood where they stand, even if they do seem to have yielded to the "dark side of the force." To be taken seriously by someone clearly invested in understanding gives hope and provides connection. Millon and Grossman (2007a) state that the essence of the truly therapeutic relationship is empathic support while conveying confidence in the people with DpPD being able to learn to both care for and care about themselves.

Treatment Provider Guidelines

McWilliams (1994) suggests that the most important condition of therapeutic intervention with individuals with DpPD is an atmosphere of acceptance, respect, and compassionate efforts to understand. Service providers must take special care, given the radar these individuals have for anything that looks or feels like criticism or rejection, to be accepting and nonjudgmental. It is particularly important not to replicate what is likely to be the response these individuals receive at home or at work; for example, "Why are you so serious?" or "Can't you see the bright side of anything?" Although this may seem obvious, subtle variations of these comments can be inserted into attempts to engage clients with DpPD by challenging their pessimistic stance of unrelenting sorrow. Service providers must not yield to feeling defeated, appear to be mindlessly upbeat, or accept the role of rescuer. It is important to engage the strength and courage these individuals show in enduring their sadness and redirect these resources toward accepting the possibility that in loving they can survive loss and in experiencing joy they can survive pain.

Professional Ethics and DpPD

Service providers with depressive dynamics may be strongly responsive to individuals with DpPD. They can overidentify, feel benign affection, or have omnipotent rescue fantasies. It is also possible for service providers to resonate so strongly with the DpPD self-deprecation and brooding preoccupation with sorrow that they either become depressed themselves or respond angrily to the impact of interacting with these individuals. Service providers who are determinedly cheerful may communicate disapproval in response to the negative attitudes held by these individuals, even suggesting that they are being willfully unpleasant. No matter what the response, if it is triggered by service provider affect, it is inappropriate. Clinical responses based upon personal need are rarely constructive. As with the other personality disorders, supervision or consultation is imperative to monitor personal responses, need to control, or need to rescue, so that the therapeutic relationship is based upon client need and interventions designed to facilitate growth.

Assessment and Treatment

Assessment of DpPD may include the following questions:

- Do you usually feel unhappy? How often do you feel unhappy?
- Does it seem like life is no fun? (or) When does life seem to be fun?
- Do you believe you are an inadequate person?
- Do you feel good about yourself very often? (or) When do you feel good about yourself?
- Do you put yourself down? (or) How often do you put yourself down? What are you doing when this occurs?
- Do you keep thinking about the bad things that happened in the past? (or) How often do you think about the bad things that happened in the past?
- Do you worry about the future?
- Do you frequently find fault with others?
- Are you critical?
- Do you expect the worst?
- Do you often feel guilty? (First, Gibbon, Spitzer, Williams, & Benjamin, 1997; P. Pociluyko, personal communication, August, 2007)

Care is needed in assessing for substance use disorders, as individuals with DpPD are likely to be self-blaming and ashamed of looking weak in relation to drug and alcohol use. Service providers must communicate understanding and acceptance of persons with substance use disorders and join with these individuals in mounting a strategy for recovery. It is alarmingly easy to sound judgmental and to ignite a need to escape the treatment setting for individuals with DpPD. It can be tempting to challenge the pessimistic stance in regard to recovery as lack of motivation; that is, "Don't you want to get better?" It is imperative that gloomy predictions of failure be responded to as anxiety or discouragement needing support rather than resistance needing confrontation.

Success in treatment for personality issues or substance use disorders may not be accepted as possible if it seems to be too difficult for these individuals. They not only know how to fail; they expect it. It is essential that service providers structure treatment intervention so that failure is actually very difficult to achieve. It is a success that these individuals are in treatment. Even if they are there by court order, they came in, and that is a success. It is a success that they are beginning to look at the consequences of their drinking or drugging. It is even a success if they are still actively using because it takes a great deal of courage to consider such a great change in their lives. There are many ways for motivational interviewing (Miller & Rollnick, 2002) to be stated in such a way that the person looking at his or her behavior can be strongly supported for doing so even if actual behavior change is not yet within reach. Even relapse can be a success if these individuals return to treatment to see what they can learn from the experience. It would be destructive to readily discharge individuals with DpPD from treatment for continuing use or relapse when such an action would only support the deepest fears they already have about their propensity to fail.

As with the histrionic, dependent, and borderline personality disorders, DpPD involves fear of abandonment. When working with these individuals, their social support system, home environment, and significant relationships are core to recovery. If people with DpPD are involved with people who either are using drugs or are willing participants in maintaining the DpPD self-derogatory stance, chances for recovery are lessened. Fear of losing significant relationships could overshadow treatment and must be directly addressed.

There is controversy about DpPD and whether the symptoms remit with the use of antidepressants. No definitive answer is yet available. It would not serve these individuals well to assume that characterological depression will not respond to medication; a psychiatric evaluation needs to be available to consider what might be possible. If medication could alleviate the painful affect of DpPD, recovery would become more attainable when working on the addiction that may be in place.

Treatment Goals

Individuals with DpPD need to overcome the maladaptive beliefs and patterns of behavior that inevitably develop as a result of their chronic depressiveness. Although overt symptoms of depression may be alleviated through the use of medication, personality factors remain. Interpersonal behavior, self-concept, habitual style of thinking, and expectations of the future may remain pessimistic and bleak. These individuals need to work toward more adaptive attitudes and behaviors to consolidate the gains from antidepressant medication (Millon & Davis, 1996). Treatment goals include replacing passivity with more active interaction with the environment, alleviating an affective and cognitive emphasis on pain, and recognizing and experiencing pleasurable events. The depressive's usual pessimism and melancholy can slowly change by practicing effective problem solving and achieving positive change as a response to disappointment or failure. A personal sense of efficacy can emerge so that anticipation of success or pleasure does not seem so futile or threatening (Bockian & Jongsma, 2001; Millon & Grossman, 2007a).

The goal of abstinence can be approached with individuals with DpPD, but if the characterological anticipation and acceptance of failure are severe enough to preclude hope, steps toward abstinence in the context of both motivational interviewing and harm reduction may be needed.

Recovery Activities for Individuals with DpPD and Addiction

Recovery that does not look possible is not recovery. These individuals need to see recovery as something they can actually achieve. They habitually lose their potential for change to the chronicity of their pessimistic thinking. Successfully completed small steps can form a foundation of recovery that can encourage people with DpPD to embrace activities that will continue their progress. Treatment providers can be strong advocates for 12-step or other peer support group attendance by pointing out the wide array of possible benefits. Many of the attitudes found in these support groups are healing not only for addiction but for the personality disorder as well. In particular, the depressive self-blame, self-derogation, and despair can be challenged within the context of AA or NA humor, self-acceptance, mutual support, and the keep-coming-back approach to addiction. It can be a remarkable experience for people with DpPD to hear someone in a peer support group talk about their humanness without self-attack and self-condemnation and then to see the support and acceptance of the group toward the person who is sharing.

Service providers can also assist individuals with DpPD in their recovery by reviewing the experiences they have had in peer support groups. Negative self-appraisal about participation can be challenged and anxiety normalized; for example, most people feel anxious when first getting started. Service providers can encourage going to a variety of meetings so that the process begins to feel manageable and there is sufficient chance to find meetings that are compatible and welcoming. Individuals with DpPD need help to look for the successes and to hear, understand, and accept the support and healing that is available in the 12-step rooms. They can be encouraged to accept leadership roles in peer support groups and to engage in active participation. They can then take in and make use of a more self-accepting path to change, abstinence, and hope.

13

Passive–Aggressive (Negativistic) Personality Disorder and Substance Use Disorders
Appendix B in the DSM-IV-TR

Passive–Aggressive (Negativistic) Personality Disorder Defined

Essential Features

The passive–aggressive (negativistic) personality disorder (PAPD) is located in Appendix B in the *DSM-IV-TR* (APA, 2000). It was included in the Cluster C personality disorders in the *DSM-III-R* (APA, 1987) but was removed from official status in Axis II in the *DSM-IV* (APA, 1994) for the following reasons:

- Passive–aggressive behaviors are often reactions to an oppressive environment.
- It appears to be too narrowly defined to be a personality category.
- It rarely exists in the absence of other personality disorders. (Frances et al., 1995)

Millon (1996) proposes expanding PAPD to the more comprehensive concept of a negativistic personality disorder characterized by:

- General contrariness
- A disinclination to do as others wish
- An irritable moodiness
- An unaccommodating, fault-finding pessimism
- Sullen malcontented complaining (Millon & Grossman, 2007b)

In Appendix B, the *DSM-IV-TR* (APA, 2000) describes the PAPD essential features as a pervasive pattern of negativistic attitudes and passive resistance to demands for adequate performance. The following characteristics are research criteria for determining the validity and utility of the proposed PAPD (negativistic) category for possible inclusion in the *DSM-V*:

- Passive resistance to fulfilling routine social and occupational tasks
- Complaints of being misunderstood and unappreciated by others
- A tendency to be sullen and argumentative
- Unreasonable criticism and scorn toward authority
- Envy and resentment toward others who appear more fortunate
- Exaggerated and persistent complaints of personal misfortune
- Alternating attitudes between hostile defiance and contrition (APA, 2000; Millon & Radovanov, 1995)

PAPD was first introduced in a U.S. War Department technical bulletin in 1945. The term was coined by wartime psychiatrists who found themselves dealing with reluctant and uncooperative soldiers who followed orders with chronic, veiled hostility and smoldering resentment. Their style was a mixture of passive resistance and grumbling compliance (Stone, 1993).

Individuals similar to those covered by the designation of PAPD in the *DSM-IV-TR* (APA, 2000) were referred to in the early literature as:

- Dissatisfied people who felt perpetually wounded
- Fussy people with sour dispositions
- Depressives with ill tempers who were spiteful, malicious, and pessimistic
- People with irritable moods
- People who took everything hard and felt the unpleasantness in every situation (Millon & Radovanov, 1995)

The *DSM-III-R* (APA, 1987) proposed that oppositional defiant disorder (ODD) in childhood or adolescence predisposed people to PAPD in adulthood. That statement was removed when PAPD was placed in Appendix B in the *DSM-IV* (APA, 1994). Whether or not ODD predisposes to PAPD, it is of interest that the behaviors, attitudes, and feelings of adolescents with ODD bear considerable resemblance to those of adults with PAPD. The *DSM-IV-TR* (APA,

2000) states that there is a similar pattern of negativistic attitudes and problems with authority figures, but ODD is diagnosed in children, and PAPD should be used for adults. The similarity between the two can be seen in the definition of ODD, which involves a recurrent pattern of negativistic and hostile behavior toward authority figures, defiance, deliberately doing things that will annoy other people, blaming others for mistakes or misbehaviors, being touchy or easily annoyed, being angry and resentful, and being spiteful and vindictive. Defiant and negativistic behaviors are expressed as stubborn resistance to directions, ignoring orders, arguing, and failing to accept responsibility for negative behaviors. These individuals justify their behavior as a response to unreasonable demands (APA, 2000).

Individuals with PAPD are also prone to anxiety disorders, depressive disorders with agitation, and chronic pain disorders. Correctional settings may have many individuals with PAPD who have committed explosive acts of violence (Richards, 1993). Alcoholism and drug dependence are associated with both PAPD and PAPD families of origin (Beck et al., 2004; Oldham & Morris, 1995).

Self-Image

Individuals with PAPD view themselves as self-sufficient but feel vulnerable to control and interference from others (Pretzer & Beck, 2005). They believe they are misunderstood and unappreciated, a view that is exacerbated by the negative responses they receive from others for their consistent defeatist stance and provocative behavior (APA, 2000; Beck et al., 2004).

Although individuals with PAPD are often disgruntled and declare that they are not treated as they should be, they are just as likely to express feeling unworthy of good fortune. They have a basic conflict concerning their self-worth; they oscillate between self-loathing and entitlement or moral superiority. The chaotic nature of this oscillation between self-hate and arrogance often leads others to avoid or minimize contact with them out of self-protection (Richards, 1993).

Wetzler (1992) believes passive–aggressive individuals think of themselves as vulnerable and powerless. Whereas their behavior reveals their hostility and aggression, their self-descriptions are of innocence and victimization by others. As these individuals age, they may accept isolation from others to avoid seeing themselves as they are and accepting responsibility for their own behavior.

View of Others

Individuals with PAPD see other people as intrusive, demanding, interfering, and dominating. They experience control by others as intolerable; they have to do things their own way (Pretzer & Beck, 2005). They resent and resist demands to meet expectations from others in both work and social settings (APA, 2000). They see most interactions as power struggles and feel justified in resistive behavior that is demeaning to others. These individuals are quite adept at inducing doubt and self-blame in others for the noxious passive–aggressive behavior they are encountering. They have an extraordinary ability to shift blame and evade responsibility.

Individuals with PAPD are convinced that they cannot get what they need from others and are in jeopardy for the very fact that they have needs. The negative responses from others confirm the PAPD self-view of powerlessness and push these individuals to a growing isolation from people they simultaneously fear and need. The isolation adds to the increasing warp of the PAPD view of others, and behavior can become more fearful or more belligerent or both.

Relationships

Wetzler (1992) states that PAPD is about one person's psychological conflict but is mostly played out in relationships. Individuals with PAPD are ambivalent about their dependency needs and have the disquieting inclination to treat nearly everyone with whom they relate as an adversary. They are sullen and deliberately rude while experiencing themselves as victims. As a consequence, they are noted for the stormy nature of their interpersonal relationships (Millon & Radovanov, 1995). These individuals can inflict so much discomfort on and become so destructive toward others that they simply cannot sustain the relationships they have filled with acrimony and perpetual conflict. They are inclined toward grumbling, moody complaints, and sour pessimism; these behaviors serve as both a vehicle for tension discharge (relieving them of mounting anger) and as a means of intimidating others and inducing guilt (providing them with a sense of retribution for the wrongs they believe they have experienced). They are able to sense the exasperation and growing animosity that others feel toward them, but they use their awareness to become even more aggrieved—without corresponding acceptance that their behavior has contributed to the situation (Wetzler, 1992).

For individuals with PAPD, being difficult, quixotic, unpredictable, and discontented allows them to control others by forcing people into an uncomfortable anticipatory stance. Individuals in relationships with people with PAPD are perpetually waiting for the next struggle, the next grievance, the next round of volatility and carping criticism. Passive–aggressive individuals are able, within their relationships, to trap people into situations wherein whatever they do is wrong. Relating to individuals with PAPD becomes a tense, edgy experience where great caution must be employed to avoid precipitating an angry incident (Millon, 1981). Wetzler (1992) describes the passive–aggressive pattern as saying something critical or barbed, looking for a fight, and then blaming the other person for being in the line of fire. He sees the "fatal flaw" of passive aggression as the inappropriate expression of hostility hidden under the guise of innocence. As a result, these individuals have relationships filled with accusations, arguments that lead nowhere, and exhaustion.

Individuals with PAPD can be very destructive parents. Child abuse, psychological or physical, is common, depending on the severity of the personality disorder and whether there is a non–passive–aggressive parent who can ameliorate the impact. Wetzler (1992) notes that passive–aggressive parents use their power to place excessive psychological pressure on their children. They make it so the children can do no right. If the child meets standards set by a passive–aggressive parent, the standards are simply set higher so that the child fails again. In the meantime, parents with PAPD hold themselves up to be flawless, loving, and always right.

Issues with Authority

Authority figures become the focus of passive–aggressive discontent. These individuals often criticize people in authority as arbitrary, demanding, and unfair with minimal provocation (APA, 2000). Although they may agree to comply with demands or requirements, they often fail to perform, or they perform while experiencing increasing resentment. When faced with the consequences of their negativity or not adequately meeting obligations, they become angry, complain of unjust treatment, and deny that their behavior has anything to do with the situation. On the other hand, individuals with PAPD also see authority figures as capable of being approving, accepting, and caring. A key issue for these individuals is the desire to get benefits from authority figures while exerting their autonomy, resisting demands, and absolving themselves from blame (Beck et al., 2004; Benjamin, 1996).

Individuals with PAPD may attempt to convince others to share their negative view of authority figures, for example, supervisors or group facilitators, and try to become negative leaders in a group situation. If the PAPD is severe enough, the behavior may become so destructive that these individuals have to be fired or removed from treatment groups.

Behavior

Behavioral features of PAPD include:

- Sullen contrariness and discharging anger with little provocation
- Inclination to be easily offended by trivial issues
- Low frustration tolerance and chronic impatience and irritability
- Vacillation between being distraught and despondent to being petty, spiteful, stubborn, and contentious
- Short-lived enthusiasm with ready reversion to being disgruntled and critical
- Begrudging the good fortune of others
- Impulsivity and explosive unpredictability
- Proclivity to engage in cruel and nasty interactions (Millon, 1981)

PAPD ambivalence is expressed behaviorally by vacillation between negativism and autonomy, and dependency and conformity. However, even when conforming, these individuals tend to be unaccommodating and pessimistic (Kubacki & Smith, 1995).

Individuals with PAPD can express their hostility overtly and directly with the intent to do harm. If their victim is aggressive in response, so much the better. That response is then used to vindicate the initial attack. The expression of the anger is dictated by the desire to wound while concealing the intention to wound or even the existence of the anger. The intent is to provoke counter-anger with such subtlety that the victims blame themselves and believe their anger is not justified. That way, people with PAPD can assume the role of innocent victim. Their skill is in never revealing their true intent (Wetzler, 1992).

Oldham and Morris (1995) suggest that individuals with PAPD experience life as dark and unpleasurable. To these individuals, thwarting the expectations of others is a victory even if they sabotage their own lives. They see compliance as submission and submission as humiliation. The opposite of the behavior appropriate to a given situation is the one most likely to be expressed.

Affect

Individuals with PAPD are vulnerable to anxiety, somatoform disorders, and depression. Major depressive episodes are not uncommon. In the PAPD depressive cycles, there is evidence of a tendency to blame others, a demanding and complaining attitude, and low self-confidence. Typically, individuals with PAPD display an agitated dysphoria, shifting between anxious futility and self-deprecation to demanding irritability and bitter discontent (Millon, 1996; Millon & Grossman, 2007b).

Individuals with PAPD experience an undercurrent of perpetual inner turmoil. They appear unable to manage their moods, thoughts, and desires internally. They suffer a range of intense and conflicting emotions that surge quickly to the surface due to weak controls and lack of self-discipline. Affect is expressed no matter what the consequences (Millon, 1981).

Passive aggression implies, by definition, some level of hostility. Negativistic individuals typically become angry about deprivation; they either do not have what they want or do not have enough of what they want. Their anger can take the form of chronic, seething hostility, sadistic carping criticism, irritability, or resentment (Kantor, 1992; Sperry & Carlson, 1993).

Individuals with PAPD feel envy and resentment of the easy life led by others. They are critical and cynical regarding what others have attained, yet covet what they have achieved. As for themselves, life has been unkind; they have been cheated. These individuals do not see their negativism, resentment, and envy as having anything to do with the dissatisfactions in their lives. Rather, they see their feelings as a reflection of what sensitive people they are (Kantor, 1992; Millon, 1981).

Wetzler (1992) states that passive aggression is a psychological pattern with anger as its driving force and fear as its hidden secret. These individuals manage their fear and anger through either covert or direct aggression. They gain perverse pleasure in raining on everyone's parade—even their own (Richards, 1993).

Defenses

Individuals with PAPD utilize displacement and opposition to defend themselves. They displace their anger from more powerful targets to those of lesser significance. They express their hostility toward others who are less likely to be able to retaliate or reject them. Their opposition functions within a very thin veneer of resentful compliance that masks their aggression. Their defenses also involve overidealization of the self and devaluation of others (Kubacki & Smith, 1995; Millon & Davis, 1996; Richards, 1993).

The Self-Created World (Altered Reality) of PAPD

Individuals with PAPD create and sustain an altered reality that, although not psychotic, increasingly compromises their ability to relate positively to others or maintain supportive relationships. Their failure to accept responsibility for their negative behaviors and inclination to see themselves as victims are both augmented by the use of alcohol and other psychoactive drugs. For individuals with PAPD, the altered reality is composed of believing:

- I am misunderstood; way down deep, I am a sensitive person.
- People try take advantage of any weakness; never let them see you bleed.
- I have been cheated all my life.
- I have the right to express myself.
- People should not get so upset when I am just telling the truth.
- I deserve to be treated better.
- Everywhere I look, I see nothing but idiots, dolts, and con men.

Substance Use Disorders and PAPD

Co-Occurring Substance Use Disorders and the Impact of Drugs on PAPD

The incidence of co-occurring substance abuse with PAPD is high, as is alcoholism among the parents of passive–aggressive individuals (Beck et al., 2004; Oldham & Morris, 1995; Wetzler, 1992). Susceptibility to substance use disorders for these individuals is exacerbated by their failure to self-regulate or accept responsibility for their behavior. They routinely seek external intervention to feel better—as much from drugs as from people. For individuals with PAPD, reality can be a very unpleasant place. Alcohol and other drugs can dim the demands of others and modulate the unrelenting pressure of resentment and envy. Mood altering substances can modify feelings without the individual changing maladaptive behaviors. The essence of the PAPD demand of the world is "make me feel better without asking anything of me." Drugs and alcohol could hardly do a better job of meeting that demand, and people could hardly do worse.

Individuals with PAPD are likely to display their addictions in a loud uproar and use them to justify their aggressive behavior or to provide a rationale for nonperformance, incapacitation, or inaccessibility (Richards, 1993). The use of alcohol and other drugs can be a means to release whatever inhibitions they may have, punish others, demonstrate that no one can stop them from doing what they want, and feel better or escape into fantasies. Ultimately, alcohol and other drug use become their own reasons. These individuals are very vulnerable to addiction.

Drugs of Choice for PAPD

Richards (1993) suggests that almost any of the drug classes suit individuals with PAPD. Prescribed pain killers and antianxiety agents, in combination with alcohol, are probably the most common pattern of abuse. Individuals with PAPD may come into treatment needing to be detoxed from benzodiazepines and other sedative–hypnotics (CSAT, 1994). These individuals feel strongly entitled to relief from either physical or psychological pain and will, in all likelihood, be furious at the suggestion that they should relinquish their Valium or their narcotic pain medication. These individuals are also likely to find over-the-counter (OTC) drugs and herbs or other preparations at a health-food store to augment what they can get from prescription or illegal drugs.

Integrated Dual Diagnosis Treatment for PAPD

Engaging in Treatment

There are two major ways for individuals with PAPD to enter treatment. The first, and most common, is externally leveraged services for individuals who do not see themselves as having a problem. Someone forced them into treatment, for example, family, employers, or the legal system. The second method for individuals with PAPD to enter treatment is via self-referral for vague complaints; for example, "I'm just not getting anywhere" (Turkat, 1990).

The PAPD personality is particularly abrasive, and interpersonal problems are readily identifiable. However, these individuals rarely want to change their own behaviors or attitudes. They are likely to demand that treatment "fix" the unacceptable behaviors in partners, supervisors, or children so that life will be easier.

Engagement in the treatment process is particularly challenging under these circumstances. Service providers must manage their own irritable or rejecting responses to the provocation, self-excusing, blaming, and generally annoying behaviors readily evident from these individuals. They do not connect to any form of treatment if they detect that they are being held responsible for their behavior or their problems. It is difficult, although not impossible, to focus on relevant concerns and express some empathy for the PAPD clients. Expressing understanding of anxiety, depression, fear, sadness, and other problems can be done while neither blaming nor absolving these clients from the negative consequences of their behavior. Expressing willingness to explore ways to resolve painful affect, manage legal problems regarding drug use, or make home life more tolerable can be an invitation to these clients to join with the treatment process. Motivation for behavior change can be enhanced in the context of gains accruing to change rather than corrections for bad behaviors. Although this may seem obvious, it can be very difficult to concentrate on this approach when sitting with individuals who are self-aggrandizing while demeaning everyone else.

Treatment Provider Guidelines

Passive–aggressive behaviors that are frequently brought forth in the treatment setting include intrusive and unnecessary telephone calls, ongoing negative evaluations of the treatment providers, absorbing nothing, engaging in denial and minimization, denying hostile motivation, absorbing everything and refusing to apply it, and using insight against themselves (Kantor, 1992). The most essential guideline for treatment providers is to remain alert to what the behaviors described above will likely elicit in their own responses. Of all the personality disorders, passive–aggressive or negativistic individuals are likely to trigger the worst the treatment providers have to offer including counter-aggression, passive–aggressive responses, sarcasm, fatigue, avoidance, and unmanageable anger. There is no other personality disorder, particularly when severe, that requires more caution, supervision, and consultation.

On the other hand, it is important for service providers to not allow themselves to feel or act apologetic for setting and enforcing limits or reinforcing boundaries between clients with PAPD and staff (CSAT, 1994). Although limits and requirements of the treatment process may elicit outrage and protestations of mistreatment, these individuals must learn to manage expectations in a positive manner if they are to be successful in changing their most maladaptive behaviors.

Service providers need to imagine what it feels like to be so resentful, bitter, and blaming. The cost is very high. Any resolution of negativistic responses can enhance quality of life for these individuals. Even though clients with PAPD test the clinical skill, personal maturation, resilience, and self-esteem of service providers, change is possible and has the potential to benefit both PAPD clients and their family members.

Professional Ethics and PAPD

No other personality disorder places as much strain on professional ethics as PAPD. The relentless criticism from these individuals is a personal assault. To be demeaned by clients who regularly self-aggrandize presses against even the most reliable professional demeanor. These individuals ask for help and then both defy it and suffer from it. It is very difficult not to become outraged and punitive.

Consultation, supervision, and peer supervision can be helpful in venting emotional responses to these individuals and planning a realistic and appropriate treatment approach. Service providers must not become so angry that they use limit setting to punish, for example, discharging from treatment when it is not clinically appropriate to do so. Treatment may need to be terminated if clients with PAPD do not curtail their spiteful behavior. The reasons for doing so must be direct, clear, and stated without rancor or counter-aggression. Decisions to limit or terminate treatment, discharge from a residential program, or report that the client has reached maximum benefit from treatment and no further effort is indicated should be made only after supervisory consultation or if a staff team makes the decision. It is harder than it may seem to avoid contaminating treatment decisions with a need to get distance from, punish, or retaliate against persons with severe PAPD. Service providers need to ensure that they have not lost their perspective and are not making intervention mistakes that can be very hard to explain at a later date. Individuals with PAPD are very prone to report what they consider professionally abusive behavior to oversight committees, supervisors, or politicians if they believe that it can either control the service providers' behavior or punish service providers for what they perceive as an abuse of power. It is a significant protection to make treatment decisions as a team or in consultation with another professional.

Assessment and Treatment

When assessing individuals with PAPD and co-occurring substance use disorders, address survival skills and self-care, use of OTC drugs, all other providers being seen for treatment, psychosocial and substance use history, mental status, coexisting anxiety disorders, medication evaluations for antidepressants, and identification of typical passive–aggressive behaviors (CSAT, 1994).

In treatment groups, clients with PAPD may engage in exploiting other group members. They can undermine the efforts, morale, and good faith of both staff and others in the group (Richards, 1993). If these individuals do not accept limits on their behavior and they substantially reduce the effectiveness of the group for all participants, termination from the group should be considered. On the other hand, group therapy provides these individuals with an opportunity to learn how to manage their hostility. When their anger and negativity emerge, group leaders can comment on the hostile behavior and encourage other group members to respond. The group leader can assist these individuals to process what it is they want or need at that moment and to rehearse appropriate behavior within the group context (CSAT, 1994).

Whether clients with PAPD are in individual or group treatment, it is important to identify and highlight examples of passive–aggressive behavior. Reflecting on the consequences of the behaviors, making clear statements about expectations, nondefensive limit-setting, and nonapologetic enforcement of boundaries are all important in treatment for PAPD. It can be a useful technique for service providers to behave like Mr. Spock from *Star Trek*. It is helpful to imagine how logical, rational, and nonemotional Mr. Spock's reactions are to situations ranging from the trivial to the life-threatening. Mostly, he states, with clarity, what the situation is and what response is available to best manage the situation. Neither his voice nor his demeanor becomes intense or angry. He communicates with as few words as necessary to be clear. However, even Mr. Spock, after tense and difficult interactions with clients with PAPD, would probably need to go down the hall, find a colleague to talk to, and allow himself to ventilate his frustration to someone he can trust.

Richards (1993) suggests that treatment failures for individuals with co-occurring disorders are often a result of neglecting to consider the function of the addiction within the context of the dominant psychopathology. Treatment for co-occurring disorders must involve recognition of needs, behaviors, and attitudes that foster addictive behavior. Individuals with PAPD feel entitled to recovery but refuse to work toward it because they believe either that they are owed normalcy or that the treatment staff are flawed and incompetent. They are easily demoralized and may feel entitled to relapse because they have been tempted by the cruel forces of fate. Recovery from either disorder will be based upon the gradual acceptance of responsibility for self, willingness to be held accountable, and diminishing blaming behaviors.

Medication for individuals with PAPD should be limited to specific targeted symptoms. These individuals are prone to depression, and it is possible that antidepressant medication will relieve symptoms enough to facilitate other treatment modalities. However, verifying all prescribed medications and working with all prescribing physicians can prevent medical emergencies. Unfortunately, these clients are inclined to demand medication and then to complain that it did not work. They then suggest that the psychiatrist who prescribed the medication is incompetent.

Finally, coercion or legal leverage may be needed to establish compliance with treatment for clients with PAPD. Drug testing is of crucial importance; these individuals are second only to people with antisocial personality disorders in insisting that they are abstinent when they are using daily. Care must be taken to be in touch with all sources of medication. Attendance in treatment should be carefully monitored. Low credibility should be given to self-reports without corroborating information (Richards, 1993). Although confrontation may be necessary to breach the sullen noncompliance in clients with PAPD, they are inclined to respond to confrontation as proof that they are being treated badly and that the staff are incompetent. It is more likely to be effective to calmly state expectations, clearly define consequences, and enforce program policies. The impact of negative consequences will likely also be blamed on treatment staff, but it is the most promising method to achieve compliance with treatment expectations.

Treatment Goals

As with any of the personality disorders, passive–aggressive treatment goals include more adaptive behaviors. To set goals that cannot be met without these clients' becoming nonnegativistic is to place them in line to fail. It may be helpful to consider harm reduction as both a treatment technique and a realistic limiter on setting goals. As with substance use, reducing negative consequences of certain behaviors may be the only place to start. What small change in passive–aggressive behavior might reduce potential or threatening consequences, for example, reduce the probability of getting fired? If PAPD clients can see that a manageable behavior change could have positive benefits, they may consider trying it. If it does not work, then exploration of what was tried and what did not work would need to be thorough. Acceptance of a treatment goal of more adaptive behavior or reduction of drug use will only make sense if it is explained in terms of the advantages to clients with PAPD; advantages to other people would probably serve as a demotivator.

Recovery Activities for Individuals with PAPD and Addiction

Individuals with PAPD may complicate their recovery with compulsive eating, spending, or other appetitive behaviors. Substance-dependent clients with PAPD must be urged to inform their physicians of their involvement in dual diagnosis treatment. As they become willing to be more open, they begin the process of accepting personal responsibility for their recovery (CSAT, 1994).

Individuals with PAPD can benefit from 12-step groups or other peer support groups, but they must be encouraged to avoid romantic involvement to escape existing bad relationships. If they will join same-sex support groups, they may be better able to avoid relationships built on a mutual need to avoid recovery (CSAT, 1994). Finally, involvement with peer support groups is self-defeating without assistance on how to use these groups without alienating other participants (Richards, 1993).

14

Final Thoughts and Future Directions

Personality Disorders and Addiction

To have a personality disorder is to engage in self-sabotaging behavior that reduces personal effectiveness, resilience, and authenticity; no facet of life is untouched by the corrosive impact of cognitive, affective, or interpersonal dysfunction. Faulty impulse control can bring serious negative consequences and a life derailed by court appearances, possible imprisonment, loss of employment, or failed relationships. To have a substance-dependence disorder is to jeopardize physical and mental health, career or employment, and significant relationships; addiction can result in the deterioration of personal ideals and values as the relentless pressure to use alcohol or other psychoactive drugs runs over everything in its path. Both personality disorders and addiction violate personal potential and compromise the future, yet they carry with them a self-sustaining adherence to the very behaviors that are the most important to change.

Personality disorders and substance dependence strongly affect both the individuals who have the disorders and those who work, live, and interact with them. Individuals with personality disorders often form relationships that are sustained by mutual pathology or the extraordinary accommodation of the disordered behavior by partners who are willing to sacrifice themselves for their own reasons. Addiction treatment can be compromised by unaddressed relationship or family issues. Developing a more resilient and adaptive personality style or changing addictive behaviors impacts the balance in significant relationships and could derail recovery. Involving partners, significant others, and family members often strengthens treatment effectiveness and facilitates recovery.

Sometimes the relationships are destructive and must be terminated for real progress to occur. Sometimes the relationships form a supportive core for persons with dual diagnosis and are essential to help these individuals tolerate the pressure of treatment and the stress of change. It is extraordinarily rare that significant relationships are irrelevant to recovery. Often family members or partners need help themselves for their own emotional pain, dysfunctional behaviors, or anxiety about the changes that are taking place in their significant others' recovery processes.

Service Provider Guidelines

To work with individuals with personality disorders is to accept the challenge to

- Form alliances with people who need help but have a compromised ability to establish authentic connections to others
- Engage with empathy and positive regard toward individuals who may know only toxic responses to interpersonal interaction
- Provide corrective feedback to individuals who may refuse to hear, see, or comprehend what is going wrong in their lives or may feel so defeated that the feedback is simply further proof of their inadequacy
- Understand one's own personality traits that may be compromising clinical effectiveness

It is important not to underestimate the pressures involved in working with individuals with co-occurring personality disorders and addiction. Professional overconfidence promotes ineffectiveness. No service providers are so experienced and skilled that they cannot lose their balance while working with individuals who alter their personal reality but are not psychotic and engage in dishonest—sometimes desperate—behaviors to protect their addiction. One very skilled clinician described herself, on one occasion, as being caught in the "magic fairy dust" of a client with borderline personality disorder and heroin addiction. Choices she would have never made under less pressure began to make sense to her when entering the world of a client who was hurt, enraged, addicted, and determined to coerce caretaking. Fortunately, the clinician was adept at rebalancing herself by seeking input from her supervisor and from her colleagues. Her true wisdom was knowing that functioning alone jeopardized her professional judgment and her client's well-being. The single greatest risk service providers can take with individuals with co-occurring personality disorders and substance use disorders is to work in isolation.

To develop the complex professional skills and personal resilience needed to be effective with co-occurring personality disorders and addiction is equivalent to joining the army to "be all you can be." The work requires uncompromising integrity, a strong commitment to ethical practice, continuous learning, interpersonal skill, personal resilience, and an unyielding honesty about feelings, reactions, and behaviors elicited from interacting with these individuals.

Nevertheless, the rewards are as great as the challenges. To facilitate change for individuals with this type of co-occurring disorder is to experience one's own clinical strength and a corresponding sense of professional achievement.

Integrated Treatment for Co-Occurring Disorders

It is unusual to encounter individuals who have only one personality disorder, substantially fit the criteria of that one personality disorder, and do not have co-occurring substance use disorders, anxiety or affective disorders, physical concerns, or trauma. To describe each personality disorder individually is important for clarity and understanding. However, to work with real people is to encounter a mix of disorders that often only marginally fit any of the diagnostic categories. The task is to understand and respond to clients as individuals and to engage in effective interventions that are informed by as substantial a knowledge base as possible.

Overall, integrated treatment of co-occurring disorders involves:

- Initial engagement and stabilization
- Symptom management
- Harm reduction or abstinence
- Learning adaptive coping skills such as affect management and positive interpersonal behaviors
- Gaining self-awareness and working toward self-responsibility
- Achieving both the ability and the willingness to help others

Treatment modalities and recovery activities that can help in this progression of treatment include detoxification; crisis stabilization; medications for both psychiatric and substance dependence disorders; psychoeducation; group, family, and individual interventions; and peer support groups. All of the treatment modalities must be able to address both disorders; the disorders do not operate independently of each other, and one cannot be effectively addressed while the other is ignored or needed intervention is delayed.

Recovery

Recovery from personality disorders and addiction is a process of building or regaining strength, growing in resiliency, becoming more adaptive when facing adversity, and living life to its fullest in the most meaningful way for each individual. Recovery can be obstructed by stigma from any source, but most particularly when there is a negative bias from service providers that individuals with personality disorders or addiction cause their own problems. Certainly these individuals engage in self-defeating behaviors and overvalue activities that cause serious negative consequences, but that does not mean people can "just say no" to craving, maladaptive defenses, destructive interpersonal behaviors, or the inability to constructively manage affect. Recovery can flourish when a partnership is developed between dually diagnosed individuals and service providers that is marked by hopefulness, determination, patience, and celebration of progress made one day at a time.

Future Directions

Personality disorders have been and continue to be the subject of debate and controversy. There are many difficulties with the concepts and constructs of the 12 personality disorders presented in this book. There are those who believe there should be more, or fewer, specific disorders. Others believe the personality categories overlap and co-occur too frequently to be useful. Considerable research is underway to better define, describe, and understand personality disorders. There are those who believe the categories of personality disorders, for example, histrionic or avoidant, should give way to dimensions, for example, aggressiveness or dependency, so that individuals can be assessed according to the degree of presence or absence of the essential dimensions instead of being placed into discrete categories (Widiger et al., 1994). Debate continues about how many or which specific dimensions should be core to this approach to personality disorders (Widiger, 2007). There are those who believe it is possible to use a hybrid construct of dimensions within categories. No resolution to the debate has emerged as yet, and it appears likely that personality disorders in the *DSM-V*, whenever it is published, will be vastly different than they are now (Fowler, O'Donohue, & Lilienfeld, 2007; Millon & Grossman, 2007a, 2007b; Westen & Shedler, 1999).

Whatever progress is made in psychiatry, psychology, or human services, knowledge will be helpful. For now, knowing that individuals struggle with personality disorders, however they are defined, and that effective interventions are available, however much they may improve in the future, is a place to start. It is possible to make a difference.

Substance use disorders also carry stigma, both in society and among service providers. There continues to be tension in regard to defining addiction as a disease, a disorder, or a volitional behavior (Hoffman & Froemke, 2007; Peele, 1985, 1989). As with personality disorders, recovery from substance use disorders is based upon hopefulness, determination, learning coping skills, developing affect management skills, and having access to effective treatment when needed.

Finally, integrated treatment for dual disorders is currently supported as an evidence-based treatment. There is reason to be optimistic about the benefits of integrated treatment; positive changes can occur with engagement, collaborative partnerships between dually diagnosed individuals and service providers, and sufficient time (Mueser et al., 2003). Continuing research and clinical experience will guide integrated treatment for co-occurring disorders into the future. It is an interesting time to embrace this complex and challenging work.

References

Adler, D. A. (1990). Personality disorders: Theory and psychotherapy. In D. A. Adler (Ed.), *Treating personality disorders* (pp. 17–42). San Francisco: Jossey-Bass.

Akhtar, S. (1992). *Broken structures: Severe personality disorders and their treatment.* Northvale, NJ: Jason Aronson.

Akhtar, S. (1995). *Quest for answers: A primer of understanding and treating severe personality disorders.* Northvale, NJ: Jason Aronson.

Akiskal, H. S. (1983). Dysthymic disorder: Psychopathology of proposed chronic depressive subtypes. *American Journal of Psychiatry, 140,* 11–20.

American Psychiatric Association. (1980). *Diagnostic and statistical manual of mental disorders* (3rd ed.). Washington, DC: Author.

American Psychiatric Association. (1987). *Diagnostic and statistical manual of mental disorders* (3rd ed., rev.). Washington, DC: Author.

American Psychiatric Association. (1994). *Diagnostic and statistical manual of mental disorders* (4th ed.). Washington, DC: Author.

American Psychiatric Association. (2000). *Diagnostic and statistical manual of mental disorders* (4th ed., text rev.). Washington, DC: Author.

Barratt, E. S., & Stanford, M. S. (1996). Impulsiveness. In C. G. Costello (Ed.), *Personality characteristics of the personality disordered* (pp. 91–119). New York: John Wiley & Sons.

Beck, A. T., Freeman, A., & Davis, D. D. (2004). *Cognitive therapy of personality disorders* (2nd ed). New York: Guilford Press.

Beck, A. T., Wright, F. D., Newman, C. F., & Liese, B. S. (1993). *Cognitive therapy of substance abuse.* New York: Guilford Press.

Benjamin, L. S. (1996). *Interpersonal diagnosis and treatment of personality disorders* (2nd ed.). New York: Guilford Press.

Benjamin, L. S. (2005). Interpersonal theory of personality disorders: The structural analysis of social behavior and interpersonal reconstructive therapy. In M. F. Lenzenweger & J. F. Clarkin (Eds.), *Major theories of personality disorders* (2nd ed., pp. 157–230). New York: Guilford Press.

Bernstein, A. J. (2001). *Emotional vampires: Dealing with people who drain you dry.* New York: McGraw Hill.

Birtchnell, J. (1995). Detachment. In C. L. Costello (Ed.), *Personality characteristics of the personality disordered* (pp. 173–205). New York: John Wiley & Sons.

Bockian, N. R., & Jongsma, A. E., Jr. (2001). *The personality disorders treatment planner.* New York: John Wiley & Sons.

Bornstein, R. F. (1996). Dependency. In C. G. Costello, (Ed.), *Personality characteristics of the personality disordered* (pp. 120–145). New York: John Wiley & Sons.

Bowler, D. M. (2007). *Autism spectrum disorders: Psychological theory and research*. West Sussex, U.K.: John Wiley & Sons.

Center for Substance Abuse Treatment (1994). *Assessment and treatment of patients with coexisting mental illness and alcohol and other drug abuse: Treatment Improvement Protocol (TIP) Series #9* (DHHS Publication No. SMA 94-2078). Washington, DC: U.S. Government Printing Office.

Cleckley, J. (1941). *The mask of sanity*. St. Louis, MO: Mosby.

Copeland, M. E. (2000). *Wellness recovery action plan*. West Dummerston, VT: Peach Press.

Craig, R. J. (1995). Interpersonal psychotherapy and MCMI-III-based assessment. In P. D. Retzlaff (Ed.), *Tactical psychotherapy of the personality disorders: An MCMI-III-based approach* (pp. 66–89). Boston: Allyn and Bacon.

Daley, D. C., & Thase, M. E. (1995). *Dual disorders recovery counseling: A biopsychosocial treatment model for addiction and psychiatric illness*. Independence, MO: Herald House/Independence Press.

Derksen, J. (1995). *Personality disorders: Clinical and social perspectives*. New York: John Wiley & Sons.

DiClemente, C. C. (2003). *Addiction and change: How addictions develop and addicted people recover*. New York: Guilford Press.

Donat, D. (1995). Use of the MCMI-III in behavior therapy. In P. D. Retzlaff (Ed.), *Tactical psychotherapy of the personality disorders: An MCMI-III-based approach* (pp. 40–62). Boston: Allyn and Bacon.

Dorr, D. (1995). Psychoanalytic psychotherapy of the personality disorders: Toward morphologic change. In P. D. Retzlaff (Ed.), *Tactical psychotherapy of the personality disorders: An MCMI-III-based approach* (pp. 186–209). Boston: Allyn and Bacon.

Dowson, J. H., & Grounds, A. T. (1995). *Personality disorders: Recognition and clinical management*. Cambridge. U.K.: Cambridge University Press.

Ellison, J. M., & Adler, D. A. (1990). A strategy for the pharmacotherapy of personality disorders. In D. A. Adler (Ed.), *Treating personality disorders* (pp. 43–64). San Francisco: Jossey-Bass.

Evans, K., & Sullivan, J. M. (2000). *Dual diagnosis: Counseling the mentally ill substance abuser* (2nd ed.). New York: Guilford Press.

Everly, G. S., Jr. (1995). Domain-oriented personality theory. In P. D. Retzlaff (Ed.), *Tactical psychotherapy of the personality disorders: An MCMI-III-based approach* (pp. 24–39). Boston: Allyn and Bacon.

Fenigstein, A. (1996). Paranoia. In C. G. Costello (Ed.), *Personality charac-teristics of the personality disordered* (pp. 242–275). New York: John Wiley & Sons.

First, M. D., Gibbon, M., Spitzer, R. L., Williams, J. B., and Benjamin, L. S. (1997). *Structured clinical interview for DSM-IV: axis II personality disorders: SCID-II.* Washington, DC: American Psychiatric Press.

Fowler, K. A., O'Donohue, W., & Lilienfeld, S. O. (2007). Introduction: Per-sonality disorders in perspective. In W. O'Donohue, K. A. Fowler, & S. O. Lilienfeld (Eds.), *Personality disorders: Toward the DSM-V* (pp. 1–20). Los Angeles: Sage.

Frances, A., First, M. B., & Pincus, H. A. (1995). *DSM-IV guidebook.* Wash-ington, DC: American Psychiatric Press.

Gabbard, G. O. (2005). Mind, brain, and personality disorders. *American Journal of Psychiatry, 162*(4), 648–655.

Gabbard, G. O. and Wilkinson, S. M. (1994). *Management of countertrans-ference with borderline patients.* Washington, DC: American Psychi-atric Press.

Gallop, R., Lancee, W. J., & Garfinkel, P. (1989). How nursing staff respond to the label "borderline personality disorder." *Hospital and Commu-nity Psychiatry, 40,* 815–819.

Golas, T. (1972). *The lazy man's guide to enlightenment.* Salt Lake City: Gibbs-Smith.

Golas, T. (1979). A perspective on LSD. Blotter zine, Santa Cruz, Califor-nia: The Psychedelic Education Center. Retrieved August 3, 1999, from http://www.highvib.org/archive1/lsd.htm

Golomb, E. (1992). *Trapped in the mirror: Adult children of narcissists in their struggle for self.* New York: Quill-William Morrow.

Grant, B. F., Hasin, D. S., Stinson, F. S., Dawson, D. A., Chou, S. P., Ruan, W. J., and Pickering, R. P. (2004). Prevalence, correlates, and disability of personality disorders in the United States: Results from the National Epidemiologic Survey on Alcohol and Related Conditions. *Journal of Clinical Psychiatry, 65*(7), 948–958.

Gregory, R. J. (2006). Clinical challenges in co-occurring borderline per-sonality and substance use disorders. *Psychiatric Times, 23*(13). Retrieved Feburary 27, 2007, from http://www.psychiatrictimes.com/Personality-Disorders/showArticle.jhtml?articleId=194500290

Grinfeld, M. (2003). Conference probes pathology of self-awareness. *Psychiatric Times, 20*(6). Retrieved February 27, 2007 from http://www.psychiatrictimes.com/Personality-Disorders/showArticle.jhtml?articleId=175802465

Gunderson, J. G., & Gabbard, G. O. (1999). Foreword. In J. G. Gunderson & G. O. Gabbard (Eds.), *Psychotherapy for personality disorders.* Wash-ington, DC: American Psychiatric Press.

Gunderson, J. G., & Links, P. (1996). Borderline personality disorder. In G. O. Gabbard & S. D. Atkinson (Eds.), *Synopsis of treatments of psychiatric disorders* (2nd ed., pp. 969–978). Washington, DC: American Psychiatric Association Press.

Gunderson, J. G., Ronningstam, E., & Smith, L. E., (1995). Narcissistic personality disorder. In W. J. Livesley (Ed.), *The DSM-IV personality disorders* (pp. 201–212). New York: Guilford Press.

Guntrip, H. (1969). *Schizoid phenomena: Object relations and the self.* New York: International Universities Press.

Hare, R. D. (1999). *Without conscience: The disturbing world of the psychopaths among us.* New York: Guilford Press.

Hare, R. D. (2003). *The Hare psychopathy checklist—revised* (2nd ed.). Toronto, Ontario, Canada: Multi-Health Systems.

Heim, A., & Westen, D. (2005). Theories of personality and personality disorders. In J. M. Oldham, A. E. Skodol, & D. S. Bender (Eds.), *Textbook of personality disorders.* Washington, DC: American Psychiatric Publishing.

Hendrickson, E. L., Schmal, M. S., & Ekleberry, S. C. (2004). *Treating co-occurring disorders: A handbook for mental health and substance abuse professionals.* Binghamton, NY: Haworth Press.

Hoffman, J., & Froemke, S. (Eds.) (2007). *Addiction: Why can't they just stop?: New knowledge. New treatments. New hope.* New York: Rodale.

Horowitz, M. J. (1991). Core traits of hysterical or histrionic personality disorders. In M. J. Horowitz (Ed.), *Hysterical personality style and the histrionic personality disorder* (rev. ed., pp. 1–14). Northvale, NJ: Jason Aronson.

Horowitz, M. J. (1996). Histrionic personality disorder. In G. O. Gabbard & S. D. Atkinson (Eds.), *Synopsis of treatments of psychiatric disorders* (2nd ed., pp. 985–990). Washington, DC: American Psychiatric Press.

Hoskins, R. (1989). *Rational madness: The paradox of addiction.* Blue Ridge Summit, PA: Tab Books.

Hyer, L., Brandsma, J., & Shealy, L. (1995). Experiential mood therapy with the MCMI-III. In P. D. Retzlaff (Ed.), *Tactical psychotherapy of the personality disorders: An MCMI-III-based approach* (pp. 210–234). Boston: Allyn and Bacon.

Ingraham, L. J. (1995). Family-genetic research and schizotypal personality. In A. Raine, T. Lencz, & S. A. Mednick (Eds.), *Schizotypal personality* (pp. 19–41). Cambridge, U.K.: Cambridge University Press.

Janicak, P. G., Davis, J. H., Preskorn, S. H., & Ayd, F. J., Jr. (1993). *Principles and practice of psychopharmacotherapy.* Baltimore, MD: Williams & Wilkins.

Kalus, O., Berstein, D. P., & Siever, L. J. (1995). Schizoid personality disorder. In J. W. Livesley (Ed.), *The DSM-IV personality disorders* (pp. 58–70). New York: Guilford Press.

Kane, E. (2006). Personality disorder: New initiatives in staff training. In J. J. Sampson, R. A. McCubbin, & P. Tyrer (Eds.), *Personality disorder and community mental health teams: A practitioner's guide* (pp. 3–20). New York: John Wiley & Sons.

Kantor, M. (1992). *Diagnosis and treatment of the personality disorders.* St. Louis: Ishiyaku EuroAmerica.

Kearney, R. J. (1996). *Within the wall of denial: Conquering addictive behaviors.* New York: W.W. Norton.

Kernberg, O. F. (1992). *Aggression in personality disorders and perversions.* New Haven, CT: Yale University Press.

Khantzian, E. J., Halliday, K. S., & McAuliffe, W. E. (1990). *Addiction and the vulnerable self: Modified dynamic group therapy for substance abusers.* New York: Guilford Press.

Klein, D. N., & Miller, G. A. (1993). Depressive personality in nonclinical subjects. *American Journal of Psychiatry, 150*(11), 1718–1724.

Kubacki, S. T., & Smith, P. R. (1995). An intersubjective approach to assessing and treating ego defenses using the MCMI-III. In P. D. Retzlaff (Ed.), *Tactical psychotherapy of the personality disorders: An MCMI-III-based approach* (pp. 159–183). Boston: Allyn and Bacon.

Kuhn, C., Swartzwelder, S., & Wilson, W. (1998). *Buzzed: The straight facts about the most used and abused drugs from alcohol to ecstasy.* New York: W. W. Norton.

Kwon, J. S., Kim, Y.-M., Chang, C.-G., Park, B.-J., Kim, L., Yoon, D. J., et al. (2000). Three-year follow-up of women with the sole diagnosis of depressive personality disorder: Subsequent development of dysthymia and major depression. *American Journal of Psychiatry, 157*(12), 1966–1972.

Laptook, R. S., Klein, D. N., & Dougherty, L. R. (2006). Ten-year stability of depressive personality disorder in depressed outpatients. *American Journal of Psychiatry, 163*(5), 865–871.

Layden, M., Newman, C. F., Freeman, A., & Morse, S.B. (1993). *Cognitive therapy of borderline personality disorders.* Boston: Allyn and Bacon.

Levy, K. N., Reynoso, J. S., Wasserman, R. H., & Clarkin, J. F. (2007). Narcissistic personality disorder. In W. O'Donohue, K. A. Fowler, & S. O. Lilienfeld (Eds.), *Personality disorders: Toward the DSM-V* (pp. 233–277). Los Angeles: Sage.

Linehan, M. M. (1993). *Cognitive-behavioral treatment of borderline personality disorder.* New York: Guilford Press.

Lish, J., Kavoussi, R. J., & Coccaro, E. F. (1996). Aggressiveness. In C. G. Costello (Ed.), *Personality characteristics of the personality disordered* (pp. 24–47). New York: John Wiley & Sons.

Livesley, W. J. (2005). The structure and etiology of borderline pathology. In J. Reich (Ed.), *Personality disorders: Current research and treatments* (pp. 21–42). New York: Routledge.

Lynch, T. R., & Robins, C. J. (1997). Treatment of borderline personality disorder using dialectical behavior therapy. *Journal of the California Alliance for the Mentally Ill, 8*(1), 47–49.

Magnavita, J. J. (1997). *Restructuring personality disorders: A short-term dynamic approach.* New York: Brunner/Mazel.

Masterson, J. F. (1981). *The narcissistic and borderline disorders: An integrated developmental approach.* New York: Brunner/Mazel.

Matano, R. A., & Locke, K. D. (1995). Personality disorder scales as predictors of interpersonal problems of alcoholics. *Journal of Personality Disorders, 9*(1), 62–67.

McCann, J. (1995). The MCM-III and treatment of the self. In P. D. Retzlaff (Ed.), *Tactical psychotherapy of the personality disorders: An MCMI-III-based approach* (pp. 137–157). Boston: Allyn and Bacon.

McCullough, P. K., & Maltsberger, J. T. (1996). Obsessive-compulsive personality disorder. In G. O. Gabbard & S. D. Atkinson (Eds.), *Synopsis of treatment of psychiatric disorders* (2nd ed., pp. 999–1002). Washington, DC: American Psychiatric Press.

McDonald, J. J. (2002). Personality disorders in employment litigation, *Psychiatric Times, 19*(4). Retrieved February 27, 2007, from http://www.psychiatrictimes.com/Personality-Disorders/showArticle.jhtml?articleId=175801731

McGlashan, T. H., Grilo, C. M., Sanislow, C. A., Ralevski, E., Morey, L. C., Gunderson, J. G., et al. (2005). Two-year prevalence and stability of individual *DSM-IV* criteria for schizotypal, borderline, avoidant, and obsessive-compulsive personality disorders: Toward a hybrid model of Axis II disorders. *American Journal of Psychiatry, 162*(5), 883–889.

McGlynn, C. (2003). New hope for double trouble: Dialectical behavior therapy targets borderline personality and addiction. *CrossCurrent—The Journal of Addiction and Mental Health, 7*(2), 16.

McWilliams, N. (1994). *Psychoanalytic diagnosis: Understanding personality structure in the clinical process.* New York: Guilford Press.

Meissner, W. W. (1994). *Psychotherapy and the paranoid process.* Northvale, NJ: Jason Aronson.

Meloy, J. R. (1996). Antisocial personality disorder. In G. O. Gabbard & S. D. Atkinson (Eds.), *Synopsis of treatments of psychiatric disorders* (2nd ed., pp. 959–968). Washington, DC: American Psychiatric Press.

Milkman, H., & Sunderwirth, S. (1987). *Craving for ecstasy: The consciousness & chemistry of escape.* Lexington, MA: Lexington Books.

Miller, W. R. (2006). Motivational factors in addictive behaviors. In W. R. Miller & S. M. Carroll (Eds.), *Rethinking substance abuse: What the science shows, and what we should do about it.* New York: Guilford Press.

Miller, W. R., & Rollnick, S. (2002). *Motivational interviewing: Preparing people to change* (2nd ed.). New York: Guilford Press.

Millon, T. (1981). *Disorders of personality: DSM-III: axis II.* New York: John Wiley and Sons.

Millon, T. (1996). *Personality and psychopathology: Building a clinical science: Selected papers of Theodore Millon.* New York: John Wiley and Sons.

Millon, T., & Davis, R. D. (1996). *Disorders of personality: DSM-IV and beyond* (2nd ed.). New York: John Wiley & Sons.

Millon, T., & Grossman, S. (2007a). *Moderating severe personality disorders: A personalized psychotherapy approach.* New York: John Wiley & Sons.

Millon, T., & Grossman, S. (2007b). *Overcoming resistant personality disorders: A personalized psychotherapy approach.* New York: John Wiley & Sons.

Millon, T., Grossman, S., Millon, C., Meagher, S., & Ramnath, R. (2004). *Personality disorders in modern life* (2nd ed.). New York: John Wiley & Sons.

Millon, T., & Martinez, A. (1995). Avoidant personality disorder. In W. J. Livesley (Ed.), *The DSM-IV personality disorders* (pp. 218–233). New York: Guilford Press.

Millon, T., & Radovanov, J. (1995). Passive-aggressive (negativistic) personality disorder. In J. W. Livesley (Ed.), *The DSM-IV personality disorders* (pp. 312–325). New York: Guilford Press.

Mueser, K. T., Noordsy, D. L., Drake, R. E., and Fox, L. (2003). *Integrated treatment for dual disorders: A guide to effective practice.* New York: Guilford Press.

Nace, E. P. (1990). Substance abuse and personality disorder. In D. F. O'Connell (Ed.), *Managing the dually diagnosed patient: Current issues and clinical approaches.* New York: Haworth Press.

Nace, E. P. (1995). The dual diagnosis patient. In S. Brown (Ed.) & I. D. Yalom (Gen. Ed.), *Treating alcoholism* (pp. 163–196). San Francisco: Jossey-Bass.

Nace, E. P., & Tinsley, J. A. (2007). *Patients with substance abuse problems: Effective identification, diagnosis, and treatment.* New York: W. W. Norton.

National Institute of Drug Abuse. (2000). *Principles of drug addiction treatment: A research based guide* (NIH Publication No. 00-4180). Washington, DC: National Institute of Health.

National Institute of Mental Health (England) (2003a). *Breaking the cycle of rejection: The personality disorder capabilities framework* (ROCR Ref: 2201). London: Department of Health.

National Institute of Mental Health (England) (2003b). *Personality disorder: No longer a diagnosis of exclusion: Policy implementation guidance for the development of services for people with personality disorder* (ROCR Ref: 1055). London: Department of Health.

National Institute of Mental Health (England) (2003c). *The ten essential shared capabilities: A framework for the whole of the mental health workforces* (ROCR Ref: 3453). London: Department of Health.

Oldham, J. M. (2005). Personality disorders: Recent history and future directions. In J. M. Oldham, A. E. Skodol, & D. S. Bender (Eds.), *Textbook of personality disorders* (pp. 3–16). Washington DC: American Psychiatric Publishing.

Oldham, J. M., & Morris, L. B. (1995). *The new personality self-portrait: Why you think, work, love, and act the way you do*. New York: Bantam Books.

O'Malley, S. S., Kosten, T. R., & Renner, J. A. Jr. (1990). Dual diagnoses: Substance abuse and personality disorders. In D. A. Adler (Ed.), *Treating personality disorders* (pp. 115–137). San Francisco: Jossey-Bass.

Patrick, C. J. (2007). Antisocial personality disorder and psychopathy. In W. O'Donohue, K. A. Fowler, & S. O. Lilienfeld (Eds.), *Personality disorders: Toward the DSM-V*. Los Angeles: Sage.

Peele, S. (1985). *The meaning of addiction: Compulsive experience and its interpretation*. Lexington, MA: Lexington Books.

Peele, S. (1989). *Diseasing of America: Addiction treatment out of control*. Lexington, MA: Lexington Books.

Perry, J. C. (1996). Dependent personality disorder. In G. O. Gabbard & S. D. Atkinson (Eds.), *Synopsis of treatment of psychiatric disorders* (2nd ed., pp. 995–998). Washington, DC: American Psychiatric Press.

Perry, J. C., & Bond, M. (2005). Defensive functioning. In J. M. Oldham, A. E. Skodol, & D. S. Bender (Eds.), *Textbook of personality disorders* (pp. 523–540). Washington, DC: American Psychiatric Publishing.

Pfohl, B., & Blum, N. (1995). Obsessive-compulsive personality disorder. In W. J. Lively (Ed.), *The DSM-IV personality disorders* (pp. 261–276). New York: Guilford Press.

Phillips, K. A., Gunderson, J. G., Hirschfeld, R. M., & Smith, L. E. (1990). A review of the depressive personality. *American Journal of Psychiatry, 147*(7), 830–837.

Phillips, K. A., Gunderson, J. G., Triebwasser, J., Kimble, C. R., Faedaa, G., Lyoo, K., & Renn, J. (1998). Reliability and validity of depressive personality disorder. *American Journal of Psychiatry, 155*(8), 1044–1048.

Phillips, K. A., Hirschfeld, R. M., Shea, M. T., & Gunderson, J. G. (1995). Depressive personality disorder. In W. J. Livesley (Ed.), *The DSM-IV personality disorders* (pp. 287–302). New York: Guilford Press.

Pilkonis, P. A. (1997). Surveying a complex domain: Research and treatment of borderline personality disorder. *Journal of the California Alliance for the Mentally Ill, 8*(1), 10–11.

Pollak, J. M. (1995). Commentary on obsessive–compulsive personality disorder. In John W. Livesley (Ed.), The DSM-IV personality disorders (pp. 277–283). New York: The Guilford Press.

Potter, N. N. (2006). What is manipulative behavior, anyway? *Journal of Personality Disorders, 20*(2), 139–156.

Preston, J. D. (2006). *Integrative treatment for borderline personality disorder: Effective, symptom-focused techniques: Simplified for private practice.* Oakland, CA: New Harbinger Publications.

Pretzer, J. L., & Beck, A. T. (2005). A cognitive theory of personality disorders. In M. F. Lenzenweger & J. F. Clarkin (Eds.), *Major theories of personality disorder* (2nd ed., pp. 43–113). New York: Guilford Press.

Rado, S. (1953). Dynamics and classification of disordered behavior. *American Journal of Psychiatry, 110,* 406–416.

Ratey, J. J., & Johnson, C. (1997). *Shadow syndromes.* New York: Pantheon Books.

Rawlings, D., & Freeman, J. L. (1997). Measuring paranoia/suspiciousness. In G. Claridge (Ed.), *Schizotypy: Implications for illness and health* (pp. 38–60). Oxford, U.K.: Oxford University Press.

Richards, J. J. (1993). *Therapy of the substance abuse syndromes.* Northvale, NJ: Jason Aronson Inc.

Rodin, G., & Izenberg, S. (1997). Treating the narcissistic personality disorder. In M. Rosenbluth (Ed.) & I. D. Yalom (Gen. Ed.), *Treating difficult personality disorders* (pp. 107–122). San Francisco: Jossey-Bass.

Rosenthal, M. Z. (2006). Dialectical behavior therapy for patients dually diagnosed with borderline personality disorder and substance use disorders. *Psychiatric Times, 25*(1). Retrieved <date> from http:/www.psychiatric times.com/Personality-Disorders/showArticle.jhtml?articleID= 17710145

Royce, J. E., & Scratchley, D. (1996). *Alcoholism and other drug problems.* New York: Free Press.

Ruegg, R., & Frances, A. (1995). New research in personality disorders. *Journal of Personality Disorders, I*(1), 1–48.

Sadock, B. J., & Sadock, V. A. (2004). *Concise textbook of clinical psychiatry* (2nd ed.). Philadelphia: Lippincott Williams & Wilkins.

Salzman, L. (1981). Psychodynamics of the addictions. In S. Joseph Mule (Ed.), *Behavior in excess: An examination of the volitional disorders* (pp. 338–349). New York: The Free Press.

Sharoff, K. (2002). *Cognitive coping therapy.* New York: Brunner-Routledge.

Shedler, J., & Westen, D. (2004). Refining personality disorder diagnosis: Integrating science and practice. *American Journal of Psychiatry* *161*(8), 1350–1365.

Siever, L. J. (1986). Schizoid and schizotypal personality disorders. In J. R. Lion (Ed.), *Personality disorders: Diagnosis and management* (Revised for *DSM III*) (2nd ed., pp. 32–64), Malabar, FL: Robert E. Krieger.

Siever, L. J., Bernstein, D. P., & Silverman, J. M. (1995). Schizotypal personality disorder. In W. J. Livesley (Ed.), *The DSM-IV personality disorders* (pp. 71–90). New York: Guildford Press.

Silverstein, M. L. (2007). *Disorders of self: A personality-guided approach*. Washington, DC: American Psychological Association.

Skodol, A. E. (2005). Manifestations, clinical diagnosis, and comorbidity. In J. M. Oldham, A. E. Skodol, & D. S. Bender (Eds.), *Textbook of personality disorders* (pp. 57–87). Washington, DC: American Psychiatric Publishing.

Sperry, L. (2003). *Handbook of diagnosis and treatment of the DSM-IV-TR personality disorders* (2nd ed.). New York: Routledge.

Sperry, L., & Carlson, J. (1993). *Psychopathology and psychotherapy: From diagnosis to treatment*. Muncie, IN: Accelerated Development.

Spoont, M. R. (1996). Emotional instability. In C. G. Costello (Ed.), *Personality characteristics of the personality disorders*. New York: John Wiley & Sons.

Stone, M. (1993). *Abnormalities of personality: Within and beyond the realm of treatment*. New York: W.W. Norton.

Stone, M. (1996). Schizoid and schizotypal personality disorders. In G. O. Gabbard & S. D. Atkinson (Eds.), *Synopsis of treatments of psychiatric disorders* (2nd ed., pp. 953–958). Washington, DC: American Psychiatric Press.

Sutherland, S. M., & Frances, A. (1996). Avoidant personality disorder. In G. O. Gabbard & S. D. Atkinson (Eds.), *Synopsis of treatment of psychiatric disorders* (2nd ed., pp. 991–994). Washington, DC: American Psychiatric Press.

Triebwasser, J., & Siever, L. J. (2006). Pharmacology of personality disorders. *Psychiatric Times*, *23*(8). Retrieved February 27, 2007, from http://www.psychiatrictimes.com/Personality-Disorders/print.jhtml?articleID=191000148

Turkat, I. D. (1990). *The personality disorders: A psychological approach to clinical management*. New York: Pergamon.

Tyrer, P., Casey, P., & Ferguson, B. (1988). Personality disorder and mental illness. In P. Tyrer (Ed.), *Personality disorders: Diagnosis, management and course*. London: Wright, Butterworth Scientific.

Tyrer, P., & Seivewright, H. (1988). Studies of outcome. In P. Tyrer (Ed.), *Personality disorders: Diagnosis, management and course* (pp. 119–136). London: Wright, Butterworth Scientific.

Unger, R. M. (1994). *Passion: An essay on personality*. New York: The Free Press.

Van Denburg, E. J. (1995). Object relations theory and the MCMI-III. In P. D. Retzlaff (Ed.), *Tactical psychotherapy of the personality disorders: An MCMI-III-based approach* (pp. 111–136). Boston: Allyn and Bacon.

Walant, K. B. (1995*). Creating the capacity for attachment: Treating addiction and the alienated self*. Northvale, NJ: Jason Aronson.

Walker, E. F., & Gale, S. (1995). Neurodevelopmental processes in schizophrenia and schizotypal personality disorder. In A. Raine, R. Lencz, & S. A. Mednick (Eds.), *Schizotypal personality* (pp. 56–76). Cambridge, U.K.: Cambridge University Press.

Weissman, M. M. (1993). The epidemiology of personality disorders: A 1990 update. *Journal of Personality Disorders, 7*(Suppl.), 44–62.

Westen, D., & Shedler, J. (1999). Revising and assessing axis II, part II: Toward an empirically based and clinically useful classification of personality disorders. *American Journal of Psychiatry, 156*(2), 273–285.

Wetzler, S. (1992). *Living with the passive aggressive man: Coping with hidden aggression—from the bedroom to the boardroom*. New York: Fireside, Simon & Schuster.

Widiger, T. A. (2007). Alternatives to *DSM-IV*: Axis II. In W. O'Donohue, K. A. Fowler, & S. O. Lilienfeld (Eds.), *Personality disorders: Toward the DSM-V* (pp. 21–40). Los Angeles: Sage.

Widiger, T. A., & Corbit, E. M. (1995). Antisocial personality disorder. In W. J. Livesley (Ed.), *The DSM-IV personality disorders* (pp. 103–126). New York: Guilford Press.

Widiger, T. A., Trull, T. J., Clarkin, J. F., Sanderson, C., & Costa, P.T., Jr. (1994). A description of the *DSM-III-R* and *DSM-IV* personality disorders with the five-factor model of personality. In P. T. Costa, Jr. & T. A. Widiger (Eds.), *Personality disorders and the five-factor model of personality* (pp. 41–56). Washington, DC: American Psychological Association.

Will, T. (1995). Cognitive therapy and the MCMI-III. In P. D. Retzlaff (Ed.), *Tactical psychotherapy of the personality disorders: An MCMI-III-based approach* (pp. 90–110). Boston: Allyn and Bacon.

Winger, G., Hofmann, F. G., & Woods, J. H. (1992). *A handbook on drug and alcohol abuse: The biomedical aspects* (3rd. ed.). New York: Oxford University Press.

Wink, P. (1995). Narcissism. In C. G. Costello (Ed.), *Personality characteristics of the personality disordered* (pp. 146–172). New York: John Wiley & Sons.

World Health Organization. (1992). *ICD-10 classification of mental and behavioural disorders: Clinical descriptions and diagnostic guidelines.* Geneva: Author.

Yudofsky, S. C. (2005). *Fatal flaws: Navigating destructive relationships with people with disorders of personality and character.* Washington, DC: American Psychiatric Publishing.

Zanarini, M., Frankenburg, F., Hennen, J., Reich, D., & Silk, K. (2004). Axis I comorbidity in patients with borderline personality disorder: 6-year follow-up and prediction of time to remission. *American Journal of Psychiatry, 161*(11), 2108–2114.

Zimmerman, M. (1994). *Interview guide for evaluating DSM-IV psychiatric disorders and the mental status examination.* East Greenwich, RI: Psych Products Press.

Index